D.C. Magazines:
A Literary Retrospective

D.C. Magazines:
A Literary Retrospective

edited by
Richard Peabody

assisted by
Gretchen Johnsen
Rachael Peabody
Zenon Slawinski

typesetting by
Joseph Lerner
Spec-Type, Inc.
Kevin Urick

Acknowledgement for Reprint Permissions in most cases goes out to the individual authors and artists whose work first appeared in either *Voyages*, *Dryad*, or *Portfolio*, and also to the following:

"Apprehension" by Mark Van Doren is reprinted by permission of Dorothy Van Doren. Copyright © Dorothy Van Doren.

Ben Belitt's translations of Pablo Neruda's Love Sonnets are reprinted from *Translations* Copyright © 1961, 1969, 1972, and 1974 by permission of Ben Belitt.

"Bats At Dusk" by Chad Walsh, is reprinted by permission of the author and the Swallow Press from *End of Nature*. Copyright © 1969.

Imogen Cunningham's photo of Theodore Roethke is reprinted from *Imogen Cunningham: Photographs* with the permission of the University of Washington Press, Seattle, WA Copyright © 1975.

"Heart, You Have No House" is reprinted from *Straw For The Fire* with the permission of the editor, David Wagoner, and the publisher, the University of Washington Press, Seattle, WA Copyright © 1972.

"The Dead Man's Room" is reprinted from *The Anonymous Lover*, new poems by John Logan, with the permission of the author and the publisher, Liveright Publishing Corp., New York, NY, Copyright © 1969, 1970, 1971, 1972, 1973 by John Logan.

"Smoke" is reprinted by permission of Macmillan Publishing Co., Inc. from *The Weather of Six Mornings* by Jane Cooper. Copyright © 1968, 1969 by Jane Cooper. Originally appeared in *Voyages*.

"We're The Only Colored People Here" from *The World of Gwendolyn Brooks*. Copyright © 1953 by Gwendolyn Brooks Blakely. Reprinted by permission of Harper & Row, Publishers, Inc.

"Every Now and Then at Night" and "High Dark" are reprinted by permission of the author and William Morrow & Company, Inc. from *The Myth Of A Woman's Fist*. Copyright © 1961, 1962, 1965, 1969, 1971, 1972, 1973 by Ann Darr.

"Bats at Dusk" is reprinted by permission of the author and the Swallow Press from *End Of Nature*. Copyright © 1969 by Chad Walsh.

"The Staff of Life" is reprinted from Henry Miller's *Remember to Remember*. Copyright © 1947 by New Directions Publishing Corporation. Reprinted by permission of New Directions.

Siv Cedering's photo on the cover of *Dryad* no. 9/10, is reprinted from *Cup Of Cold Water*, New Rivers Press. Copyright © 1973, Siv Cedering.

"The Later Caresse Crosby; Her Answer Remained 'Yes'" by Harry T. Moore is reprinted from *ICarbS* III:2 (Spring-Summer, 1977), 127-134. Copyright © 1977.

The excerpt from *Children of the Albatross* by Anais Nin is reprinted by permission of the Author's Representative, Gunther Stuhlmann. Copyright © 1947, 1959 by Anais Nin. Copyright renewed © 1975 by Anais Nin.

Wilfredo Lam's painting "The Caribbean Parade," is reprinted with the permission of the Visual Artists and Galleries Association, Inc. © S.P.A.D.E.M., Paris/V.A.G.A., New York, 1981.

First Edition
Printed in the USA

Copyright © 1981, by Richard Myers Peabody, Jr.
All rights revert to the individual authors
and artists upon publication.

Library of Congress
Cataloging in Publication No.: 81-82082

ISBN: 0-9602424-5-7 (vol. 1)
0-9602424-4-9 (series)

The Paycock Press
P.O. Box 57206
Washington, D.C. 20037

Foreword

by Richard Peabody

The first decent history I ever read on the local literary scene was Jack Foley's "A Bank of Violets," published in *Aleph* no. 1 in 1975. The piece was good at putting the 60s explosion of local magazines and literary presses into perspective, but hardly touched on what had gone before, save to trot out Walt Whitman, Charles Olson, Ezra Pound, and St. John Perse as writers who lived here for a time. Bill Walker's Coffee 'n Confusion Beat-era coffeehouse (which was written up in greater detail in Dick Dabney's profile of Walker in the May 1981 *Washingtonian*) also got a brief mention. My interest in putting together this book grew from a desire as a D.C. native to know more about what had gone on before in the city's literary history. Of course, it's impossible to cover all the local literary activity in 150 pages, so it was decided to do one volume in a possible series of historical books focussing on the DC literary scene, the first volume of which would feature the magazines that were the most international in scope and longest running of the lot—*Portfolio, Voyages,* and *Dryad*. Not that it's any easier to do justice to these magazines in a book this size; they each deserve an anthology of their own. But I hope to demonstrate in the space allotted, that the city of Washington has never deserved the bad press it has received as a "literary backwater."

The actual impetus for the project and the eventual focus on Caresse Crosby's magazine grew from two incidents in 1977. The first was stumbling across a copy of *Portfolio V* at David Southern's Bull City Studio in North Carolina, and second was Tom Lacey's loan of Geoffrey Wolff's *Black Sun: The Brief Transit and Violent Eclipse of Harry Crosby* later that same year. Wolff's biography, though sensationalized, did lead to my discovery that Caresse's first husband and I, while not at all related, shared identical names—Richard Peabody. After that it was a combination of luck, locomotion, and curiosity which led to the retrospective as presented.

I regret not being able to include work by Kay Boyle, close friend of the Crosbys, who declined to participate; as did Sterling A. Brown, surely poet laureate of this city, and another *Portfolio* contributor. Many others were left out who either couldn't be located, never responded to my letters, or for whom reprint rights or permissions could not be obtained. The permissions as they stand took nearly two years to gather, and yet this book remains far from perfect.

I had to put this book together and locate the source materials in order to learn exactly what it was I wanted to do. Now I'm prepared to tackle the book I really want to see come out of this research, and envision a cross between Lawrence Ferlinghetti and Nancy J. Peters' *Literary San Francisco* and William Rose Benet's *Reader's Encyclopedia*, that would cover the Washington area. The book would be crammed with interviews, photos, reprints of covers, articles from the *Post, Star,* and *Washingtonian*, plus excerpts from the literary magazines listed in the back of this volume.

Useful sources for the historical research were: Jack Foley's aformentioned piece; Helen Nicolay's *Sixty Years of the Literary Society* (privately printed, 1934); Carrington Bonner's "Already Out: A Historical Analysis of the Black Small Press Movement in the Baltimore/DC area, 1963-1979," (*The Black Review*, Vol. 2, No. 1); *The Little Magazine: A History and a Bibliography* by Frederick Hoffman, Charles Allen, and Carolyn F. Ulrich (Princeton University Press, 1946); Constance McLaughlin Green's *Washington: A History of the Capital* (Princeton University Press, 1962); James Boyer May's *Trace* magazine, issues no. 1-72/73, June 1952-Autumn 1970; Marion Sader's *Comprehensive Index to English-Language Little Magazines 1890-1970* (Kraus-Thompson Organization); Stephen Goode's four volume *Index to American Little Magazines*; and Len Fulton and Ellen Ferber's *International Directory of Little Magazines and Small Presses* no. 1-16, 1965-1981; *Magazines in the Twentieth Century* by Dr. Theodore Peterson (Univ. of Illinois Press, 1968); John Tebbel's *The American Magazine: A Complete History* (Hawthorne Books, 1969); and Frank Luther Mott's excellent five volume *A History of American Magazines* (Harvard Univ. Press, 1967).

Special thanks for information, history, assistance, advice, permissions, and other sundry items goes out to the following:

Polly Peabody Drysdale
Harry T. Moore
Rufus King II
Mrs. Logue, American University Archives
Elizabeth Miller, Curator, Columbia Historical Society Library
Roxanne Dean, Washingtoniana Division, Martin Luther King Library
Thomas D. Grischkowsky, Rights & Reproductions, The Museum of Modern Art
Mary E. Janzen, Curator of Manuscripts, Morris Library, Southern Ill. Univ.
Tom Kilpatrick, Morris Library, Southern Ill. Univ.
David V. Koch, editor of *ICarbS*, Southern Ill. Univ.
David Kresh, Library of Congress
Mary S. Duffy, Dover Publications
Juanita B. Pike, Univ. of Washington Press
Valerie Harms, Magic Circle Press
Sasha Newborn, Mudborn Press
A.D. Winans, Second Coming Press
Kevin Urick, The White Ewe Press
Lise Ferber, National Gallery of Art
Professor A.E. Claeyssens, George Washington University
Mrs. Anette D. Steiner, George Washington Univ. Archives
John Reynolds, Georgetown University Archives
Nick Scheetz, Georgetown University Archives
Elmer Kayser—G.W.U. Historian
Mary Kay Schall—G.W.U., Special Collections
Maria-Gaetana Matisse, Pierre Matisse Gallery
Russell Cox
Irene Rouse
V.V. Rankine
Rupert Pole
Gunther Stuhlmann
D.H. Melham
W.D. Snodgrass
Jane M. Dow
Kay Boyle
David Wagoner
Stark Biddle
Philip Herzbrun
Philip K. Jason
Eric Baizer
Diane Ward
Josephine Jacobsen
Mark Jenkins
Mary-Averett Seelye
Susan Lee

Thanks also to those editors, writers, and artists who helped me add to my history of the DC literary scene:

Paul Lawson, Charioteer Press
Deirdra Baldwin, Word Works, Inc.
Alan Austin, Watershed Foundation
Anne Becker, Watershed Foundation
William E. Garrison
Frank & Cathy Gatling
Richard Harrington
Peter Noterman
Elisavietta Ritchie
Will Inman
E. Ethelbert Miller
Michael Lally
Walt-Christopher Stickney
Walter H. Kerr
Phyllis Rosenzweig
Betsy Wollaston

Grace Cavalieri
Charles Fenyvesi
Joe Stewart
Howard Friedman
Mac Wellman
Jim Everhard
Charles Bernstein
Octave Stevenson
Betty Parry
Peter Coates
Simon Schuchat
William F. Ryan
Faye Moskowitz
Doug Lang
Linda Pastan
Sam Blate
Michael Winston

And most of all, thanks to Bill Claire, Merrill Leffler and Neil Lehrman without whom this book wouldn't have been possible.

James Boyer May
1905-1981

Contents

Thomas Merton Cover
Romolo Marcellini *Portfolio in Rome* 12
Harry T. Moore *The Later Caresse: Her Answer Remained "Yes"* 13
Gwendolyn Brooks *We're the Only Colored People Here* 15
Pablo Picasso *Portrait of Paul Verlaine* 16
Henry Miller *The Staff of Life* 17
Francis Coleman Rosenberger *Manet In Merkers* 21
Wilfredo Lam *The Caribbean Parade* 22
Charles Bukowski *20 Tanks From Kasseldown*
J.J. Grandville *Civil Marriage* 24
Anais Nin *from Children of the Albatross* 25
Jean Moralis *Wood Cut 1940* 26
Niko Engonopoulos *Room for Rent* 27
Eliot Porter *Bird in Flight* 28
William F. Claire *An Interview* 30
Pablo Neruda *Two Love Sonnets* (tr. by Ben Belitt) 34
Ben Belitt *Fat Tuesday* 35
Robert Lax *Two Poems* 35
Robert Lax *Photo* 36
Robert Lax *from the Journals I* 37
Daisy Aldan *Friday the 13th: YWCA* 38
Josephine Miles *Chairman* 39
Jane Cooper *Smoke* 39
Deena Metzger *What Rough Beast* 40
Ann Darr *Every Now And Then At Night* 42
Harriet Zinnes *E.D.* 43
Carolyn Banks *Idyll* 44
Linda Pastan *The Last Train* 44
Josef Erhardy *The Dance* 45
H.R. Hays *Keep Off The Grass (A divertissement for the poetic theatre)* 46
Richard Snodgrass *from The Lamp* 48
Samuel Hazo *Where It Was* 49
Marvin Cohen *An Amicable Solution* 49
Hiram Haydn *from Amos Bailey* 51
Jorge Luis Borges *The Unending Gift* (tr. by Robert Newcomb) 52
Reed Whittemore *A Dream of an Attic* 54
Henry H. Roth *President Richard Nixon Has Destroyed South Nyack* 55
Theodore Roethke *from The Notebooks (arranged by David Wagoner)* 58
Imogen Cunningham *Portrait of Theodore Roethke* 59
Martin Steingesser *Automobile & Pigeon 1968* 60
John Logan *The Dead Man's Room* 61
Brian Swann *Deer Head* 63
Joyce Carol Oates *How Another Child Came To Be Born* 64
Mark Van Doren *Apprehension* 68
Michael Biddle *Etching* 69

Catherine Frisch   *Cover issue #1*   70
Merrill Leffler   *An Interview*   72
Neil Lehrman   *An Interview*   74
Leonard R. Garzotto   *Etude: The Morning*   77
Chad Walsh   *Bats At Dusk*   77
Philip Appleman   *A Word To Socrates*   78
L. Suzanne Gordon   *from The Eastern Seaboard*   79
James Scully   *Letter to David*   80
Bill Holland   *Birthday in Monrovia, 1965*   81
Ann Darr   *Night Drive*   82
Roderick Jellema   *On Seeing Perhaps Miss Marianne Moore in the Library of Congress*   83
Gene Fowler   *Two Sides Of This Rolling Coin*   85
Irving Weiss   *She*   85
Ann Slayton   *After Too Many Intervals Of Rain*   86
Reed Whittemore   *The Fall of the House of Usher*   86
Myra Sklarew   *Departures*   87
Roderick Jellema   *Because I Never Learned the Names of Flowers*   87
Siv Cedering   *Directions*   88
Siv Cedering   *The Souls of the Hares*   89
Richard Forsythe   *Sense and Sentences: On Getting A Computer To Write Poems*   90
Sandra Slayton Namias   *Graphic*   92
Ann Darr   *High Dark*   93
Robert Carlson   *Drawing*   94
Roger Aplon   *The Spring of '59*   95
Saundra Maley   *War Bonds*   95
Morton Marcus   *How Would You Touch the Body of God*   97
Linda Pastan   *To A Second Son*   97
Barbara Frank   *Drawing*   98
Clarinda Harriss Lott   *The Doctor*   99
Margaret Gibson   *Scenes*   100
Roland Flint   *His Oyster*   101
Edward Gold   *Fish*   102
Denis Boyles   *off the Edgeware Rd and near to Brittany Elisabeth she made tea nice*   103
Robert Carlson   *Drawing*   104
Merrill Leffler   *Partly Pandemonium, Partly Love*   105
Doug Flaherty   *Lover's Leap*   107
Adelaide Blomfield   *After, Love*   107
Philip Dacey   *The Mermaid Crashed Upon The Mind*   108
W.V. Moody   *The Hung Buck*   108
Kathleen Jeffrie Johnson   *Tortoise Birthday*   109
Rodger Kamenetz   *Program Notes*   109
Tom O'Grady   *Sallie Sitting A Chestnut Mare*   110
Cumulative Indexes   111
Portfolio Index   112
Voyages Index   114
Dryad Index   117
Contributors Notes   121
D.C. Magazines: A List in Progress (1784-1981)   126
Other D.C. Anthologies   135

Portfolio

Caresse Crosby was born Mary Phelps Jacob on April 20, 1892, in New York City. She married Richard Rogers Peabody in January 1915, and had two children. Known as "Polly," she met Harry Crosby on July 4th, 1920, in Boston. After a six month separation she divorced Richard Peabody in February 1922, and married Crosby in September of that year. In December of 1924 they changed her name to Caresse. And then in December 1929 Harry shot another man's bride of six weeks and himself. Caresse later remarried to Selbert Young, a man 19 years her junior. It was after her divorce from Young that she came to Washington, opened a gallery, and started *Portfolio* magazine.

The magazine was always international in conception. She published six issues from 1945 to 1948. Issues 1, 3 and 5 were printed in the US, but issue 2 was published in Paris in December 1945 and featured primarily French writers and artists; 4 was published in Rome and did the same thing for Italian writers and artists; issue 6 was a Greek issue. Caresse planned to do issue 7 on Black American writers and artists, and issue 8 on the Irish, with material collected towards that end. Issue 9 was to include an anthology of poems by Seferis and Elytis with prose by Kanzantzakis and Vanezias. Issue 10 was to be a Near East issue.

Every issue of the magazine consisted of a mix of different size sheets of paper printed by various printers on every colored stock imaginable, and stuffed in a large folder. The folders were 11½ in. by 14 in. 1,000 copies of every issue were printed with 100 or so deluxe editions featuring original artwork by Matisse, Romare Bearden, or others.

For the curious—*Portfolio*'s editorial offices were at 2008 Q Street, N.W. and the Dupont Circle gallery was located at 1606 20th Street, N.W., present home of the Smull Gallery. Caresse's autobiography *The Passionate Years* was reprinted in 1979 by the Ecco Press. The book sells for $6.95 and is available from 1 West 30th St., NY, NY 10001.

Photo by Romolo Marcellini

The Later Caresse Crosby: Her Answer Remained "Yes"

by Harry T. Moore

At the end of her lively autobiography, *The Passionate Years*, Caresse Crosby tells of driving into Washington early in World War II. With the New York, Boston, and Paris phases of her life receding into the background and yet always present in her magnetic personality, she began a new career with the Crosby Gallery of Modern Art, which became the artistic-intellectual headquarters of wartime Washington.

At first associated with David Porter, she set up her gallery on "G" Street near Ninth, in downtown North West, eventually moving to the Dupont Circle area, a district much later to be dominated by hippies. Her gallery parties were attended by members of the government, the diplomatic corps, and the military set, all of them delighted to have a relaxed evening after intense work that often took up all the daylight hours, sometimes seven days a week.

Various notable figures who had never met before became acquainted at Caresse's parties; for example, Henry J. Kaiser, the industrialist who was so prominent in the war effort, first encountered Vice President Henry Wallace at the Crosby Gallery: they were introduced, greeted each other cheerfully, and immediately staged a mock wrestling match. That's the way it was at Caresse's.

She had an exhibition opening every month. She served nothing but martinis, and they were always at hand. But other parties took place several nights each week, and usually Caresse and her friends would go out to eat afterward, to the Salle du Bois, to the Mayflower, to the Occidental, to the Balalaika, to O'Donnell's, or to one of the seafood restaurants on the Potomac. Occasionally we went to my favorite little restaurant, the Trianon, on Seventeenth Street just above Pennsylvania Avenue. It was a small place, with red-checkered tablecloths and a little, old, jovial headwaiter from Luxembourg, Joseph, who always dressed formally, white tie and tailcoat. The cuisine was excellent, particularly the boeuf bourgogne. Once in a while some of my colleagues at the Pentagon ate there with me, and they usually found the place a bit too "native," hence dirty. But Caresse loved the place, and so did one visitor who often joined us there, Henry Miller, an old friend of hers who was on his way to the West Coast, spending some time in Washington with Lepska, the Polish girl he was to marry.

Another friend of Caresse's, the actor Canada Lee, often came to Washington but couldn't eat with us at the Trianon because he was black. Nor could he eat in any "white" restaurant, or attend any white theater, in that center of activity of the second large-scale attempt to save the world for democracy. When we went out to eat with Canada, we would go to an African restaurant, the Bengazi, whose proprietor had no prejudice against whites. Ironically, the largest theater in town, which never let a black onto its stage or into its auditorium, was called the National Theatre.

Caresse determined to break down this barrier. She began by staging *Othello* at her gallery, with Canada magnificently tragic in the title role (I was lucky enough to be cast as Iago, and Caresse was a luminous Desdemona). Canada, now alas too much forgotten, was a superb actor who had scored his greatest success in Richard Wright's *Native Son*. In 1944 Caresse decided to flout the segregation laws and customs by opening a theater in Washington which would have blacks on its stage and in its audience. Those of us who wore uniforms in the daytime were going to put on costumes at night to take part in the defiant project. The first play was to be the Restoration tragedy *Oroonoko* (1695), the drama which Thomas Southerne had adapted from Mrs. Aphra Behn's novel about African slaves revolting against their British masters in the West Indies. Caresse tried to purchase or rent a defunct movie house on Ninth Street, but regrettably was unable to do so. If she had, she might have caused some huge trouble; but it might have been good trouble.

As the war in Europe drew near its end, Caresse wanted to return there, particularly after the Allied troops took over Paris. But the leading figure in the passport bureau of our State Department, a woman known as Ma Shipley, wouldn't let Caresse go to Europe then. One evening when she was grieving over this at one of her cocktail parties, I suggested that she start a new cultural magazine with international overtones—she blazed up at once and began organizing the project. Since paper was difficult to obtain in bulk, she cleverly bought papers of different sizes and colors which would be put into cardboard folders; and she called the magazine *Portfolio*. This was issued for several years under the imprint of the Black Sun Press, taking over the name of the avant-garde publishing house Caresse and Harry Crosby had started in Paris in the 1920s. Soon after the first appearance of *Portfolio*, Ma Shipley had granted the passport, and Caresse brought out editions featuring European writers: one number was devoted to the new French authors, another to Italians, still another to Greeks, introducing to America many of the authors who were to become famous in their own lands and throughout the world in the postwar years. Caresse edited all their work brilliantly and also included that of notable artists. She invited several of us to become associate editors, in some issues calling us assistant editors: Henry Miller, Samuel Rosenberg, and Selden Rodman. I was fortunately able to serve as literary editor, which meant that new books poured in for several years.

The first number of *Portfolio* was ready in the summer of 1945, and Caresse set up a party to celebrate it; the day before the party, V-J Day broke upon us, and there was dancing in the sedate streets of Washington. In a wild crowd at the Balalaika I saw an old friend, Thornton Wilder, in the uniform of a lieutenant colonel. I asked him whether I could bring the girl I was with over to meet him, but with his eager politeness he said he would come over to our table. I took the liberty of inviting him to the *Portfolio* party at Caresse's gallery the next night, where he would for the first time meet David Daiches, who had come to teach at the University of Chicago just after Wilder had left. Wilder appeared at Caresse's, met David Daiches, and even suggested a book to him—which David then proceeded to write. Such episodes were typical of Caresse's gatherings, at which the air was electric with potential creative activity.

A year after the War I married, while still in the Air Force, and my wife and I invited Caresse to visit us for Christmas at Craig Air Force Base, Alabama. She accepted and, at military parties, was as brilliantly successful as ever in conveying her magnetic geniality. In the daytime we virtually closed her in her room, telling her that she must write her autobiography; I even gave her a title, *The Passionate Years*. She wrote a good many of the opening passages of the book there, finishing it not too long afterward, to the benefit of us all. (Eventually the Southern Illinois University Press brought out a paperback edition.) It concluded, Molly Bloomwise, "The answer to the challenge is always '*Yes.*'"

Until her death in 1970, Caresse lived in different parts of the world, untiringly active in furthering her Citizens of the World movement. For a few years she operated out of Greece, from Delphi, the classical-mythical navel of the world. But the Greek government, becoming increasingly reactionary, finally expelled her from that country.

My wife and I sometimes stayed with her in Washington, where she kept her residence, and she came to see us in Wellesley Hills, Massachusetts, and in Carterville, Illinois, where we moved after I had joined the SIU-C faculty; and one or both of us would see her in London, Paris, or Rome. On one of Caresse's several visits to Southern Illinois, she addressed my Fitzgerald-Hemingway class, a special treat for the students. On an earlier occasion she had agreed to talk with the students of my James Joyce course about her old Paris acquaintance, Joyce. But just before we left for Carbondale, a neighbor telephoned and said, "Turn on the TV—quick." We did so, and discovered that President Kennedy had been assassinated. Caresse said, "I won't be able to talk to your class," and I assured her that I would certainly cancel the session on such a day. We went over to Carbondale, and on the way to the classroom I stopped to collect my mail at the English department, where the departmental secretary, Betty Mitchell, said that all classes had been called off for the day.

So Caresse, my wife, and I were left in Carbondale on a terrible day: what could we do? Caresse said, "Why don't we go see Bucky Fuller?" It was a marvelous idea, and we drove to Bucky's dymaxion house which stands out oddly among the Grant-Wood-Midwest-Gothic houses of Carbondale. We were going to see old friends (for, like Caresse, I had known Bucky before either of us came to SIU-C), and it was the best possible thing anyone could have done on that day, for we sat talking quietly with Bucky and Anne Fuller. We had scheduled a party for Caresse in Carterville the next night, and that morning every one of the guests telephoned to ask whether we were going to have the party, and we said we would. And everyone came, except one couple who soon afterward were divorced, and everyone said it was a wonderful gathering, because it was a dreadful time and people needed to be together. Caresse was grand as always, becoming an unforgettable part of the SIU-C community.

Her connection with the university was made permanent when the Morris Library acquired her papers, for the most part connected with the Black Sun Press. The library in those days had money to spend, and Ralph McCoy, then the Librarian (and later Dean of Libraries), decided to try to obtain as much twentieth-century material as he could for Special Collections— why pay thousands of dollars for a one-page letter by a Restoration or Regency author when more recent material was considerably less expensive and would grow in value? I suggested various authors I knew personally or by correspondence, including Lawrence Durrell, Kay Boyle, Richard Aldington, and Francis Stuart. Caresse's papers would make a very fine acquisition, what with all the Black Sun Press's limited editions, original manuscripts, and letters from Hemingway, Joyce, D.H. Lawrence, Hart Crane, Pound, and others, as well as the portraits of Caresse by noted painters. But Caresse was cagey.

I can recall that Ralph McCoy and I once telephoned her from his office to the castle she had bought in Italy. Later she wrote me a letter saying that she didn't want her papers to be deposited at any library where black students couldn't have access to them. This was in the early 1960s, when civil-rights advocates were battling for desegregation—much of their work has recently (late 1970s) been undone by Nixon and Ford appointees to the Supreme Court—and perhaps Caresse felt that the term "Southern" in Southern Illinois was suspicious; she hadn't met any black faculty members at our parties (I don't think there were any then), and when we had gone to Carbondale restaurants she hadn't seen any black students eating in them. I wrote a letter telling her that there was no segregation on the SIU-C campus, that black students were allowed access everywhere. Caresse finally sold the papers to SIU-C, and various scholars have come here to consult them, crediting SIU-C in their books for whatever use of them they made.

When Caresse wanted to sell her castle, Roccasinabalda, she suggested that SIU-C might wish to buy it. President Delyte Morris heard that I was about to leave for Europe and invited me to breakfast to discuss the castle; he asked me to make a report on it. I said I knew nothing technically about buildings, particularly castles, but he assured me that that didn't matter: he wanted to know what kind of summer school it might make. So, from Rome, I went with Caresse in her chauffeur-driven car to Roccasinabalda, about an hour's drive northeast. The castle, set wonderfully on mountainside cliffs, has towers and battlemented walls that provide a massive view of the valleys of the Sabine Mountains. When we arrived at the castle gate, members of Caresse's household staff came down to the car and carried her up the sloping entranceway to the castle itself. This might seem a revival of the tradition of welcoming the grand lady, but the ceremony was performed only because the condition of Caresse's heart made it impossible for her to walk uphill.

The castle was full of young people staying there, painting and writing; Caresse had even put in a swimming pool. My report to President Morris was non-technical, merely a subjective appreciation of the place, but the next time he went to Europe, he and Mrs. Morris went to see it, along with several other people, including John Rendleman, then Vice President at the SIU-C campus. Caresse liked the Morrises and Rendlemans, but she mischievously and considerably raised her originally-quoted price, so the party left politely, but without further discussion of the matter. Years later, Bucky Fuller's daughter told me why Caresse had virtually doubled the price, but let it not be mentioned here.

Caresse died in Rome on 24 January 1970, at the age of seventy-seven. I learned of her death almost at once by telephone, and wrote the obituary for the *Times* (London). On 18 February, a group of us met for a memorial gathering at the Gotham Book Mart, with Bucky Fuller (who had been active with Caresse in her Citizens of the World movement) as master of ceremonies. Frances Steloff of the Gotham said that Caresse always represented the joy of life, and her gaiety and charm should always be remembered, among her positive achievements. Many of her other friends spoke of her reminiscently, always mentioning her brightness; Sam Rosenberg pointed out that she was never malicious. Three friends who couldn't attend sent tape recordings from California: Kay Boyle, Henry Miller, and Anais Nin. Bucky Fuller's son-in-law, Rob Snyder, showed his evocative film of Caresse at Roccasinabalda, with Ezra Pound and others, and with flashbacks showing Caresse at other places, with companions ranging all the way from Salvador Dali to Bob Hope.

When I returned to SIU-C a few days later, Ed Brown invited me to appear with him on the university's television station, and we talked about Caresse and showed a film made of her on one of her visits to Carbondale, in which Ralph Bushee (former Rare Books Librarian) and I discuss adventurous publishing with her. We are fortunate in having these films of her, and the title of Rob Snyder's provides a perfect epitaph for its subject: *Always Yes, Caresse*. □

We're the Only Colored People Here

by Gwendolyn Brooks

When they went out to the car there were just the very finest bits of white powder coming down with an almost comical little ethereal hauteur, to add themselves to the *really* important, piled-up masses of their kind.

And it wasn't cold.

Evelina laughed happily to herself: it was pleasant out, and tonight she and Paul were very close to each other.

He held the door open for her—instead of going on around to the driving side, getting in, and leaving her to get in at her side as best she could. When he took this way of calling her *lady* and informing her of his love, and he took it only on special occasions such as these movie Saturdays, she felt precious, protected, delicious. She gave him an excited look of gratitude. He smiled indulgently.

"Want it to be the Eagle again?"

"Oh, no, no. Paul. Let's not go there tonight. I feel too grand inside to be going there tonight. Gum-smacking. Haw-hawing. Cursing. Feet. Let's go downtown?"

She had to suggest that with a question mark at the end, always. Usually he had three protests. Too hard to park. Too much money. Too many white folks. And tonight she could really expect a *no* because he had come out in his blue work shirt. There was a spot of apricot juice on the collar, too. His shoes were not shined . . . But he nodded!

"We've never been to the World Playhouse," she said timidly and all in one breath. "They have a good picture. I'd feel like I was—somebody—going there. On Michigan and all. Around all those high and mighty stores. And at night, too."

"You really wanta?"

"Oh. Please!"

"Sure."

It wasn't like other movie houses. People from the Studebaker Theatre which, as Evelina whispered to Paul, was "all locked-arms" with the World Playhouse, were strolling up and down the lobby, laughing softly, smoking with gentle grace.

"There must be a play going on in there and this is probably an intermission," Evelina whispered again.

"I don't know why you feel you got to whisper," whispered Paul. "Nobody else is whispering in here." He looked around, resentfully, wanting to see a few, just a few, colored faces. There weren't any—other than his own.

Evelina laughed a nervous, defiant little laugh, and spoke loudly this time. "There certainly isn't any *reason* to whisper. Silly, huh?"

The strolling women were cleverly gowned. Some of them had flowers or "flashers" (Evelina) in their hair. They looked—*cooked*. Well-cared-for. And as though they had never seen a roach or a bed bug or a rat in their lives. Or gone without heat for a week. And the men had even edges. They were men, Evelina thought, who wouldn't stoop to fret over less than a thousand dollars.

"We're the only colored people here," said Paul.

She got mad at him—a little. "Oh, hell. Who in hell cares?"

"Well, what I want to know is, where do you pay the damn fares."

"There's the box office. Go on up."

He went on up. It was closed.

"Well," sighed Evelina. "I guess the picture has already started. But we can't have missed much. Go on up to that girl at the candy counter and ask her where we should pay our money."

He didn't want to do that. The girl was lovely and blonde and cold-eyed, and her arms were akimbo, and the set of her head was elegant. No one else was at the counter.

"Well. We'll wait a minute. And see . . . "

Evelina almost hated him. Coward! She ought to flounce over to the girl herself—show him up . . .

The people in the lobby tried to avoid looking curiously at two shy Negroes wanting desperately not to seem shy. The white women looked at the Negro woman in her outfit with which no special fault could be found, but which made them think, somehow, of close rooms, and wee, close lives. They looked at her hair. They liked to see a *dark* colored girl with long hair. They were always slightly surprised, but agreeably so, when they did. They supposed it was the hair that had got her that tall, yellowish, good-looking Negro man.

The white men tried not to look at the Negro man in the blue work shirt, the Negro man without a tie.

An usher opened a door of the World Playhouse part and ran quickly down the few steps that led from it to the lobby. Paul opened his mouth.

"Say, fella. Where do we get the tickets for the movie?"

The usher glanced at Paul's feet before answering. Then he said coolly, but not unpleasantly, "I'll take the money."

They were able to get in.

And the picture! Oh, Evelina was so glad that they had not gone to the Eagle! Here was technicolor. And the love story was sweet. And there was classical music that silvered its way into you and made your back cold. And the theatre itself! It was no palace, no such great shakes as the Tivoli out their way, for instance (where many colored people went every night). But you felt good sitting there, yes, good, and as if, when you left it, you would be going home to a sweet-smelling apartment with flowers on little gleaming tables; and thick rich rugs; and wonderful silver on night blue velvet, in chests; and crackly sheets; and lace spreads on such beds as you saw at Marshall Field's. Instead of back to your kit'n't apt , with the garbage of your floor's six families in a big can just outside your door, and the gray sound of little gray feet scratching away from it as you drag up those flights of narrow complaining stairs.

Paul pressed her hand. "We oughta do this more often."

And again. "Yes, we'll have to come here often. And go to plays, too. I mean, at the Blackstone, and Studebaker, and Opera House."

She pressed back, smiling beautifully to herself in the darkness. Though she knew that once the spell was over it would be a year, two years, more, before he would return to the World Playhouse. And he might never to a legitimate play. But she was learning to love moments. To love moments for themselves.

When the picture was over, and the lights revealed them for what they were, the Negroes stood up among the furs and good cloth and faint perfume, looked about them eagerly, They hoped they would meet no cruel eyes. They hoped no one would look intruded upon. They had enjoyed the picture so, they were so happy, they wanted to laugh, to say warmly to the other outgoers. "Good, huh? Wasn't it swell?"–If only no one would look intruded upon . . . . . .

Pablo Picasso

Paul Verlaine. Paris, June 5, 1945.
Wash, pen and ink, 11 5/8 x 8 1/4"
On extended loan to The Museum of Modern Art, New York.

The Staff of Life

by Henry Miller

Bread: prime symbol. Try and find a good loaf. You can travel fifty thousand miles in America without once tasting a piece of good bread. Americans don't care about good bread. They are dying of inanition but they go on eating bread without substance, bread without flavor, bread without vitamins, bread without life. Why? Because the very core of life is contaminated. If they knew what good bread was they would not have such wonderful machines on which they lavish all their time, energy and affection. A plate of false teeth means much more to an American than a loaf of good bread. Here is the sequence: poor bread, bad teeth, indigestion, constipation, halitosis, sexual starvation, disease and accidents, the operating table, artificial limbs, spectacles, baldness, kidney and bladder trouble, neurosis, psychosis, schizophrenia, war and famine. Start with the American loaf of bread so beautifully wrapped in cellophane and you end on the scrap heap at forty-five. The only pace to find a good loaf of bread is in the ghettos. Wherever there is a foreign quarter there is apt to be good bread. Wherever there is a Jewish grocer or delicatessen you are almost certain to find an excellent loaf of bread. The dark Russian bread, light in weight, found only rarely on this huge continent, is the best bread of all. No vitamins have been injected into it by laboratory specialists in conformance with the latest food regulations. The Russian just naturally likes good bread, because he also likes caviar and vodka and other good things. Americans are whiskey, gin and beer drinkers who long ago lost their taste for food. And losing that they have also lost their taste for life. For enjoyment. For good conversation. For everything worth while, to put it briefly.

What do I find wrong with America? Everything. I begin at the beginning, with the staff of life: bread. If the bread is bad the whole life is bad. Bad? Rotten, I should say. Like that piece of bread only twenty-four hours old which is good for nothing except perhaps to fill up a hole. Good for target practice maybe. Or shuttlecock and duffle board. Even soaked in urine it is unpalatable; even perverts shun it. Yet millions are wasted advertising it. Who are the men engaged in this wasteful pursuit? Drunkards and failures for the most part. Men who have prostituted their talents in order to help further the decay and dissolution of our once glorious Republic.

Here is one of the latest widely advertised products: Hollywood Bread. On the red, white and blue cellophane jacket in which it is wrapped, this last word in bread from the American bakeries, it reads as follows:

BAKED WITH

whole wheat flour, clear wheat flour, water, non-diastic malt, yeast, salt, honey, caramel, whole rye flour, yeast food, stone ground oatmeal, soya flour, gluten flour, barley flour, sesame seed, and a small quantity of dehydrated (water free) vegetables including celery, lettuce, pumpkin, cabbage, carrots, spinach, parsley, sea kelp, added for flavor only.

The only thing missing from this concoction is powdered diamonds. How does it taste? Much like any other American product. Of course, this is a reducing bread of which one should eat two slices a day three times a day and not ask how it tastes. Grow thin, as in Hollywood, and be thankful it doesn't taste worse. That's the idea. For several days now I have been trying to get a whiff of some of those ingredients—sea kelp especially—which were included "for flavor only." Why they were not added for health too I don't know. Naturally all these delicious-sounding items amount to about one ten-thousandth part of the loaf. And on the second day, stale, flat and unprofitable, this marvelous new bread is no more attractive to the palate or the stomach than any other loaf of American bread. On the second day it is good for replacing a missing tile on the roof. Or to make a scratchboard for the cat.

The second day! If the first is given to creation, to light, let us say, the second (in America) is given up to garbage. Every second day is garbage day in America. I know because I have had lots to do with garbage. I've hauled it, for pay, and I've eaten it upon necessity. I learned to distinguish between one kind of bread and another by salvaging dry crusts from the garbage can. I don't know which is worse—the day of creation, when everything turns to gas and bilge, with its concomitants dandruff, constipation, halitosis, false teeth, artificial limbs, psychic impotency, and so on, or the second day, given up to garbage, when all creation turns out to be nothing but a mirage and a disillusionment. It has been said, and I have no doubt it is true, that the garbage accumulated by one big American city would feed certain of the little countries of Europe handsomely. I know no quicker way to kill off the warring nations of Europe than to feed them our garbage. The pygmies might thrive on it, possibly even the Chinese coolie, who is supposed to thrive on anything, but I cannot see the Danes, the Swiss, the Swedes, the Greeks, the Albanians, or the Austrians thriving on it. No Sir. I would sooner feed them buzzards than the left-overs from the American table. Already, with our canned food products, our cold storage meat, our dehydrated vegetables, we have brought about a tremendous deterioration in these sturdy people of Europe. From these to the machine and thence to war is but a step. Then, famine, plague, pestilence, dung heaps. And monuments, of course. All sorts of monuments. Done by second or third rate artists.

The care and affection which once was bestowed on the human body now goes to the machines. The machines get the best food, the best attention. Machines are expensive; human lives are cheap. Never in the history of the world was life cheaper than it is today. (And no pyramids to show for it either.) How natural, then, that the staff of life should be utterly without value. I begin with bread and I shall end with bread. I say we make the foulest bread in all the world. We pass it off like fake diamonds. We advertise it and sterilize it and protect it from all the germs of life. We make a manure which we eat before we have had time to eliminate it. We not only have failed God, tricked Nature, debased Man, but we have cheated the birds of the air with our corrupt staff of life. Everytime I fling the stale bread over the cliff I beg forgiveness of the birds for offering them our American bread. Perhaps that is why they are not singing any more as they used to when I was a child. The birds are pining and drooping. It's not the war, for they have never participated in our carnages. It's the bread. The stale, flat, unprofitable bread of the second day. It shortens their wing-span, weakens their umbrella-ribs, reduces the scope of their swoop, blunts their beaks, deteriorates their vision, and finally—it kills their song! If you don't believe me, ask any ornithologist. It's a known fact. And how Americans love facts!

Another fact.... Food, when it is not enjoyed, kills. The best diet in the world is useless if the patient has no appetite, no gusto, no sensuality. On the whole, Americans eat without pleasure. They eat because the bell rings three times a day. (I omit mention of the clay eaters of the South and other poor whites who live on rats, snakes, and cow-dung.) They don't eat because they love food. To prove it you have only to shove a glass of whiskey before them. See which they reach for first! And now, with vitamins and all the other life-savers, food has become even less important. Why bother trying to squeeze a bit of life out of our worn-out products of the soil? Why pretend? Throw anything down the hatch to stop the gnawing and swallow a dozen vitamins. That way you'll make sure you've had your proper dose of the vital essentials. Should the vitamins fail, see a surgeon. From there to the sanitarium. And from there to the nut-house—or the dung heap. Be sure to get a Hollywood funeral. They're the loveliest, the duckiest, the most sanitary, the most inspiring. And no more expensive than ordinary ground burial. You can, if you like, have your dear lost one propped up in a natural reclining position, her cheeks rouged, a cigarette to her lips, and a phonograph record talking to you just as she once talked to you in life. The most wonderful fake imaginable. Jolly, what? O death, where is thy sting? What's more, she can be kept that way for an unspeakably long period; the cigarette is guaranteed not to rot away before the lips or the buttocks. You can come back and have a second, a third, a twenty-fifth look at the beloved. Still smoking a cigarette. Or you can have her reading a book, the *Iliad*, say, or the *Bhagavad Gita*—something uplifting like that.

I remember when I used to be served a slice of home-made bread with butter and sugar smeared over it. Glorious days! That bread really had a taste. *Schmecht gut, nichtwahr? Yah! Sehr gut. Wunderbar. Ausgezeichnet.* With a piece of bread like that I used to sit and read *Pinocchio* or *Alice Through the Looking Glass* or Hans Christian Andersen or *The Heart of a Boy*. Mothers had time in those days to make good bread with their own hands, and still do the thousand and one things which motherhood demands of a woman. To-day they haven't time to do anything, and hardly a bloody mother in the bloody land knows how to bake a loaf of bread. Mother gets up early now to work in an office or a factory. She's busy doing nothing all day, which is to say—earning a living. Earning a living has nothing to do with living. It's the belt line to the grave, without a transfer or a stopover. A one-way passage via the frying pan and the cookerless cooker. A child is an accident—bad rubber goods or else too much drink and recklessness. Any way, it's there and it has to be fed. You don't bake bread for accidents, do you? And why bother to produce milk from the breast when the cows are working over-time for the dairy companies of America?

Day by day the morons, epileptics and schizoids multiply. By accident, like everything else. Nothing is planned in America except improvements. And all improvements are for the machine. When a plenum is reached war is declared. Then the machine really gets going. War is a Roman Holiday for the machine. Man becomes even less than nothing then. The machine is well fed. The food products become plastics and plastics are what make the world go round. Better to have a good steering wheel than a good stomach. In the old days an army advanced on its stomach; now it advances in tanks or spitfires or super-fortresses. Civilians never advance. Civilians always rot and help make insurance companies richer.

But bread.... Let's not forget, it's bread we want—and children that are not accidents brought about by defective rubber or bathtub gin. How to get it? Bread, I mean. By putting a monkey wrench in the machine. By going backwards on all fours, like giraffes with broken necks. By praying for life now and not hereafter. By exercising freedom and not inventing four, five or six freedoms won by the slaughter and starvation of twenty or thirty millions. Begin today by baking your own bread. First of all you need a stove. A wood or a coal stove. Not a gas range. Not an electric apparatus. Then let the flies in. Then roll your sleeves up and get your hands in the dough. Lick your fingers. Never mind if you lose your job. Eat your bread first, then maybe you won't want to work in an office or a factory. Life begins with bread. And a prayer. Not a begging prayer, but a prayer of thanks. Don't bless the block-busters. Bless God for his favors—air, water, sun, moon. God wants you to enjoy the bread of life. He never meant you to go out all day working at a job you loathe so that you can buy a loaf of store bread wrapped in cellophane. God gave us germs as well as air and water and sun. Germs attack only what is already rotting. Man is rotting in every fibre of his being: that is why he is a prey to germs. And that is why he is allergic to everything that is for his own good.

Before Communism was there was Communion and before that there was God and God said let there be light and there was light. And what a glorious light it was. It lasted for aeons, and then came the scientific age and darkness fell upon the land everywhere. Now everything can be proved backwards and out of existence and instead of soaring with our own wings or on the backs of our giant birds we make things of metal and plastics which spread havoc and destruction in their wake. We throw bones to the dogs and eat the dogs instead of the bones. Not one step has been taken towards improving the flow of milk from the mammary glands. Only mothers and wet nurses give milk, whereas with time and experimentation every one could give milk and the food problem would be solved for eternity. We wouldn't even need to sit down to eat: now and then a step-ladder might be necessary, but nothing more. Why hasn't any one thought of that? Is it so improbable? Ants have their milk cows—how did that happen? Anyway, with human milk the universal food, with manna falling from heaven, and nectar and ambrosia for dessert, think what a lot of work would be eliminated. Think too of the gratitude the animals would show, once they got on to the new scheme of things. All we would need, men and animals, would be one huge grass plot. No more dairy companies, no more containers, no more bottles, plates, knives and forks, spoons, pots, pans, stoves. The solution of the food problem would throw a monkey wrench into the entire economic and social system; our mores would change, our religions would disappear, our money become valueless. One can hardly imagine what the cause for war would then be, though doubtless a good excuse will always be found.

Outside of the foreign quarters, then, take it for granted that there is no good bread to be had. Every foreign group has introduced into our life some good substantial bread, even the Scandinavians. (Excepting the English, I should add, but then we hardly think of them as foreign, though why we shouldn't I don't know, for when you think of it the English are even less like us than the Poles or Latvians.) In a Jewish restaurant you usually have a basket filled with all kinds of bread from which to choose. In a typical American restaurant, should you ask for rye, whole wheat or any other kind of bread but the insidious, unwholesome, and unpalatable white, you get white bread. If you insist on rye bread you get whole wheat. If you insist on whole wheat you get graham bread. Once in a great while you come upon nut bread; this is always a sheer accident. Raisin bread is a sort of decoy to lure you into eating unpalatable, perifidious and debilitating white bread. When in doubt go to a Jewish restaurant or delicatessen; if necessary, stand up and eat a sandwich made of sour rye, sweet butter, pastrami and pickle. A Jewish sandwich contains more food value than an eighty-five cent meal in the ordinary American restaurant. With a glass of water to wash it down you can walk away feeling fit. Don't sit down and eat a Jewish meal, because the Jews are bad cooks despite their great concern about food, which amounts to a neurosis. It is curious, though, how the desire to survive has made the Jews keen about preserving the staff of life. It is even more curious that they are just as much riddled with disease as the other members of the community—more so, in fact, judging purely from personal observation. They not only have all the physical ailments which other white peoples are heir to but they have all the mental and nervous ailments. Often they have everything at once, and then they concentrate upon food with even greater acuity and despair. It is only when they become revolutionary that they begin to lose interest in food. The real American, on the other hand, though totally unrevolutionary at heart, seems born with an indifference to food. One can serve a white American food which would make an Igorote turn up his nose. Americans can eat garbage, provided you sprinkle it liberally with ketchup, mustard, chili sauce, tabasco sauce, cayenne pepper, or any other condiment which destroys the original flavor of the dish. On the other hand, olive oil which the French eschew when preparing salads because it has too strong a flavor, Americans hardly ever use in their salads. Nothing on God's earth is more uninviting, more anaemic, than the American salad. At its best it is like refined puke. The lettuce is a joke: even a canary would refuse to touch it. This concoction, mind you, is usually served before the meal, together with the coffee which is cold by the time you are ready to drink it. The moment you **sit down at a table** in the ordinary American restaurant, the moment you begin scanning the menu, the waitress asks you what you wish to drink. (If by chance you should say "cocoa," the whole kitchen will be thrown out of gear.) To this question I usually counter with another: "Do you have anything but white bread?" If the answer is not a flat No, it is: "We have whole wheat," or "We have graham bread." Whereupon I usually mumble under my breath: "You can stick that up your ass!" When she says, "What did you say?" I reply, "Do you have rye bread by any chance?" Then, before she can say no, I launch into an elaborate explanation of the fact that I don't mean by rye bread the ordinary rye bread, which is no better than white, graham, or whole wheat, but a succulent, tasty, dark, sour rye such as the Russians and the Jews serve. At the mention of these two suspect nationalities a scowl spreads over her face. While she is saying in her most sarcastic voice that she is sorry but they do not have that kind of rye bread or any rye bread, for that matter, I begin asking about the fruit, what kinds of fruit, fresh fruit, they have on hand, knowing damned well that they haven't any. Nine times out of ten her answer will be: "We have apple pie, and peach pie." ("Stick it up your ass!") "I beg your pardon?" she says. "Yes, fruit . . . you know, the kind that grows on trees . . . apples, pears, bananas, plums, oranges . . . something with skin on it that you peel." Whereupon a light dawns and she hastens to interpolate: "Oh, but we have apple sauce!" ("Fuck your apple sauce!") "I beg pardon?" Here I look leisurely round the room, surveying the shelves, the counter, the pie plates. Finally, resting my gaze upon a bowl of artificial fruit, I exclaim with glee: "Like that over there, only *real*!"

Sometimes, upon scanning the menu and knowing that it will only give me a belly-ache, I ask immediately if they can serve me a large bowl of fresh fruit. Here, incidentally, let me call attention to the dishes of mixed fruit prepared early in the morning which stand rotting in disgusting sweet canned juices until lunch or dinner hour. In the Automat type of restaurant one sees the counter piled with these vile stews. These, like the salads mentioned a moment ago, and like the pies frabricated by the wholesale bakers (who are probably responsible for more deaths than all our wars **put together**), are peculiar to the American temperament. There is not the least food value in any of them. The salad is at its worst when served in one of those delightful little inns run by spinsters in villages of imaginary charm, such as one is supposed to find in Vermont, Maryland, or Connecticut. Here everything looks immaculate and is immaculate, and therefore without value, without flavor, without joy. One suddenly feels like a canary which has been castrated and can no longer warble or differentiate between seed and salad. **Beginning with this obscene salad** one just knows that the meal is going to end with a charming little dessert such as prune whip or vanilla ice cream. To ask for a grape or a herring in one of these places is like committing sacrilege. There are certain things you must never ask for in an American restaurant. Never. One is good sour rye such as the Russians and the Jews make. Another is a cup of strong coffee. (Exceptions: French and Italian restaurants, and Louisiana. In Louisiana you can get a cup of coffee that is like liquid dynamite. But it tastes good; it has chicory in it. And chicory is excellent, despite all opinion to the contrary.) A third is cheese. A fourth is grapes. A fifth is nuts. Never have I seen a bowl of assorted and uncracked nuts put on the table in an American restaurant. Now and then, rarely, very rarely, one sees nuts in an American home. Usually, however, they are there as decoration. The fruit likewise. Fruit and nuts belong on the sideboard for the children, when there are any, to nibble at. The mixed fruit, or fruit salad, as they have the impudence to call it in America, reaches the height of abomination in the arm-chair Automat type of restaurant. Have you ever noticed the derelicts who frequent these eating places, sitting in the show window munching their lunch or dinner? Is there any more lugubrious sight on earth? (The corollary to it is the cheap traveling salesman type of hotel where all day long the weary commercial traveler sits in an enormous leather armchair staring vacantly out on the street. This is the type who gets orders for useless commodities which the American slave toils his ass off to accumulate, which he sells to his own kind and pretends thereby that he is earning an honest living. This is the type that votes the Democratic or Republican ticket year in and year out, in lean years and fat years, in war and in peace, and is always complaining that business is bad. This is the most traveled man in the world, and yet he knows nothing, absolutely nothing, and brags about it. This is the type who when you mention China says immediately—"coolies." If there is any more ignominious coolie than the traveling salesman I have yet to know him. The fact that he reads the "Digest" or some other compilation of facts gives him the illusion that he is informed and a useful member of society.)

But it's the pie that takes the cake. The pie is at its worst in the Greek restaurant, often called "New York Cafe," and encountered in every village and hamlet throughout the length and breadth of the land. In fact, every**thing is at its worst in** this type of eating place. But it's here that the pie becomes positively obsessive. Often there is nothing to offer the weary traveler but pie. There they stand, row upon row of pie plates, all filled with gangrene and arsenic. The crust looks like scurf and is scurf, usually of the finest rancid grease made by the Criscomaniacs of America. Here and there one can detect in a whole pie a piece of fruit, such as apple or peach; it is surrounded by a clot of phlegm swimming in a mess of undefinable paste. The piece of apple or peach is sourish, bilious, gaseous, having no more resemblance to the apple or peach in its native state than corn whiskey has to corn on the cob. The Greek proprietor delights in serving white Americans this unholy dish; he despises them for eating it, but, canny businessman that he is, he believes in giving them what they ask for. He himself has a totally different cuisine, a damned good one, too, I must say, if you ever make a friend of him and get invited to his home. On his table you will see olives, real olives, okra, olive oil, fruits of all kinds, nuts, rice, vine leaves, the tenderest lamb imaginable, wines of all kind, including retsina, and cognac, Greek cognac, and other delicacies.

Let us digress here a moment. . . . How is it that Americans, composed of nothing but foreign nationalities, living amongst people accustomed to the most varied cuisines, people who have made an art of cooking from time immemorial, continue to be the worst cooks in the world, continue to open one foul restaurant after another? Explain it, if you can. To me it's an enigma. The more mixed becomes the blood in our veins, the more American we become. And by American I mean the more set, crass, conservative, prejudiced, stupid, narrow-minded, unexperimental and unrevolutionary. In every big city we have Chinese, Italian, French, Hungarian, Russian, German, Swedish restaurants. Do we learn anything from these skilled restaurateurs? No, not a thing. We go our way, serving pies, mixed fruit salads, hamburgers, baked beans, steak and onions, vicious veal cutlets, whether breaded or unbreaded, and so on. Has any one ever had a good stew in an American restaurant? The peasants of Europe have thrived on stews for centuries. Here a stew means a couple of spoonfuls of superannuated meat swimming in a tiny pool of grease and bilge with bloated potatoes as a garniture. One hasn't begun to eat when the meal is over. It's an imaginary stew at the best. And the most imaginary part of it is the vegetables without which no stew is complete: leeks, carrots, turnips, onions, celery, parsley, and so on. If you find a tiny piece of any other vegetable than the potato you are indeed a lucky individual.

All right, steak then! Steak is the great American dish. Steak and onions. Fine. Nothing better, I say. Where can you get it? I mean without paying $2.50 per person! The first and only time I got the real flavor of steak was when I passed through Denver. Up till then I never knew what a real steak tasted like. The meat companies are for convincing us that meat from the refrigerator, meat that has been on ice several years, is the best meat of all. The whole world is being shipped and fed the cold storage meat, thanks to Armour & Co. and their subsidiary hog-butchers. In France I used to eat *filet de boeuf* practically every other day. It cost, for one person, a good portion, mind you, from twelve to eighteen cents, at the rate of exchange prevailing in the late thirties. It was delicious meat, and I knew how to prepare it. (Americans as a rule know only how to spoil a good piece of meat in cooking it.) When I came to America, in 1940, I went to the butcher one day and asked for my customary *filet de boeuf*. A piece for two people came to $1.10, so help me God. I couldn't believe my ears. And this was in a cheap butcher shop on Third Avenue, New York. Christ only knows what it would have cost in the Park Avenue neighborhood. I took it home and I fried it. I did everything just as I used to at the Villa Seurat. I had wine with it too, the best I could buy for $1.25 the bottle. I also had grapes and nuts, and a salad prepared with the best olive oil. I had several kinds of cheese, including roquefort and camembert. Despite all precautions the meal didn't taste the same. There was something lacking. As a matter of fact, all the essentials were lacking. A piece of lettuce grown in America is like a piece of lettuce grown in France only in looks and name. American fruit, the most sensational looking fruit in the world (barring the tropics), is practically tasteless compared to the sicklier looking European fruits. American cheeses look delicious, and God knows the Kraft brothers have tickled them up inordinately, but they do not have the flavor of the cheeses they are made to imitate. A stale piece of camembert in a dirty French restaurant is worth a whole box of beautiful looking fresh Camembert put out by the crafty cheese-makers of Wisconsin. The flat Dutch cheeses are of course still more flat and tasteless when you eat them in America, being as they are the product of the most pampered cows in all the world. Wines, even when they are good, and in the realm of ordinary table wines America makes some of the best, do not taste as good as in Europe, perhaps because the atmosphere, the violence, the tempo of American life destroys whatever blessings wine confers.

Wine with the meal, in America, produces the wrong result. What is required, when attempting to digest American food, is strong spirits—whiskey, gin, cocktails. The correct procedure is to get soused beforehand; this enables one to eat without noticing how vile the food is. It gets one flushed and excited, and the food is forgotten. It makes one argumentative, which aids in bringing on indigestion and dyspepsia, flatulence, constipation, hemorrhoids, and finally the operating table. Whichever road you take, in America, you always wind up at the surgeon's door. If you buy an automobile it's the surgeon you have to reckon with eventually. If you take a good-paying job, it's the surgeon who will bleed you to death. If you economize and eat in arm-chair restaurants, or the Greek restaurants (where American food is served—not the real Greek restaurant!), you meet the surgeon sooner or later,

generally sooner. If you take to the soil and live the outdoor life, you first must have all your teeth pulled out and plates inserted. Farmers have about the worst teeth of all, even worse than factory workers. They have all the physical ailments, too, and are often as not undernourished. Farmers die of inanition in the midst of plenty. There isn't anything you can do, in America, by way of earning a living whereby you can escape dire taxation, disease, accident, misery and humiliation. At the end of every road stands the surgeon, who is for Americans what Nemesis was for the Greeks. The whole culture of America springs from two lunatics: the Marquis de Sade and Sacher Masoch. Justice, always retributive, is apotheosized by the surgeon. His henchmen are the dentists. If you have an ache or pain never mention it to the dentist, or he will immediately extract all your teeth. Nowadays even cowboys are proud of their false teeth. Scarcely any hardworking American, however splendid his physique, is without plates or bridges after forty. Hardly any normal American has a full head of hair after forty. Hardly any American over twenty-one, whether he works hard or takes it easy, is without eye-glasses. Almost every American suffers from hemorrhoids. Practically every American over forty has a bad heart. Cancer, syphilis, arthritis, tuberculosis, schizophrenia are so prevalent that we accept them as part of the bargain—i.e., the American way of life. Nearly every family boasts of one moron among its members, one lunatic, one drunkard, one pervert. All the food advertisements boast of the vitamin contents of their products. All the medicaments advertised boast of their cure for every thing under the sun. It is obvious that our foods lack the proper vitamins, just as it is obvious that in employing these health foods so rich in vitamins we nevertheless are afflicted with all the diseases known to man. We die young, mortgaged to the hilt, insolvent, despite all the insurance policies issued by all the insurance companies whose tentacles reach into every avenue of commercial and industrial life. It is also evident that, despite the fact that this is the land of opportunity where freedom reigns, where every one has the right to worship and the right to vote for the wrong candidate, that the zest for life is so low that less than one child per family is now produced, except among certain Indian tribes, certain religious communities, certain strata of poor whites, and among the Negroes as a whole. Even the Jews, known for their big families as well as their good bread, are beginning to have less children—in America. And when the Jew loses his desire to perpetuate his own kind there must indeed be something seriously wrong with the national life. In the poorest countries of Europe the Jew still remained fertile; here, with everything in his grasp, except recognition by the Gentiles, he withers away. Only among the American Indians, and there only in certain tribes, is the population on the increase. It is said that this is due in part to the practice of polygamy. And here we touch another tender subject, one almost as potent as bread. I mean the fear among native white Americans of indulging in any other form of marriage but that sponsored by the Christian churches. Why not polygamy? Why not polyandry? Why not any kind of marriage, including love marriages? With polygamy the Mormons were fast on the way to building an empire. Nobody can say that the Mormons are, or ever were, an undesirable element in the great American community. They were and still are one of the few communities in this country where poverty is relatively unknown. They produce less criminals than other parts of the country—and less morons, and less idiots, and less trouble of any nature. And God knows they were never, never more immoral than the other members of the community. On the contrary, they were not only more law-abiding, more peaceful, more prosperous, more social-minded and far-visioned than the other communities of America, but they were absolutely more moral in the strictest sense of the word, that is, in the sense that they actually practised what they preached.

But to get back to bread ... Today the mailman brought three kinds of bread: Italian bread, a milk loaf, and pumpernickel. (No sour rye, of course, no corn bread.) The bread comes from Monterey, the nearest town, which is fifty miles away. In Monterey there is no Jewish grocer or delicatessen, worse luck. In Monterey there are Mexicans, Portuguese and Filipinos . . . well, among other things they have all our bad habits. Nobody in Monterey has a good slice of bread to eat. Nor in Carmel either, unless it's Robinson Jeffers, and that would be a sacramental bread. Just outside of Carmel lives Edward Weston, the photographer. And that leads me to speak of another kind of bread: photographic bread. Have you ever noticed that even the photographic bread tastes poorly? Have you ever seen a piece of bread photographed by our advertising maniacs which you would like to bite into? I haven't. Edward Weston could undoubtedly make you the most wonderful photographic bread conceivable—*but could you eat it?* The bread you hang on your wall is not the bread you want to eat at table. Even a piece of **bread by Man Ray** would prove unpalatable, particularly if he just happened to be reading his favorite author, the Marquis de Sade. Sacher Masoch might have made a good bread, if he had lived long enough. It has a Kosher sound, *Sacher Masoch*. But in the long run I have a feeling it would make one morbid and introspective, this Sacher Masoch bread.

I have now found that the only way to eat our most unwholesome, unpalatable and unappetizing American bread, the staff of our unsavory and monotonous life, is to adopt the following procedure. This is a recipe, so please follow instructions to the letter.

To begin with, accept any loaf that is offered you without question, even if it is not wrapped in cellophane, even if it contains no kelp. Throw it in the back of the car with the oil can and the grease rags; if possible, bury it under a sack of coal, *bituminous coal*. As you climb up the road to your home, drop it in the mud a few times and dig your heels into it. If you have a dog with you, let him pee on it now and then. When you get to the house, and after you have prepared the other dishes, take a huge carving knife and rip the loaf from stem to stern. Then take one whole onion, peeled or unpeeled, one carrot, one stalk of celery, one huge piece of garlic, one sliced apple, a herring, a handful of anchovies, a sprig of parsley, and an old toothbrush and shove them into the disembowelled guts of the bread. Over these pour first a thimbleful of kerosene, a dash of Lavoris and just a wee bit of Clorox; then sprinkle guts liberally with the following—molasses, honey, orange marmalade, vanilla, soy bean sauce, tabasco sauce, ketchup and arnica. Over this add a layer of chopped nuts, assorted nuts, of course, a few bay leaves (whole), some marjoram, and a stick of licorice cut into fine pieces. Put the loaf in the oven for ten minutes and serve. If it is still lacking in taste whip up a chili con carne piping hot and mix bread with it until it becomes a thick gruel. If this fails, piss on it and throw it to the dog. But under no circumstances feed it to the birds. The birds of North America are already on the decline, as I pointed out earlier. Their beaks have become dull, their wing-span shortened; they are pining and drooping, moulting in season and out. Above all, they no longer sing as they used to; they make sour notes, they bleat instead of tweeting, and sometimes, when the fogs set in, they have even been heard to cackle and wheeze. □

Manet In Merkers

"Soldiers looking at a painting by the French impressionist Edouard Manet in the collection of gold, SS loot and art treasures removed by the Germans from Berlin to a salt mine vault in Merkers."
 Caption of a photograph in the *New York Times*, May 4, 1945.

This too, in its way, is their signature:
Less than the burned bodies, the charnel houses, Belsen
    and Buchenwald,
The starved dead, the abomination that appalls,
But the small item, easily understood,
The pickpocket mind, the murderer's take:

Fat Hermann and quick Heinrich as the connoisseurs
Of tooth fillings,
Judges of the quality of gold in wedding rings,
Testers of spectacle rims,
Masters of the new Exhibition of the Rejected,
The grotesque burglary of a continent,
This is their signature and a sign:
The Manet in the salt mine at Merkers.

—*Francis Coleman Rosenberger*

Wilfredo Lam   **The Caribbean Parade, 1945**

20 Tanks From Kasseldown

by Charles Bukowski

He sat in his cell tapping his fingers on the bottle, thinking, it's very sporting of them to give me this bottle. When he tapped at the glass it felt good on his fingers, spreading them a bit so, and getting the cool, clean touch. He had used whiskey before, found it made life bearable; took off the edge; was a good wash for minds that turned too fast: culling it, slowing it, settling it to a visible mark.

A roach moved across the floor, click-fast, then click-stopped before one of his shoes. It stood there and he stopped tapping, and watched. From the still fingers on the bottle to the very shape of the shoe by the roach, his lines were slim, pliable, womanish without being feminine; and there was a dignity that made you think of kings, of princes, of sheltered and spoiled things, and if you hadn't known, you'd think he'd been untouched by life. (He stepped out and crushed the roach.) He was about thirty and the face, like a thinker's face, looked at the same time younger and older. His movements were restrained and quiet, always subservient to the mind, and sometimes when in crowds, falsified and churned up bluntly so as not to attract attention. During the trial, when he was news, the cell was piqued with reporters. He smiled continually when they questioned him, yet they could see he wasn't the least happy—as if he *should* be! And yet it wasn't a mocking smile. It was pleasant in a sense. There didn't seem much hatred in him; just a vagueness, an inconsistency. He hadn't bothered to shave and had a fine-grained beard, thin, like the hair under the armpits. It *did* give him that martyred look, that beard, the ghost eyes, and he would lean back against the wall, light his cigarette in soft-handed movements, looking down. Then he would smile at the reporters: "Well, friends, what can I do for you?"

"Just keep the priests away . . ." he said . . .

He sat in the cell and the fingers began tapping again, tapping the bottle. Still, it was the second time, and it wasn't as good because he expected it. He began to smile.

Had time to write a book. Should have written a book. Print on pages, you know. The first letter of each chapter very fancy. Done up with a rose or a leaf or a maiden's knee. Should have written a book. They all do it. "Treason . . . is only being on the losing side of revolution." This is a small country, but I could have written a large book . . . This is a small country, but with 20 more tanks, just 20, I would be at Kasseldown and Curtwright would be here—writing a book. Hell, even with 100 horses . . .

But now you are the peculiar target to make the glory of country more armorous in the history textbooks. You see, you have killed a roach and they have too—that is, they will today when the sun goes down . . . See the little ones reading, reading, and there the teacher with her long wooden stick and her blackboard, pointing to a colored map. The notebooks, the fat ink in desks . . . memorize, memorize this. A whole movement, a whole flow of word and thought and idea . . . hours of talk and counter-talk, examination, tradition bent in hard on soft minds, and forever unchanged. And now they sing, sing, and march out of classrooms and bounce balls and believe . . . and grow and read the newspapers, and believe . . . all this, on the difference of 100 horses, 100 chunks of beast flesh, fed and dunged; dumb, dumb mass of beast flesh that made the notes of song . . . *Curtwright's* horses.

He sucked at the bottle again, feeling very lonely but not because of four wet and arenaceous walls.

But *still* . . . you tried it. And if you had won, it would have been the same thing at the other end . . . Why did you bother with it? Didn't you know that beyond the numbered few, even slight meaning ends? . . . No, it wasn't ambition—in that sense . . . It was just the people, all lives running, all lives running so weak, plunged through with fear. Everything was a ritual of no-do, no-hurt, no-chance. He had just gotten a hunger, a hunger for *doing* . . . doing anything at all to break the suffocating shell.

He sat in the cell and held the bottle before his eyes. The light was poor but still he could make out the branded words in the glass: FEDERAL LAW FORBIDS SALE OR REUSE OF THIS BOTTLE . . .

He stood up and found he was looking at the walls. Walls funny grey, sweating cold, thick—yet bunched through with a drama of their own—and so old . . . Old. Funny about women, too . . . How they got old. Sad, really sad. You saw the young ones walking all tight and high . . . and you hated their proudness, for proudness had no right in things mechanical and momentary. Proudness only belonged to those who created new forms, and won . . . He smiled again and stood looking at the walls. They seemed pleasant and meaningful and he touched a finger to the rough edge, grey and wet.

His throat felt dry and he went over to the tap and filled his tin cup. The water came hard and made a swirling, white rising of foam in the cup. He shut the tap, but too late, and there was a splash of overflow making a blotch of clean, porous leather on one shoe. Something turned slowly in his forehead and he thought, it is too quiet. He drank the water but it tasted badly of tin, and all of a sudden he felt sick, very sick. He sat down again on his cot, the room all shadow and cement, and he was conscious that he was breathing, and through each inhale came the taste of tin. He drank what was left of the whiskey bottle, then set it very quietly on the floor. The settling down of a bottle was one of the few independent actions he had left. He leaned back against the wall, closed his eyes, opened them, and knew he was just perhaps really frightened, the mind trying to work up some apology for the death of the flesh.

As the thought set in, a chill began in the fingers and went up both arms, making him jerk his shoulders spasmodically to shake it out of his back. It is very quiet, he thought again, and all of a sudden his mind found an outlet, a base, and he hated the swirl, the meaning-drenched swirl, the vast mass and press of unchanneled and baseless things that could kill without a glisten, a sigh, a tick.

But here, he thought, never let passion deform the frame. Passion, unmoulded, is a sign of inferiority! Listen. Take this, all this, and for *them*—make numerals, symbols, hard and fought-out, well-balanced formulas.

Then he, at last, began laughing—not laughing but sniggering, womanish, only half-understood, semi-mad.

"Guard!"

"Guard!" he yelled.

The guard came and stood there, outside the bars. "Do you want the priest?" he asked.

The guard was bald and fat, and looking at him he

thought: bald and fat, his face is crossed between brutality and humor and can't make up its mind, and the eyes are so small, so small.

"You mustn't accuse me of crassness or bitterness, guard, but a man like you—makes no difference when he lives: now, or two thousand years hence, or some place in between. You make no marks, no sounds, no new entrances... Still, it's grand to be alive, grand, even as you. Grand to stand there and ask me if I want a priest, grand to play your little safe game and watch the larger clash going on. After all, you do absorb something, even standing aside... but I'm sick of hearing my voice. You say something. What do you think, guard?"

"What do I think?"
"Yes."
"Do you want the priest?"
"No. Go away."
He sat in his cell, sick.

I try, I try... I *try* to see. But the whole god damn world seems fake, *fake*... Oh, I should have stayed at the hospital, tinkering with people, painting at night. I could have made my own world at night. But I wanted to stir the whole pond, shake the base. Oh hunger—hunger.

He looked down at the floor, at the spot that had once been a roach, and smiled again.

J. J. Grandville

Civil Marriage
Engraving, 1845.
from *The Private and Public Life of the Animals.*

from Children of the Albatross

by Anais Nin

Lawrence had finished the phosphorescent painting. He closed the curtains and the cage shone in the dark. Now he decided to paint with phosphorescence everything paintable in the room.

The next day Lawrence appeared with a large pot of paint and he was stirring it with a stick when Paul telephoned: "I can get away for a little while. May I come?"

"Oh, come, come," said Djuna.

"I can't stay very late . . . " His voice was muffled, like that of a sick person. There was a plaintiveness in it so plainly audible to Djuna's heart.

"The prisoner is allowed an hour's freedom," she said.

When Paul came Lawrence handed him a paint brush and in silence the two of them worked at touching up everything paintable in the room. Then they turned off the lights. A new room appeared.

Luminous faces appeared on the walls, new flowers, new jewels, new castles, new jungles, new animals, all in filaments of light.

Mysterious translucence like their unmeasured words, their impulsive acts, wishes, enthusiasms. Darkness was excluded from their world, the darkness of loss of faith. It was now the room with a perpetual sparkle, even in darkness.

(They are making a new world for me, felt Djuna, a world of greater lightness. It is perhaps a dream and I may not be allowed to stay. They treat me as one of their own, because I believe what they believe, I feel as they do. I hate the father, authority, men of power, men of wealth, all tyranny, all authority, all crystallizations. I feel as Lawrence and Paul: outside there lies a bigger world full of cruelties, dangers and corruptions, where one sells out one's charms, one's playfulness, and enters a rigid world of discipline, duty, contracts, accountings. A thick opaque world without phosphorescence. I want to stay in this room forever not with man the father but with man the son, carving, painting, dancing, dreaming, and always beginning, born anew every day, never aging, full of faith and impulse, turning and changing to every wind like the mobiles. I do not love those who have ceased to flow, to believe, to feel. Those who can no longer melt, exult, who cannot let themselves be cheated, laugh at loss, those who are bound and frozen.)

She laid her head on Lawrence's shoulder with a kind of gratitude.

(Nowhere else as here with Lawrence and with Paul was there such an iridescence in the air; nowhere else so far from the threat of hardening and crystallizing. Everything flowing . . .)

Djuna was brushing her hair with her fingers, in long pensive strokes and Lawrence was talking about the recurrent big problem of a job. He had tried so many. How to work without losing one's color, one's ardor, personal possessions and freedom. He was very much like a delicate Egyptian scarab who dreaded to lose his iridescence in routine, in duty, in monotony. The job could kill one, or maim one, make one a robot, an opaque personage, a future undertaker, a man of power with gouty limbs and a hardening of the arteries of faith!

Lawrence was now working in a place which made decorations for shop windows. He liked to work at night, to go on strange expeditions in the company of mannequins, papier mache horses, to live on miniature stages building jungles, sea landscapes, fabulous animals. To flirt with naked mannequins whose arms came off as easily as other women's gloves, who deposited their heads on the floor and took off their wigs when they took off their hats. He became an expert at dismantling women!

Lawrence lived and breathed color and there was no danger of his dying of drabness, for even accidents took on a most vivid shade and a spilled pot of gouache was still a delight to the eyes.

He brought Djuna gifts of chokers, head dresses, ear rings made of painted clay which crumbled quickly like the trappings for a costume play.

She had always liked objects without solidity. The solid ones bound her to permanency. She had never wanted a solid house, enduring furniture. All these were traps. Then you belonged to them forever. She preferred stage trappings which she could move into and out of easily, without regret. Soon after they fell apart and nothing was lost. The vividness alone survived.

She remembered once hearing a woman complain that armchairs no longer lasted twenty years, and Djuna answered: but I couldn't love an armchair for twenty years!

And so change, mutations like the rainbow, and she preferred Lawrence's gifts from which the colored powder and crystals fell like the colors on the wings of butterflies after yielding their maximum of charm.

Paul was carving a piece of copper, making such fine incisions with the scissors that the bird which finally appeared between his slender fingers bristled with filament feathers.

He stood on the table and hung it by a thread to the ceiling. The slightest breath caused it to turn slowly.

Paul had the skin of a child that had never been touched by anything of this earth: no soap, no wash rag, no brush, no human kiss could have touched his skin! Never scrubbed, rubbed, scratched, or wrinkled by a pillow. The transparency of the child skin, of the adolescent later to turn opaque. What do children nourish themselves with that their skin has this transparency, and what do they eat of later which brings on opaqueness?

The mothers who kiss them are eating light.

There is a phosphorescence which comes from the magic world of childhood.

Where does this illumination go later? Is it the substance of faith which shines from their bodies like phosphorescence from the albatross, and what kills it?

Now Lawrence had discovered a coiled measuring tape of steel in Djuna's closet while delving for objects useful for charades.

When entirely pulled out of its snail covering it stretched like a long snake of steel which under certain manipulations could stand rigid like a sword or undulate like silver tipped waves, or flash like lightning.

Lawrence and Paul stood like expert swordsmen facing each other for a duel of light and steel.

The steel band flexed, then hardened between them like a bridge, and at each forward movement by one it seemed as if the sword had pierced the body of the other.

At other moments it wilted, wavered like a frightened snake, and then it looked bedraggled and absurd and they both laughed.

But soon they learned never to let it break or waver and it became like a thunderbolt in their hands. Paul attacked with audacity and Lawrence parried with swiftness.

At midnight Paul began to look anxious. His luminosity clouded, he resumed his hesitant manner. He ceased to occupy the center of the room and moved out of the focus of light and laughter. Like a sleep walker, he moved away from gayety.

Djuna walked with him towards the door. They were alone and then he said: "My parents have forbidden me to come here."

"But you were happy here, weren't you?"

"Yes, I was happy."

"This is where you belong?"

"Why do you think I belong here?"

"You're gifted, for dancing, for painting, for writing. And this is your month of freedom."

"Yes, I know. I wish . . . I wish I were free . . . ."

"If you wish it deeply enough you will find a way."

"I would like to run away. But I have no money."

"If you run away we'll all take care of you."

"Why?"

"Because we believe in you, because you're worth helping."

"I have nowhere to go."

"We'll find you a room somewhere, and we will adopt you. And you will have your month of life."

"Of life!" he repeated with docility.

"But I don't want you to do it unless you feel ready, unless you want it so much that you're willing to sacrifice everything else. I only want you to know you can count on us, but it must be your decision, or it will not mean anything."

"Thank you." This time he did not clasp her hand, he laid his hand within hers as if nestling it there, folded, ivory smooth and gentle, at rest, in an act of trustingness.

Then before leaving the place he looked once more at the room as if to retain its enfolding warmth. At one moment he had laughed so much that he had slid from his chair. Djuna had made him laugh. At that moment many of his chains must have broken, for, nothing breaks chains like laughter, and Djuna could not remember in all her life a greater joy than this spectacle of Paul laughing like a released prisoner. □

Jean Moralis   **Wood cut 1940**

"Ce que j'ai vu dans une chambre vide d'une vieille maison abandonnee"

Niko Engonopoulos **Room for Rent, 1947**

Voyages

A NATIONAL LITERARY MAGAZINE
WASHINGTON, D.C. $1.50
VOLUME 1   NUMBER 1 • FALL, 1967

BEN BELITT ISSUE • THOMAS MERTON DRAWINGS • CAROLYN KIZER INTERVIEW
M. YOUNG on ANAIS NIN • ROGER HECHT POEMS • E. de GRAZIA • J. PAUKER

Voyages

William F. Claire's *Voyages* was published in a uniform edition of 6 inch by 9 inch books which averaged from 100-150 pages in length. The numbering system became a little eccentric (see note at beginning of index), but every issue featured white/beige covers.

An Interview with William F. Claire

William Claire was born in Northampton, Mass. in 1935. Since retiring *Voyages* in 1973, he has published six books or chapbooks, the first of which, on Alan Swallow, received a "Best Title Award" from *Library Journal*. The most recent, *The Essays of Mark Van Doren, 1924-1972*, was selected by the *New York Times* as one of the best books of 1980. His poems and essays have appeared in over fifty journals and anthologies, including *The Antioch Review, The American Scholar, The Nation, The New Republic* and the *New York Times*.

After *Voyages*, three sad occasions developed with former advisory editors of the magazine, and he organized memorial services, for Mark Van Doren at the Folger Shakespeare Library, introduced the first Katherine Garrison Chapin Memorial Lecture Series at the Guggenheim Museum in New York City, and coordinated "A Celebration for Anais Nin" at the Cosmos Club in conjunction with the French Embassy.

Bill has read his poems widely in a variety of forums but since last year, when he received a Rockefeller Foundation residency in Bellagio, Italy, he has been working on a novel titled *So Deep A Measure*.

He is currently director of the Washington Office of State University of New York.

Peabody: How did you first get involved in small press publishing?

Claire: Well, I can't remember what the germinal idea behind a magazine was—I wanted to fill a need in Washington at the time: it was somewhat analogous here to T.S. Eliot's first segment of *The Wasteland*; the war was going on, there wasn't any kind of literary intelligence or sense of community that I was able to discern, other than the Library of Congress. There was a very elitist group who met for readings... something called the Institute of Contemporary Art, which brought major figures like Eliot and Dylan Thomas to Washington, but I don't think the events were publicized, and very few people knew about them; and I had been involved, in a way, with writers, and others, and I thought that it would be the time to do it ... Why do you do something like this? It's a mixture of idealism and insanity; you don't know the problems you'll run into. I just launched it, and I was very lucky to attract fine writers (it was never intended to be specifically a Washington publication). I had new translations of Pablo Neruda in my first issue; Thomas Merton sent me some letters from his monastery in Kentucky; I had an extraordinary combination of luck and some excellent people who were interested in the magazine, and then—some people like Frances Smyth who were involved in design and photography also seemed to coalesce at that time. Eliot Porter sent me a spectacular photograph for my first issue, and somehow—we were flying, and when the magazine came out it surprised everybody in being quite as nice as it was, and with such an array of important writers. And by naming those great names I didn't mean to preclude others who were unknown, of course, that I also published. I published Edward de Grazia, who was then the attorney for Grove Press, living in Washington (and was also William Burroughs' lawyer, and Allen Ginsberg's, and Mailer's—and others in very important censorship cases.) But he was also a playwright, and I published his first play, I believe, in my first issue. And so on—there were always Washington writers in each issue, but I never intended it to be just a Washington magazine; I wanted it to be in some sense national and international.

Baizer: I'm curious about what your background was going into that... Had you majored in writing? Had you published or edited anything before?

Claire: Yes, I had had somewhat of a career in writing and I had published some poems and literary essays along the way ... my earlier background was not excessively literary, though. This was my first effort; I thought I was marching against the czar, as I think most magazine editors do. I didn't know that much, really, about technical matters—that's why I put such a strong emphasis in my first answer on luck, the fact that people interested in layout and design came along and helped me. I was truly surprised with the way it came out, I must say. And once it was out and received such a good response, well that, of course, gave me the incentive to continue.

Elsberg: What about the reaction here in Washington? You said the magazine was not meant to be a regional magazine ... but did you get significant encouragement from this community itself?

Claire: Not really ... it was much better received in—strange places, and not necessarily large cities. I was astonished ... people from Montana ... all word-of-mouth, we never put a cent into publicity or anything of that sort. Somehow the word traveled around—but, no, most people in Washington were mystified by it. —And I must tell one story— when a large story appeared about it in the *Post*, I was gainfully employed somewhere else, and my employers were so stunned by this, and wondering what kind of weird person was working in their Washington office, that they had secret meetings to find out what was going on here.

But, no, it was really bad here ... but good anywhere else, it seemed.

Elsberg: What about distribution? That is always a problem with any small press. How did you manage to get copies out to the areas where the magazine was getting a good response?

Claire: Well, for the first few years it was as crude as you could imagine—you sent them out where you found people who would take them. About halfway through the game, I got a major distributor on the West Coast, where the magazine was quite well-known—in San Francisco—so that took care of several states out there. I never could put together anything here on the East Coast, so it was mainly sending packets of the magazine to selected bookstores. And I must say wherever it went, it sold out—whether it was the Gotham Book Mart in New York, or Boston, Cambridge—so I was always pleased with that. But it was agony getting together ten or twenty issues and just mailing them out. I'm sure that there are more sophisticated means now, since so much attention has been given to distribution . . .

Baizer: I would imagine . . . you started in '67 . . . in other east-coast cities of the time, Boston, New York, I would imagine there was quite a lot of small press publishing. Any theories about why so little in Washington at that time?

Claire: No, except I think it's a company town—a government town—and everything here seems to be at a level of chi-chi, or what will be attractive, and so on. Although in subsequent years there's a very strong literary community here, there just didn't seem to be then. Rod Jellema, at the University of Maryland, had gathered together a group of people, writers, many of whom did not know they knew each other, who did not know they lived here, to come to an important conference, and then from that . . . and Merrill Leffler's magazine *Dryad* started not too long thereafter, so that the beginnings of a community, I think, were established then. There was some communion with black writers here, both in music and art—but that came to an end after the Martin Luther King assassination, and that fell apart for a while. And it's, I guess, just starting to come back now.—But I spent time explaining the magazine once to somebody and they said, "Is it going to be like *Time* magazine?" I mean, the variance between what I was trying to do and how it was accepted here was astonishing. Which is not to put down the fact that there are a lot of good people here—but, in broad terms, it was misunderstood, right from the beginning, I thought.

Peabody: How did you assemble the advisory board? This board of associate editors?

Claire: Just through the literary community, and so forth. Mark Van Doren had been a teacher of mine at Columbia; Carl Bode was from the University of Maryland, I simply asked him . . . Roger Hecht's a poet, New York; John Pauker's a Washington poet; Anais Nin was a friend of mine from long standing; Francis Murphy was a professor of English at Smith—I thought I ought to have one academic; Tram Combs is an unusual figure, a poet . . . I don't know where he is. Some people think he's dead. He's got a story like Weldon Kees—he'd owned a bookstore in the Virgin Islands, and was a very important figure in the San Francisco renaissance. Then he disappeared. Jim Wright I had known through Roger Hecht in New York. So I wanted to balance it, with people I knew, but most of them—with the exception of Nin—were to be names, it was agreed; it was to be my magazine, and I would call upon them from time to time. Nin was to become an active advisory editor.

Elsberg: To do what? I was wondering what sort of involvement did they have?

Claire: Well, advisory editors can send other writers your way, they can suggest certain themes . . . they should never have, it seems to me, any editorial say over what you publish. It's window dressing, for the most part, to have names like that. Anais Nin was an exception; in every single issue there are manifestations of her willingness to send writers to me, to have me look at certain things, and so on. So they can be very valuable; they can open a few doors for you here and there. With any board, you have to know how to use them, I think.

Baizer: Why did you stop doing the magazine?

Claire: Well, by 1972 I had a very strong belief and faith in the validity of the literary magazine movement of America. They come and go, and I don't think they should last too long. I think that once an editor feels he has done what he set out to do, it's a good time to get out. It's a kind of cycle . . . I left at the time the reputation of *Voyages* was at its highest point.

Elsberg: Let me ask you straight-forwardly. What in your own mind did you set out to do?

Claire: Well, I set out, first of all, to gather and pay homage to certain writers that I didn't think were being paid attention to in our excessively commercial kind of society. I think everybody I featured was in some way an outsider, even if, in some cases, they had presumably large names, and I wanted to pay a certain kind of tribute to them, before they died, if you will; and then I also wanted to discover other writers, I wanted to do some experimental things, I did some early concrete poetry, and visual poetry; I did a women's issue long before the so-called movement got its official start. Things of that sort. Each issue seemed to me to be an event; it was almost like putting together a book, an anthology. Its coherence was in the homage to two writers, and then, the balancing kinds of things.

Elsberg: Did you expect someone to carry on? I mean I get the sense that you were doing something that you felt needed doing and when you came to the conclusion that you'd done your share of it did you expect somebody to carry on?

Claire: No, not in this context. This was my personal thing, for better or for worse. I regret that it didn't get around more; that's the distribution problem you alluded to earlier. But at that time, too, the development of magazines in the Washington area and elsewhere seemed to me to be greatly on the increase. And you can't feel vain—that what you've done will be missed that much. There are enough others coming along

Photo by William Stafford

William F. Claire circa 1967

to take its place. And that's what's great about the movement. And it's all over the United States....

Baizer: Getting back again to the Washington literary climate when you started *Voyages*, were there any other magazines being published in Washington? You were the only one, small press?

Claire: Yeah, absolutely the first. And then *Dryad* came not too long thereafter....

Peabody: What was your circulation with *Voyages*? I know that printing costs have escalated like everything else but I'm curious what it cost you to print the magazine back then?

Claire: Gee... it went up through the years, clearly... and everything was volunteer, there weren't any salaries involved, but it was always sort of expensive. I think it started around twelve or thirteen hundred, per issue, and got up to—"

Peabody: For how many copies?

Claire: We were always around two thousand, twenty-five hundred, from the beginning, and we ended up sort of right there, too. But the costs did increase... fortunately postage was lower then than it is now.

Baizer: What percentage of expenses did you get back from sales? A quarter? A third?

Claire: I would say a third, maybe—it sold pretty well when I got it around. I was extremely lucky; in my first issue I had Wesleyan, Grove Press, Random House—I can't imagine why they took ads, but they were paid ads. University of California at Berkeley was another... I also ran free ads; that is part of the tradition.

Baizer: Did you get any grants along the way?

Claire: Yes. The most important one for me was a Washington-based foundation called the Meyer Foundation which really helped out at one time. And I won two or three awards from the Endowment, an editor's award; they sponsored an anthology that was edited by George Plimpton, who selected the best of literary magazines, something like an early *Pushcart*. And they paid not only the writers, but the editors, so I received a few of those along the way. You tie together different things....

Baizer: How did you get around this funding problem? Did you stage benefits for the magazine?

Claire: Never had a single benefit or a fund-raiser in Washington, although I could have... No, I wanted to keep it pretty independent of anything or anybody. But I'm not decrying others who can raise money any way they want.

Peabody: We've touched on your funding, and it is pretty much of a fact that none of the small magazines published here locally made a profit last year or broke even for that matter. Did *Voyages* break even?

Claire: No, absolutely not, every issue was a loser, unfortunately.

Peabody: That seems to be a small press tradition... Did you have many library sales?

Claire: Quite a few. That helped, too. There were some subscription agencies that came to me, after the magazine was around, and asked if they could advertise the magazine, and they did that on their own. And abroad—the astonishing thing to me was that libraries in Australia, Brazil, Great Britain, and Ireland, subscribed, and I felt terrible, sometimes I didn't answer their letters—you know the time it would take to have a magazine go by boat—and I feel guilty to this day that I wasn't more responsive, because again how the word got around to these places just escaped me. And I also had some interesting things happen: because it was called *Voyages*, some people thought it was a travel magazine, so I got several subscriptions from people who believed that; and one, an institute of oceanography in Brazil, ordered five subscriptions, thinking perhaps it had to do with underwater exploration. But that was all right with me—I got the magazines off to them....

Elsberg: Did you get any feedback from the librarians? That they were perhaps more interested in your magazine than in another one because you had the featured poets?

Claire: Well, I think so, and I think that, however you break these things down, the decision-making process of a librarian, the way a publication looks has a real, a powerful pull; there are so many valuable and valid magazines that are nonetheless put together with mimeograph sheets, or what have you, that when a librarian has a tight budget, and looks at something, clearly the better-looking publications will often make it... that may be unjustified, because we've seen what trash can come between slick covers in the publishing world—but I know that helped a great deal.

Baizer: Any plans to get back into publishing?

Claire: No, I don't think so. No, I had a good time while I was in, but I think the problems now are even worse than when I was there. The cost of postage, and printing, and so on... I'm really happy with what I was able to accomplish—and so I leave it to others....

Peabody: Quite willing to sit on your laurels?

Claire: Yeah, if you can call it that.

Peabody: Do you have any final advice for magazine editors?

Claire: Well, keep plugging away, don't worry too much about the marketplace; don't ever worry about going out of business, because you're not in business (you may be in circulation); print what you think is necessary and important to print, no matter what anyone says... That's the only justification in the final analysis.

—Interviewed by Eric Baizer, John Elsberg, and Richard Peabody

Voyages

A NATIONAL LITERARY MAGAZINE
WASHINGTON, D.C. $2.00
VOLUME II   NUMBERS I & II
(DOUBLE ISSUE)   WINTER, SPRING 1968

ROBERT LAX SPECIAL ISSUE • POEMS • JOURNALS • PHOTOS • MERTON-LAX LETTERS • MARK VAN DOREN • D. LEVERTOV • S. BANN

Voyages

A NATIONAL LITERARY MAGAZINE
WASHINGTON, D.C. $1.50
VOLUME II NUMBER IV SPRING, 1969

ROY P. BASLER ON ROBERT FROST • HOMAGE TO H. R. HAYS • JAMES T. FARRELL
HENRY ROTH • LINDA PASTAN • JOHN UNTERECKER • WILLIAM PACKARD • OTHERS

Voyages

Interview with
William Jay Smith, p. 89

A NATIONAL LITERARY MAGAZINE
WASHINGTON, D.C. $2.00
VOL. II NOS. 1 & 2   WINTER 1970

HIRAM HAYDN CELEBRATION • JAMES SCHEVILL SECTION • DANIEL HOFFMAN
WILLIAM JAY SMITH INTERVIEW • M. YOUNG ON MARK VAN DOREN / SHORT
STORIES • POEMS • PHOTOS • REVIEWS

Voyages

A NATIONAL LITERARY MAGAZINE
WASHINGTON, D.C. $1.50
VOLUME II • NUMBER 3 • FALL, 1968

CAROLINE GORDON AND C. PEEBLES • ANAIS NIN • M. MIHAJLOV • JOSEPHINE
MILES • JANE COOPER • P. WHIGHAM • F. FIELD • D. METZGER • S. EISENSTEIN

Two Love Sonnets by Pablo Neruda

XXXII

Morning in the house: the truth is ours again,
feathers and linens, the sources of a day
intent on nothing, a leaky barge adrift
within a double-skyline: dream and order.

Things root in their rubbish, in search of their vestiges—
a clinging jetsam going nowhere, unloved bequests,
a papery noise of hidden corrugations,
dregs in a bottle in search of the night before.

Dear Orderer, who moves with a passing bee's pulsation,
it is for you to touch the vanishing realm of shadow
and force your way to the light, with the power of white.

Definition returns in you: all is rebuilt again,
the things of the wind respond to the life of the world,
and order apportions its dove and its daily bread.

XC

I dreamed that I died: that I felt the cold close to me;
and all that was left of my life was contained in your presence:
your mouth was the daylight and dark of my world,
your skin, the republic I shaped for myself with my kisses.

Straightway, the books of the world were all ended,
all friendships, all treasures restlessly cramming the vaults,
the diaphanous house that we built for a lifetime together—
all ceased to exist, till nothing remained but your eyes.

So long as we live, or as long as a lifetime's vexation,
love is a breaker thrown high on the breakers' successions;
but when death in its time chooses to pummel the doors—

Ay! — there is only your face to fill up the vacancy,
only your clarity pressing back on the whole of non-being,
only your love, where the dark of the world closes in.

—Translated by Ben Belitt

Fat Tuesday

(Homage to Antonio Machado)

Yesterday's
seven-thirty still clots the band-stand
clock. A child sleeps near the tinsel and papier-mache
in a kerosene ring under the wavering flies.
The lovers embrace on the grand-stand

as slowly
the machinery of celebration engages
its spokes and wheels around the incandescent center
of their pleasure. The plazas sparkle like stages
with a blind bicarbonation, and the masquers enter.

How simply
their dangerous reversal
is accomplished, the permutations of concealment
turning the cheese-cloth and the mica of their disguises
into the dramatis personae of a dress rehearsal

and showing
the eye-hole's razor edges framing the double ovals
of the masquer's eyes, like buckets rearising in a well, glowing
with vagrant spontaneities, the amateur's surprises
caught in the act of his improvisations.

Knowing
those Tuesdays of the flesh, reptilian
in their hungers, Antonio Machado, dragging his horse-hair
great-coat, his *Irregular Verbs for French Beginners*, the chalky
bastinado of his calling.

through the parched
Castilian school-day, in ear-shot of a parish's explosion,
scribbled a maxim in his Marginalia:
"Not to put on one's mask, but to put off one's face: that
is Carnival; the face alone in the world—that is appalling!"

And watched
from a cindery tussock how the masquers circled
a fountain in Baeza, putting off his cheekbones, eyes, the sensuous
underlip, emptying his skull of what it held
under the make-believe regalia,

leaving only
the arm-band of the widower's long deprival,
the school-teacher who had "studied under Bedier and Bergson"
counting martlets between the bell-tower and horizon,
intent on the apocryphal and lonely.

And noted:
"The poet is a fisher in time: not of fish
in the sea, but the whole living catch: let us be clear about that!"
He put off his face, facing away from Madrid; the Tuesday of the guns
                                                            grew fat;
he crossed the border into France, put on his mask, and died into his wisdom.

—Ben Belitt

flee-
ing

from

bridge-
port

—

don't forget
the fish-sticks
love

remember to
bring the frozen
avocado

there may not
be a toddle house
in new haven:

we'd be lost

sandra's danc-
ing lessons all
on tape

she'll need 'em
when we get there

don't forget your
ear-plugs, love

here's your sleep-
mask, sandor

don't forget to
bring the dog

don't forget to
bring the dog

—*Robert Lax*

—

it is good
to keep

the secrets
of a king

but right
to recount

the wonders

of the

Lord

—
—

—*Robert Lax*

Photo by Robert Lax

april 24 afternoon

by Robert Lax

i talked just now to a sponge-diver named constantinos who comes from rhodes, got married here, and now, at 29 lives in chora with his wife and one child, he'll be going, too, to bengazi with the caiquis a few days after easter.

like everyone else, he says the work's no good; but he was able to tell me more about it than most of the divers i've talked to. (i think i've seen him at the younger night-club in chora; he may have been the first of the dancers i saw; he's blond and blue-eyed and wears his cap with style; the movie company fastened on him immediately as typical).

i tried to ask him what it was like down there, and at first he hardly understood. soon, though, he was telling me.

(but first he talked about the rigors of life at sea. nothing to eat all day: cigarettes and a little coffee: you eat at night and then not again til the next night. do you come back after the seven months very thin? it all depends: one man gains weight at sea, another loses it. (it all depends on how they're made). do you like the sea? I do.)

each diver has his own limit of depth and time. he dives thirty arm-lengths—the length of your outstretched arms from tip to tip: (about 6 feet) and stays down fifteen minutes at a maximum. Others may go down less and stay down longer.

he dives (as they all do) three times a day: once for fifteen minutes, once perhaps for 11 and once for 8. the most in the beginning when he's strong, the least when tired. he tells the boy who handles the rope how long he intends to stay; the boy has a watch, the diver hasn't (but on a well-equipped caiqui, he has a (micro-telephone) inside the helmet); the boy keeps his eye on the watch (a casual vigilance, as I've seen it) and when it's time, he pulls him back. if on the way back he sees a sponge, and wants to stay to pick it up he signals to the captain (with rope pulls), or tells him by phone; the captain approves or disapproves; the diver stays or comes back up.

but it must be bad to stay when you're on your way up? It's bad. (when you know you've only got so many minutes) it must be better to come straight up. it is.

(then what do you think makes a person) stay down any longer? the sponge. he said: he sees a sponge and he wants it.

but wouldn't it be better to come back up, and then go down for it later?

it would be better to come back up and then go down for it later, he said. (as though he had said it to himself, and to other divers a thousand times)

Then why would he stop? the sponge, he said: it's hard to explain it. you may be standing here with sponges all around you. and you see one over there: it's like a *raggazina* (a little girl), it's like a sister (he said, for want of any other word in italian): you will go over there and *then* come back for the others. (that one is little (and sweet) and these are big (and gross); the sponge: i can't explain it: it's like a magnet.

do you like it down there? (is it beautiful?) it's beautiful, but the work's no good. you come back after seven months and you can hardly walk: one foot is here, and one is there: your legs are like water, from walking up and down the deck, and from walking under the sea.

(when you've been down too long, or too deep, he said, you don't die down there; you don't die while they're pulling you up. you die when you're up: when they unscrew the helmet. and the air rushes in; when you take your first breath of oxygen: that's when you die.

i walked around last night and it all seemed different. the pastry shop had put some tables up outside across the road (it's pretty much the social center of town); there were still some divers and their wives (and the rest of the townies) to fill up the tables, and at first it all seemed more crowded than ever. but it wasn't. only a few people seemed to have left on the boats (and yet a major element was missing). the tables and celebrants outside made it look as though they had been saving summer until the divers had left.

and later, walking past the cafes, the same abandoned look and feeling: they had been decimated, nothing more; only a part of the crowd had gone, but it was the livelier part.

another (lively) part was at the church, as I realized later. two major events have kept the town on the move (and their spheres keep intersecting); the coming of easter is one; the departure of the fleet is the other. yesterday as the boats were leaving three girls walked down fisherman's wharf carrying a flower-laden image of Christ (to approach and kiss); it was palm sunday, and this was Christ's triumphal entry into jerusalem: the beginning of holy week. last night, the churches were crowded.

Friday the 13th   YWCA

Sometimes, alone on Friday the 13th, you may be facing a dark room
where lone women are sitting at blue tables.
You must do this to keep in touch with the Great Spirit of ALL Things. For example:
the green glass skyscrapers in whose reflections evening clouds are gliding
seen through the windows of the 13th floor (called the 14th) of the YWCA
where the Cafeteria is, and where there are good steak dinners for $1.50;
and courses in Painting, Modern Dance, and Learning a Language.

Why do "Y" women, though Young — Women — Christian — and an Association,
all attributes on the road to Joy, look so lonesome?
Is it because they take the Friday courses:

> PREPARATION FOR MARRIAGE WITH IRMA SWIFT; JUDO FOR WOMEN
> safeeasyfun;
> FACTUAL WRITING FOR CAREER MINDED SECRETARIES;
> PERSONAL MONEY MANAGEMENT; WRAP LOVELY GIFT PACKAGES COURSE;
> ENTREES AND VEGETABLES; LOOKING FOR NEW HORIZONS?
> FIVE STEPS TO DISCOVERY AND SUCCESS FOR WOMEN WHO SEEK
> GREATER JOB SATISFACTION
> DESSERTS — PLAIN AND FRENCH; AFRICA IN A WORLD CRISIS —
> Up—To—The—Minit Facts To Challenge Your Thinking;
> *THUS TO SHOW KNOWLEDGE AND LOVE OF GOD?*

> Today in South India, devotional dark-eyed girls in iridescent saris
> accompany men in skirts of feathers, carrying long lances.
> Or in Kerala, where caparisoned gold and red umbrella-shaded elephants and
>   loping camels stroll,
> where the Tiger not the Lion is King of the Jungle,
> lusty-voiced girls in maroon and purple, are dancing in mango groves.
> Some are picking berries; others following the lure of sweet pomegranates.
>   (*Flow gently, River, for my man is on the other side.*)
> The minarets of Mosques, tall and slim and white, rise over the bottle-green
>   foliage
> where peacocks trail their long tails, or unfurl them, multiple-eyed, to gaze
>   upon the world;
> for it is said the eyes of peacock tails *see* those who behold them.

Oh "Y" Women, (penultimate letter of the alphabet — the Name of God),
so sad and alone at blue tables in a darkened room:
   Do you know that the Stars are your older brothers?
   That the Sun can set a house on fire?
   That if you think of Fire, you will become Fire:
   You have only to say: I AM THE SUN!

—Daisy Aldan

Chairman

Now the old men are getting nervous.
They are shedding so much blood not theirs
That they begin to taste it, and the acrimony
Colors their tongues.
In the board room
Freshly shaven
They vote, ten or eleven to seven
To kill.

They feel in their age a tenderness for the young,
So they set at the head of the table,
Blond to the grey at his left and his right, a charismatic
Youth, a lightfoot babe,
Early mellow
Who, nodding to left and to right,
Will move the previous question,
To kill, and to kill.

—*Josephine Miles*

Smoke

An air of departures. Silences.
Again the pines are sheathed in a wet snow.
The chimney breathes its slow, transparent smoke.

Everything has been offered, nothing given.
Everything, not the first thing has been said.
After me who will sit here, patiently writing?

Words over a page: a slow smoke
scrolling across the sky what is unconsumed
by the deep, thunderous fires of the house.

An air of departures. Now the tall city
stoops to receive us, where we blur like snow
leaving behind a breath of loves and angers.

—*Jane Cooper*

What Rough Beast

by Deena Metzger

... Finally he emerged in a small clearing and settled back on his haunches to find himself surrounded once again by his friends the dogs and by four white quacking geese.

How white they were. And how soft. The yellow horn of their bills were trumpets he wished to suck into his mouth to blow some blaring song. The notes extending abrupt and sharp under the tufted feathers at the tail. He took a goose in his hands and played its back, finding stops along its ribs to alter tunes. The wings fluttered uselessly but that was a song too and he held tight. It was tucked white and soft under his arm and filled with his own breath as a bag pipe and then the air so gently pressed out so that it sang not its own twisted bleat but as a swan might sing if it were played, or a round melon hollowed and struck with soft hands, or a full pregnant belly if it were strung to the neck and plucked. He was no longer on his knees but sitting cross legged and straight backed and playing to these beasts as if they understood how notes could sharpen and strike like a horn into the breast. And even the wings softened and stopped flapping, tremored only a little now and then when he found the heartbeat of the goose and played that. And then the wings fluttered because the rhythm was too strong to bear and the feathers flung the notes away.

And then he played its neck, stroking the feathered pipe so gently as though it were a flute through which the sound twisted into a mournful knot. His hands caressed the soft tube. His thumb probed the slight arch of the neck and his fingers ran deep onto the back reaching the skin. They were buried beneath the feathers and burrowed into the soft cover, emerged and stroked down again. After some moments it was an act he could not stop. When in the air his fingers tingled to be back again in the warmth. They rose up reluctantly and urgently rubbed their way down to be blanketed, submerged in the flesh at the end of the white down. Unexpectedly the goose which had been silent cried a little. A short flat piercing cry, a voice of its own, which was like a wing struggling to be free, or feet running, and he could not bear it and before he knew it his stomach reached into his fingers and pressed them closed that they might never have to leave that neck and pressed them tightly about the soft neck. His hands rubbed away from each other. The palms ran stiffly about the neck seeking to escape their own grip. But he could not let go. His hands only wound about the neck which bent and folded like clay does when it is twisted and soon it began to tear so that the feathers dulled in bright red blood spurting from the white flute which he drank thirstily from the bowl of his hands as the goose collapsed onto his lap in a last song.

Hunger had done it to him, had held him to it. He sat there before his dinner, thinking of a fire and the sweet smell of roasting flesh, thinking of the cold limp feathers in his lap and the blood taste. He set it up on its web feet and tried to balance it that it might walk again but it fell directly again into his stained lap. His hunger was a sharp pain, his guts writhing emptily, the flesh stretching open to be filled. Only warm air from his stomach filled his mouth, and the sharp taste of nausea settling inside of him, so that he heaved emptiness within him. He opened to and closed against the goose, sat stupefied amid the barking dogs, shaking his head at his choice, for he had made it as surely as if his stomach had hands of its own to pull plunder with. He was revolted, nauseated, twisted by the pain in his belly and the bird's pulse still beating on his palms, though he had dropped it, and which might always beat, that they could not both live, that he could not fill his mouth with sand and water but needed always to pull some plant up by the roots or chew the red heart of another beast.

Leo sat still for a long while. The dogs lay down also near him. Not quite at his feet but not at a distance. The other geese wandered off. The night sat too. And soon everything settled. The warm life of the goose slowly departed until the flesh was cold, the feathers limp, and the meat only food. Nothing that resembled life remained.

Leo got up, and started walking. He crouched under the branches and headed toward the street. The dogs followed at a polite distance. He had seen an empty lot on the next block and he was heading toward it. There were sticks in the gutter which he picked up and some paper and he broke some dry twigs from the maple trees. Most of the branches were covered with too many leaves and a few dry, naked twigs were wintering beside the leaves. He was doing the tree a service by trimming it.

At the lot he found whatever else he needed, even matches. He piled rocks together, and started his fire. There were enough pieces of wood in the area to cook his meal. He pulled the goose apart with his hands and plucked one part at a time, dropping the feathers into the fire and then spearing the meat on a wire which he had bent over the flames. The fat dripped onto the fire and yellow flames jumped and surrounded the meat. The smells of burnt feathers and oils, wood and paper and leaves all mixed pungently and rose in a black smoke which blended into the air. The coals were red hot and sparks spun into the night. He was finished and the goose was clean and roasting over his fire. Leo leaned in to adjust it and his arm passed into the flames. His hairs burned and the smell was familiar. Just for an instant he returned his arm until the hair seared again and then he pressed it to his nose. The black stumps smelled like the feathers he had burned. And he liked the smell. He pulled some long hairs from his head and held them over the fire, watching them pull back from the heat and then succumb, bubble for a moment into ashes and then disintegrate. Nothing was left.

If it were that easy to keep evil from him. Only burning his past and he was safe. If it took only that then he would send yesterday to ashes in a great red pyre. But tomorrow felt heavy to him. Tomorrow had been light for those brief hours in the woods, light tomorrow while rolling in the grass, while standing on a hill and seeing nothing but the spirit wind swirling dust into spires. Dead men traveling across the plain. He preferred those spirits and ran into them and let the wind wind about him so that he was clothed in it. Tomorrow was heavy, and though he burned all his nails and hair, though he swept his past from him, stamped out its sandy footprint in his mind, though there was nothing left that could be used against him, though he walked into it new and freshly born, and even his cord buried and the afterbirth burned, though all precautions would be taken, tomorrow was heavy, he knew.

The goose was ready. All the feathers were gone and soon the bones would be clean and buried and the skin eaten and the flesh too and the grease soaked into the ground and even the ashes blown away and then no harm could come to it. That was the only way. To be wound forever into the wind, to hoot out from the dark night into some cloistered corner and then hide again for years, to be the smoke coming up from the fire and fade out into the air living in the lungs of a scorpion or the gills of a fish or nesting in hot hummingbird heat. Yes that was the best way, better than slipping slowly into the ocean or hardening into stone or being wrapped by the white threads of roots pushing into the mouth and ears and eyes for food.

His feet had made him bitter. He looked at them reproachfully. So the death thoughts came from his feet and the death of the goose came from his stomach and there was nothing for him to do, wherever he was, for he did not feel that he was in his feet or his stomach but floating powerlessly knocking through the window at a deaf mute, nothing to do but sit by with all his buttons pushed until his body was satisfied. But with his feet looking the way they were, bloody and swollen and dripping and the dirt rubbed into every crevice so he could not tell scab from sand, how else was he to feel? But that he was meat and subject to spoil, just like the goose turning on the spit. And how was he to feel about it when he saw his feet looking the way they did and he knew that they would be more useful turning on the spit with the goose. For they were only flesh too. And roasted pretty fast and there was nothing more to it when his feet hurt. It doesn't make a difference, it or me, his feet thought and his stomach agreed and Leo lost somewhere outside of them protested in muffled tones but his tongue refused to move. There was a total insurrection. Even his arm refused to move anywhere but to get that goose. So it reached out and took the goose from the fire and broke off a leg and brought it to his mouth. It went into his mouth and the grease ran down his chin and in a moment the bones were clean and hastily buried so the dogs wouldn't get them and choke on the splinters. He threw them some meat to distract them and dug a hole with his nails. Some more dirt under them wouldn't matter.

The dirt packed under his nails and he could feel the grit of it as it pushed the nails away from the flesh. But he dug and buried and covered it up knowing they could smell the bones through the dirt but hoping they would be deceived by his own smell and think that something else was buried there. He hunched up close to the fire and threw another log on and watched the sparks explode up again. He had nothing to do but watch the fire. Never before had he done that, had he seen a fire so uncontrolled. Only the circle of stones held it together now. And if he wished to put it out he would need to shovel sand on it or stones or pound it with his feet or piss on it. And even then he could not be sure that it was really out. The rocks would stay hot and a coal might be blown out by the wind or a leaf might land and burst into flame and there it would go up to the sky and out but perhaps catching the dry brush as it rose and making torches of the grasses until the rains came.

There was an oak nearby and Leo did not want it to burn, nor the grass nor even the stickers which still caught in his skin. The red crackle within his stones was enough. But it wasn't certain that the rocks would hold it or that they themselves would not fill up and explode into the dry leaves or that the fire wouldn't leap over anything to catch the hair perhaps on Leo's own head and he would have to roll and roll in the dirt until it was out. It was a fight between them and one could destroy the other with a blow.

He was warm now and did not want to move. When had he sat like this before? Never. Previously he had seen only little blue beads of fire—which burned on gas and turned on and off by command. There was nothing to watch there. And once in a stone niche he had seen a fire. But not open like this, not free. Not cracking and leaping and red hot but mostly not changing. These flames moved and licked about the wood, curling one hot claw after another around the twigs, as if in love. As if they did not know the tree would wither from that touch. And they curved closer and closer to the bark which itself shrank from the touch and cried ashes until it broke and fell and the flame leaped up into the night and died. But there was still wood left and where one flame died another stepped forward on a yellow paw and grew fat and orange and then red or bristled with a blue tongue at the sap sputtering out of the wood to be consumed.

As the wood fell he scooped the coals quickly back into the fire so nothing would be left, so he could sit longer and be warm. And the dogs too seemed to like it for they lay close to him and dozed. And he felt contented and perhaps he even felt hopeful for the first time since he had determined to come down from the hills. Yes, if there were spots like this, then he could live. He was encouraged. If there were moments where the cement was broken and the earth came through and the trees grew wild and the leaves were not severed into shapes by shears but allowed to grow whole, then he could live. If he could build a fire and cook his food and burrow into dry leaves to sleep, then he had been mistaken. He had seen his adventure as a suicide. But now he was hopeful. It was possible that he would live.

The fire leaped about him and his face burned and the blood in his feet was warm and running through his veins and healing his wounds. There wasn't much wood left, only leaves and he threw them on though they smoked and some papers too, and he sat down again. Such a fire without the bells going and the wavering screams in the night promising disaster. Now what had made him think of that. The house going up in flames and the inarticulate animal screams and the bells going in the night, the bells sounding themselves like running water or drops on the tin roof and ringing now so that the sound of them would break the sky and suck the water down.

But the water never came. Never came in time and the fire roared louder as if it were the anger coming up from the mountain and shoving the earth aside to spill on everything and the bells dripping on the tin roof sizzled and went out. And the fire roared louder, sucking the air from everything into itself, sucking nothingness and living on that and deadening all other sound but itself so even the cries could not be heard nor the walls collapsing nor the roof falling into the flames. Only the bass of the fire and the thin bells tinkling uselessly in a higher key and a voice sometimes yelling unintelligibly. The bells going were the most vivid, ringing and ringing, and ringing like they did now. He could hear them again as if it were then. He could hear them now getting louder and louder as if the past were down the street and rushing on some engine toward him.

He jumped up. The fire had mesmerized him and the bells were real. And coming toward him and even in his confusion he understood. Coming toward him and his fire to put them both out. There was some brush at the end of the lot and a brick wall and some hibiscus in heavy bloom and he leaped toward it, climbed the wall and hid shaking in the bushes. He could see nothing and if they were coming for him he would not know. But he could hear the bells coming closer and then the engines stopping but the bells ringing nevertheless and the voices strange and angry and speaking in unison. A roarpack of voices. All together.

"Someone's crazy around here," they yelled.

Was he crazy who was so cold now trying to get warm before who had been so cold and was so again.

"Starting a fire in the middle of the block."

He could not see them, only hear their harsh voices which pimpled his skin and made him shiver with fear. He shook and the leaves shook and the big pink blossoms trembled as to a hummingbird and his heart stung as the yellow flower center must sting when priced by that sharp bill. They will think it a wind, only a wind caused by the fire, he thought.

If only the dogs would come to keep him warm. The dogs which had deserted him. The dogs which had gone immediately to their friends, which stood, Leo knew, nearby, watching, seeing the yellow snakes unwind and spit out his fire. The dogs which stood dumbly near the angry voices, no party to them but no foe. The dull dogs with tails down and incurious eyes staring at the marchers.

Leo did not need to see to know how they walked about the fire, staring, shouting, "Crazy man. Crazy. Where is he?"

"Just starting it and leaving it."

"I saw him. I don't know who it was. Just sitting and warming himself. With all these dogs around."

"Don't come to me now," Leo thought. He was so cold, but don't come to me now.

"Just a form?"

"I don't know. How could I tell from far. It was that damned smoke I smelled. Autumn smoke. Not spring smoke. Who burns leaves in spring. Only in Autumn. On Sundays. Crazy loon."

"Why make a fire at this hour? Crazy. Must be crazy."

"Well, put it out. You, put it out. Get that pumper going."

"Burning leaves at this hour."

"There must be a law against it. Know it must be illegal."

"No law? Well, there ought to be a law, Sunday's for burning leaves, everybody knows. Why, if I hadn't seen it it would be burning still."

"It's out now?"

"Are you sure?"

"Well, he must be nuts. We'll find it. Nuts can't keep covered long. They sprout sooner or later. Let's go home."

And the bells still clanging slipped away and the voices and then a few last steps and it was quiet. But for a long time Leo wouldn't move, thinking that there was someone there waiting for him, stalking him, knowing he had hidden close by in a place he couldn't see from, knowing the branches were digging in his back but he wouldn't move because there wasn't enough wind to cover him, and he was sure he was going to sneeze or cough or fall and tensing his muscles and relaxing them alternately because he didn't know which was best. His legs were aching and his neck hurt and his eyes threatened to close and leave him asleep, but he fought his body this time. And soon he knew he was right for there were steps near him. He could hear shoes kicking at stones, cans, looking for footprints. Then silence. They listened to each other. Leo didn't breathe. And then the footsteps again. Going away and the dogs with him. Down the street they went and soon he couldn't hear them anymore. There was a garage and a narrow alley behind with some trash cans there and he squeezed among them, being careful not to disturb anything. Two garages were back to back without touching and a small space between filled with barrels and boxes and rags and paint cans. He squeezed into the area, made a space for himself to curl into it. Gently he lowered his body onto the ground. He would sleep now. For the moment he was safe. □

Every Now And Then At Night

Every now and then at night
when a billowed cloud this side the moon
rides black and madam-like, I think of her.

Standing against the velvet draperies
in the almost pitch dark room, she
was the only shining thing.

Bulbous woman who peddled booze
in a dry county in a checkerboard wet dry state
in a wet war country, and all

that rot-gut she sold us
should have been pure silver
for the price we paid.

And we drank ourselves to lunacy
on our one night off the base.
We knew nobody but ourselves for a thousand miles.

So we dreamed she
was our black and shining mother,
and she was.

—Ann Darr

E.D.

Even the legend of Emily has died—
that shy recluse of Amherst
dressed in white.

Now we know
there was a Ben
Newton and
a Reverend
Charles Wadsworth:

but one died young
the other married.

And Emily?

Her *life closed*
twice before its close.

E.D.
Emily Dickinson
Born 1830
Died 1886
Given to America 1890.
Coded, edited, revised:
3 vols., *The Poems of*, 1955
3 vols., *The Letters*, 1958

And for excellent accounts of
the poet
major
American
(woman)
who bears the name
Emily Dickinson
see
George F. Whicher, *This Was a Poet*, 1938
Thomas H. Johnson, *Emily Dickinson: An Interpretative*
 Biography, 1955
and still acceptable
(and sound)
by a woman
(also poet, American)
Genevieve Taggard
The Life and Mind of Emily Dickinson, 1930

Emily Dickinson
once body
once frail
once having had
no more than seven
poems
slipping into print
during her lifetime
now duly saved
in 3 vols.
neat
coded
beautifully embalmed.
I'm nobody! Who are you?
Are you nobody, too?

—*Harriet Zinnes*

Idyll

by Carolyn Banks

They avoided the glass glitter of the greenhouse and walked into the shed. The light fell curiously, striating their clothing and their features. Looking at the striped columns she thought of Cordova. She would have said so, but he spoke.

"My mountain ash died," he told her. "A great catastrophe in my family."

"My mother had a mountain ash. Two of them. You need two, don't you? For berries?"

"Oh, no. Mine bloomed very nicely alone. I think a willow would be nice. The dampness killed the other, you know." He led her to a plot where the young trees grew unsheltered.

She tried to concentrate. "Willow will get into your water pipes, won't it? Don't willow trees look for water?"

He spoke evenly, "I shall be gone by then." He was in his sixties.

The trees were weak and narrow, their leaves choked with roadside dust. She frowned at them, "They look sick, these trees."

He bent to the ground, turning a tiny pale egg with one finger. There was a small mucoid pool where it had rested. She looked up, expecting to find a nest in the wan branches overhead.

They walked single-file through the slatted shed again, down the long green rows. The dark smell of earth grew heavier. The strips were too closely zoned to permit them to walk abreast. Here and there were hanging baskets, so low that he stooped to avoid jarring them. She read the names, smiling.

The herb table stopped her and she leaned to the peppermint, saddened by its fading aroma. "Shouldn't mint be . . . ?" but he had passed beyond her, through the greenhouse door. She watched him for a while, until he saw her.

"Sweet William," he called at her approach.

Later they sat on the bench of a picnic table facing a pond. A split rail fence held off the road, but not the sound of traffic. Five ducks swam toward them.

"Oh," she placed her hand on his forearm, "I wish we had something to give them."

The Last Train

"The long-distance passenger train has moved one step nearer to extinction: on July 26 The New York Central said it intends to discontinue all trains running over 200 miles . . ."
                        U.S. News & World Report

There may have been a boy,
lying in a cabin in the subtle place
where field and plain each goes its separate way,
who fell asleep to the muffled drumming of buffalo,
as, dark and shaggy as sleep itself,
they travelled past his window towards extinction.

Now in a house at the edge of the same plain,
another boy lets consciousness recede
on the receding whistle of a train
passing his open window for the last time,
leaving behind a spike or rusted nails
like arrowheads or pieces of dried bone.

So we are left,
each boy, each sleeper,
to the single, abstract tone of the jet plane.
We follow sleep as well as we are able
along disintigrating paths of vapor,
high above the dreamlike shapes of clouds.

—Linda Pastan

Josef Erhardy

The Dance
Marble with inlaid color, 1966.
Collection: Madame Annick Rollin-Roth-Le-Gentil, Paris

Keep Off The Grass (A divertissement

(The two performers should be dressed in black leotards. The ball can be an eight foot inflatable weather balloon, or, if space is limited smaller. Preferably the movement should be choreographed by a dancer.)

       He
(Enters stage right pushing the ball. He looks at it admiringly and turns to the audience.)
It's round.
       She
(Entering stage left.)
Like the world.
       He
You're not supposed to be here.
       She
Why not?
       He
This is mine.
(Caresses the ball.)
       She
What difference does that make?
       He
I want to think about it.
       She
Can't we both think about it?
       He
(Considers this.)
Yes.
       She
How?
       He
(Pushes the ball and lets it roll stage Left.)
A snowball.
       She
(Runs across and rolls it stage right.)
A ripe peach.
       He
(Retrieves it and sends it upstage.)
Sunset.
       She
(Runs up and sends it downstage.)
Sunrise.
       He
(Spins it in one spot.)
The wheel of life.
       She
(Kicks it away.)
Disaster.
       He
(Runs after it, stops it and holds it still.)
Buried treasure.
       She
(Crosses toward the other side of the ball and pushes toward him. They push against each other during the following lines.)
I'm the queen of summer.
       He
I'm the king of the castle.
       She
I'm crossing the Sahara on a dromedary.
       He
I'm flying over Spain.
       She
My father was a deep sea diver.
       He
My mother was a harem beauty.

(As they both push hard the ball escapes and goes upstage. The Momentum carries them into each other's arms. There is a long kiss. They break, go to opposite sides of the stage and sit facing each other. They do not move. This lasts as long as the audience can stand it. Then she goes up stage to the ball and places her ear against it.)

       She
I can hear it breathing.
       He
(Also comes up and listens.)
I don't hear a thing.
       She
That's because you have six toes on your right foot.
       He
I do not have six toes on my right foot.
       She
How do you know? When did you last look?
       He
I looked this morning.
       She
That doesn't prove a thing. You might have had a birthday since then.
       He
You imagine things. You imagine a black cat jumped in the window.
       She
It did jump in the window.
       He
You imagine this ball is here.
(He caresses it.)
       She
Well it is.
       He
It is and it isn't. I made it up.
       She
You're wasting time. I'm the one who knows what's happening.
       He
(Listen to ball again.)

for the poetic theatre)

by H. R. Hays

I don't like this. It will cost a lot of money.
    She
Oh no it won't. A few nice fresh
words every day will be enough.
    He
Like what words?
    She
Like blue and yellow. Like ice cream soda
and harpsichord. Like forever and ever.
    He
Those are no good. If you said oleomargarine
and melted lead or electromagnet and fire
hydrant, I'd feel much better.
    She
Anyway, we must be very careful.
    He
We'll only drink bottled water.
    She
And never go to the toilet when it rains.
    (They move over side by side
    and begin to push the ball in a
    circle about the stage together
    as they talk.)
    He
Do you think we'll need a sphygnomanometer?
    She
Perhaps if you just put your pants on backward . . .
    He
But then I'll be sure to find frogs
in the morning mail.
    She
Only tadpoles.
    He
It was bad enough when all the blood
ran out of my watch.
    She
That was because you forgot to dip
it in flour before you wound it.
    (There is a long pause as they
    roll the ball silently.)
    He
Shall we communicate with the old
birdcages left in the attic?
    She
Mayflies and other winged creatures.
    He
Or compose odes to the subway?
    She
Especially at night when all the trees
have folded their leaves.
    He
There may be a passage beyond the alphabet.
    She
When I was only seven a fairytale
wiggled its ears at me.
    He
Answer when spoken to, using either yes or no.
    She
Spaghetti, dyed pale blue and used
for making chairseats.
    He
    (Stops abruptly.)
I've had enough! I will not give
haircuts to screechowls!
    She
I was expecting that! I was even expecting
you to shoot my grandmother!
    He
How could I do that? She has a castiron leg!
    She
    (Sends the ball violently away.)
And your uncle raises armadillos.
    He
    (He retrieves ball and drives it
    back at her. This continues with
    acceleration during the next lines.)
It's not true! They're Australian anteaters!
    She
I hate you! Ever since I discovered
you eat pickles!
    He
And what about those newspapers you're
always burning in the bathtub?
    She
You made that up! You made that up just to
take my middle name away from me!
    He
You mislaid your middle name last
Wednesday in the supermarket!

    She
    (As the ball goes faster they hurl
    the following words at each other.)
Carpet sweeper!
    He
Fryingpan!
    She
Hootowl!
    He
Carburators!
    She
Hacksaw!
    He
Microscope!
    She
Gingerale!
    (They both freeze for a minute.)
    She
I always have my hair done on
Friday morning.
    He
Keep off the grass!
    (They fling the ball into the audience.)
    Both
It's all yours!
    (They walk offstage in opposite directions.)

From *The Lamp*

"All adolescence sputters and flares
Like a lamp overturned in the rain."
                      (Pablo Neruda)

The tract darkens in the dusk;
Streetlights, burning but with
No effect, bobble in the wind;
Leaves pirouette along the curbs;
And the last child heads home.

And in your house, your home,
You see your mother's face
Above a tall lace shade
Grow pale in the sudden light
She sets against the evening.

She lingers for a moment, then
Is gone; while in another room,
Another light, your father slouches
Watching cowboys, filling time
Until the time for sleep.

You hurry to the car, left
Waiting for you in the drive,
Start the engine, readjust
The seat, mirrors, radio
To make it yours again,

Then floor it. And once again,
With screaming tires, sucking
Carburetors, inside glass and steel,
A world, moving among worlds.
You hurl yourself towards town.

The engine winds to Eighty
Before you ease off, relax a bit,
Roll down the windows, and let

A smile break across your face.
You guess you showed them.

Overhead, the sky closes
Tight above the valley's hills,
A promise of approaching winter
When colors are reduced to grey:
Red-grey, blue-grey, green-grey.

You don't care; passing seasons
Only mark a change of sports:
Another jacket, another year.
You stand your collar upright
And scan the radio for songs.

At the edge of town you
Pull into a service station.
A boy your age leaps up
At the first bell, then slows
A little, seeing who it is.

"Fill it," you call, digging
For the credit card, and getting
Out to stand and watch,
Hands jammed into your pockets.
A passing car honks; you halloo.

"Big night tonight," you grin,
Expecting everyone feels that way.
The boy, kneeling, looks up from
The tank and shrugs: "Guess so."
You think to ask about his wife

And kid, but what the hell.
The tag signed, stamps collected,
Stashed away with all the rest,
You roar away, proud of burning
Rubber half a block. . .

                      —Richard Snodgrass

Where It Was

An echelon of ducks veers
    overswamp like some lost
    squadron from the world's last
war.
        Unstuttering they go
before and after buckshot
buckles one.
            Crumpling, it
falls from a white flakburst
of feathers.
            It leaves the memory
of where it was.
            The feathers,
one by three by five
coming fallingleafing down
The echelon ascends.
            The place
where the duck would have been
rises and soars with the flock.

—Samuel Hazo

An Amicable Solution

(PEACE OVER BEASTLINESS)

A crocodile and a hippopotamus met one dark afternoon on the muddy bank of an uncertain river. They looked each other balefully in the eye, under lids scaly with protective leather. This confrontation was timeless, for time had no meaning for either of those hide-bound animals. The hippopotamus confused the crocodile for a snake. The crocodile confused the hippopotamus for an elephant that likes to travel light and so has deposited its trunk with an immovable porter. These confusions grew out of ignorance, and simply added to what they grew out of. "Goodbye to your fat and thick ugliness," assured the crocodile, casting a cordial look upon the mud-baked hulk and graceless bulk of the bulging, blunt, and brutish hippopotamus. The hippopotamus was not a beast to take an insult lightly. (Not for nothing does it weigh a useless ton.) "Farewell, you sea-snake stuck to a dried-up river hole with nothing slimy to slither on," wished the unpleasant hippopotamus. On that unfriendly note, those decided enemies parted, having outdone man in wisdom: war and bloodshed had not been resorted to.

—Marvin Cohen

Voyages

A NATIONAL LITERARY MAGAZINE
WASHINGTON, D.C. $2.00
VOL. III NOS. III & IV SPRING, 1970
ISSUE # 8/9

REED WHITTEMORE ISSUE • HOMAGE TO DAVID GALLER • ALAN C. PURVES
WILLIAM STAFFORD • BORGES • POEMS • REVIEWS

Voyages

A NATIONAL LITERARY MAGAZINE
WASHINGTON, D.C. $2.00
VOL. IV NOS. I & II WINTER, 1971
ISSUE # 10/11

JOHN UNTERECKER SECTION • DANIEL STERN • HENRY H. ROTH
V. LLONA ON FITZGERALD • H. WITHERSPOON • JOHN TAGLIABUE • POEMS • REVIEWS

Voyages

A NATIONAL LITERARY MAGAZINE
WASHINGTON, D.C. $3.00
VOL. IV NOS. III & IV ISSUE # 12/13
SPRING 1971 – SPRING 1972
(a combined issue)

JOHN LOGAN ISSUE: ROBERT BLY, SISKIND PHOTOS • JOYCE CAROL OATES
M.J. BOSSE • K. FORT • ROETHKE NOTEBOOKS • C. HALLETT • W. McEVILLY

Voyages

A NATIONAL LITERARY MAGAZINE
WASHINGTON, D.C. $3.00
VOL. V (NOS. I–IV) ISSUE #14/15
1973 FINAL ISSUE

MARK VAN DOREN MEMORIAL ISSUE: NEW POEMS, TRIBUTES • BARTHELME
THREE ARTISTS: BIDDLE, SULLIVAN & PEREIRA • FLYTHE • NIN • REVIEWS

from Amos Bailey

by Hiram Haydn

It was the grocer. It took him two trips to bring in the packages, the while he whistled like a bobolink. He arranged all the items, as precisely as though setting up a new store.

Amos watched with curiosity his quick, nervous but efficient movements. I have never really looked at this man before, he thought, and felt an unexpected pang. He had never seen that his hair was a tight curly red mat, that he was abundantly freckled, that he was a wiry man of forty or so, and that his biceps bulged below his short sleeves. Until now, Amos realized, he had really observed only his eyes: a strange slate color, but flecked at moments of interest with a brighter light.

On impulse Amos said, "Do sit down, Mr. _____. Have a drink with us."

For a moment the rufous man froze on tiptoe, as though about to break into flight. Then he relaxed and said with a thin, frosty smile, "Don't mind if I do. It's slow at the store. And that bourbon you buy is good."

Amos bustled about, preparing their drinks, wondering as he worked how Jill would appear this time, and why he had invited this man to stay. When —

"Name's Clarke, T.E. Clarke," said the grocer as he accepted his glass. "With an *e* at the end."

They lifted their glasses politely, and then sat in awkward silence.

Finally Mr. Clarke ceased his bright, birdlike contemplation of object after object.

" 's clearing. The sun will be out less'n hour." He looked sharply at Amos, as though expecting to be contradicted. "And then," he added portentously, "the whole sky'll flush clean, and it'll be that after-storm blue. Blue as Mrs. Delafield's eyes."

Amos choked on his drink, spluttered and coughed. With her unerring timing, Jill entered the room, wearing her one dress, her silky hair loose over her shoulders.

"Hello," she said.

The men rose, Amos with difficulty.

"Mr. Bailey's having trouble with his larynx," T.E. Clarke said drily. "Let me make you a drink, Mrs. Delafield, and I'll maybe just freshen up mine while I'm about it."

Jill's soft arms and scented cheek proved an antidote to Amos' choking spasm, but not to his confusion. Yet she seemed cool, unperturbed. A suspicion spun through his mind. She had predicted the knock, apparently knew Clarke much better than he did, possibly—He blew it away and settled for the generalization that she was a witch.

"Thanks, groceryman," said Jill, and took a first sip.

Clarke looked at her flintily.

"Why d'you call me that?" he demanded.

She batted her eyes at him.

"I'm sorry if you're offended, but that's the way I always think of you. As *The* Groceryman, actually. Like The Walrus or The Carpenter."

"What sort of talk is that?" The Groceryman asked, but more in amusement (derision?) than in anger, it seemed to Amos.

"Straight talk," said Jill. "I'm not a canny New Englander."

Amos was studying them.

"Apparently you've known each other longer than I realized?"

"Haven't exchanged the time of day more'n seven-eight times in the store," said The Groceryman shortly. "But Mrs. Delafield knows my knocker gets all inflamed whenever I see her, and I expect she's putting me in my place."

Jill let out a snort of laughter, but Amos stood up, red-faced.

"I won't have you talking to Mrs. Delafield like that." His voice was strong, controlled. What *was* happening to him? "This is my house, Clarke, and you'll apologize or get out."

"Pish," said the Groceryman. "It's not your house, but Everett Saunders'. And for that matter, we're in the twentieth century, where Islanders and off-Islanders can talk together like humans. And it's off-season, so you're not summer visitors, and I don't have to be polite to you. But—just a minute, Mr. Bailey—I'll do as you wish, for you're a nice man. A muddler, perhaps, but a true gentleman. So I'll say, Mrs. Delafield, that I'm sorry I spoke like an uncouth Islander a word or two you've no doubt heard about a thousand times."

"That's no—" Amos began angrily, but Jill put her cool palm over his lips.

"Hush, darling. He doesn't mean any harm, or anyway I don't care what he says."

"I mean harm, all right," said The Groceryman, "But not to Mr. Bailey. And that's why I offered to bring the groceries out. To warn him a bit. Not about His Lordship your husband, who's left the Island claiming he's glad to be rid of you. But this here's the Commonwealth of Massachusetts, you know, and there be an antique statute or two about adultery that some of the older Island heads remember. And you couldn't know, Mr. Bailey, but Island justice in the winter bears precious little resemblance to the kind you're used to, be it Boston or Philadelphia or Shutwell's Corners."

"Are you threatening us?" Amos' voice was firm again, cold. "What business is it of yours what we do? Can no one live his life here without old gossips making up lies and slander?"

"Mmm." The slate eyes turned almost humorous. "I think you've summed it up pretty well, Mr. Bailey, with your questions. It could be put even stronger, though."

Jill rose briskly.

"Amos, I think I understand The Groceryman. So let me make us another round, and I'll do a little questioning."

She collected the glasses. The back view of her was even more distracting than usual, Amos noticed darkly. I'm over my depth, he thought.

He set his fresh drink aside, but the other two sipped for a moment in silence. Then Jill spoke, with a sharpness new to Amos.

"You've come to negotiate, Groceryman. What do you want?"

His face seemed to grow sharper, But he chuckled.

"Right to the point, eh? All right, better so, for I'll be on my way when I finish this drink. It is *good* bourbon, Mr. Bailey.

"Well, Mrs. Delafield, as I said, I wouldn't have harm come to Mr. Bailey, nice as he is and here to get over his heart attack. But there's not much misses the Islanders' eyes. We know about the goings on between you and your husband and that other summer couple, and we're as horny as the next one. But we have our own law and order, too, and there's those as would rather see you facing trial for your shenanigans than teaching us old party games that we know anyhow from way back. So whatever you think of The Groceryman, he's been looking out for you. And all I ask you now is to be hospitable tomorrow night when I'll bring over a friend or two that's ready to help you out of this jam." He rose. "Now, Mr. Bailey, I can see that you're taking me wrong, misreading my meaning. Tomorrow night's talk will be quiet and proper as Methodist prayer meeting."

He was gone. Like that. Leaving a gaping door that framed the shining blue world of after-storm.

* * *

The Unending Gift

by Jorge Luis Borges

Un pintor nos prometio un cuadro.

Ahora, en New England, se que ha muerto. Senti como otras veces, la tristeza y la sorpresa de comprender que somos como un sueno. Pense en el hombre y en el cuadro perididos.

(Solo los dioses pueden prometer, porque son inmortales.)

Pense en un lugar prefijado que la tela no ocupara.

Pense despues: si estuviera ahi, seria con el tiempo esa cosa mas, una cosa, una de las vanidades o habitos de mi casa; ahora es ilimitada, incesante, capaz de cualquier forma y cualquier color y no atada a ninguno.

Existe de algun modo. Vivira y crecera como una musica, y estara conmigo hasta el fin. Gracias, Jorge Larco.

(Tambien los hombres pueden prometer, porque en la promesa hay algo inmortal.)

*Jorge Luis Borges
"Nueva Antologia Personal"
Emece Editores, Buenos Aires, 1968, p. 83

The Unending Gift

A painter promised us a painting.

Now, in New England, I learn that he has died: I felt as other times, the sadness and surprise of comprehending that we are as a dream. I thought on the man and on the lost painting.

(Only the gods can promise, because they are immortal.)

I thought on a predetermined place where the canvas will never reside.

I thought afterwards: if it would be there, there would be with time that thing more, a thing, one of the vanities or customs of my house; now it is unbounded, unceasing, capable of any form and any color, not tied to any thing.

It exists in some mode. It will live and will grow as a musical piece, and will remain with me to the end. Thanks, Jorge Larco.

(Yes, men can promise, because in the promise there is something immortal.)

Translated by Robert Newcomb

A Note on Landscape

by John Unterecker

1.

Ghosts that attempt to escape the hold of life haunt places made unnaturally vivid by intensity of passion. A haunted house traps ghostly lovers in one corner of a room where centuries before a heap of rumpled quilts defined their lives; a murderer haunts open fields that once had been dense forest; a vaporous terrified spirit still hovers above the cliff that marked his suicide. Such ghosts surround us, fill the breathing landscape with breathless agony. We brush past them, of course, unconcerned, indifferent to passions not our own. At most, we experience an inexplicable chill at sunset, the long light brightening the cliff we stand on. Or so we say, trying to believe ghost stories for the sake of the ghosts.

2.

Ghosts of a different kind—infinitely more vivid, their landscapes places I have walked—people memory. The streets they brightened dominate dream and daydream. They are the unforgettable bright figures who drive us, if we are lucky, into art.

For Wordsworth was at least partially right: violent emotion (in my experience, never recollected in tranquility) dominates us until we discover forms that permit us almost to cope with it. We find those forms in the world around us. Light that moves along an elm restores us to the only August vineyards memory owns. A child calling from across a stream plunges us—we think forever—into a forest overgrown in brambles and fern, over and over returns us to April's white flare of wild orchids, July's lizard-crusted walls, February's sea anemones and urchins, again and again to the first musky breath of March acacia or the dark miraculous flow of January seas.

Feelings restore the event; the event restores its landscape—and I am on a narrow cobbled street. Mobylettes lean against flaked stucco walls. Mike, Francois' dog, darts out between forge and anvil. "Jour, Francois." "Jour. Travaille bien, monsieur." "Oui." Half a dozen Catalan ladies, net sacks in hand, crowd the counter of Madame Maillol's butcher shop. Paul, seven years old, holds a kitten in one hand and a toy rifle in the other. Our street—the Rue du Soleil—twists one more time, then opens out abruptly onto beach, harbor and bay and, beyond bay, onto the luminous flat reaches of the Mediterranean.

3.

Painter and poet share, I think, an attitude toward landscape. At least, I hope they do. But I can speak only for myself. It as if a double action moves between the real remembered place and another similar one that I invent. Here, in an area between two worlds, the ghost walks. I sometimes call him you, and when I do that, I think I know who you are. But in fact, of course, you may in those moments become only what I need you to be.

4.

It is in these rarest of times, when you engage the two landscapes, that a dialogue of then and now begins, the past seeming to remember the present, almost to demand it, and the present offering itself to the past as to a lover. Mountains, canyon, and cliff rearrange themselves to permit one figure to emerge against a blossoming tree. I am breathless from the musky odor of bright blossoms.

5.

Perhaps the painter's forms that seem to me reminiscent of flesh are nothing more than what they ought to be: the abstract pattern of cloud on sky, reflected cloud on water. Certainly an abstract rhythm moves the painting, confining my eye yet manipulating it through a series of echoing interrelated planes. Nevertheless, I should like both to discover and to deny a body, or the memory of a body, in the landscape. I should like to feel and to reject and yet respond to a muscular sort of tension in the abstracted shape of mirrored cloud, castle, and sea wall. The painting is a sensuous rhythm made out of planes of space and of affection and of color—affection, perhaps, only for the place itself, or for the processes of painting, or for a way of being that has nothing to do with overt subject matter.

The subject matter of the poem, more literal, is always the sleight of hand that distracts us from the workings of the poem. I say, "The poem is about Collioure." And of course it is. But it is more significantly about feelings that happened there. The subject matter is the vehicle for a set of interrelated significant images. The images are the vehicle for emotion.

6.

It is not especially important, it seems to me, that Collioure —which does have almond trees, anemone, and the true musky yellow mimosa blossoms of the acacia, which does have grey lizards sunning on grey sea walls—it is not especially important, I think, that Collioure does not have a canyon made dangerous by spring rains. I have seen a canyon thirty miles inland from the coast. It cuts into the rough mountains behind Amelie-les—Bains. I remember no acacia on any of the sea cliffs near Collioure but I do remember Collioure acacia. The poem distorts the real landscape for the sake of the poem's truth.

7.

Feelings seem to me always to call up darkness and light, the vacillations of sea, the drainage and renewal of tide pools. Feelings live in the quick mortality of cut flowers. It is as if the visible world were an orchestration of natural symbols and as if our feelings were a melody woven in and of them.

There seems always to be an implicit dancer in the poem. You find yourself reflected in the poem as if miracle had taken place, your arms, legs, and torso full of a still motion.

The rhythms of the poem are only superficially the rhythms of the spoken words. Another rhythm moves against spoken rhythms: the feelings silently balance out dark/light; sea/land; canyon/seascape; blossom/stem/root. A rhythm of statements— of ideas—is also ultimately superimposed on the insistent rhythm of the spoken word and the hovering rhythm of emotion. The dancer's head remembers rhythms of the heart; the dancer's heart explores the variations hammered on a drum.

8.

The painter's landscape involves us in a set of planes flattened out on canvas; near, more distant, most distant become elements of one design on a two-dimensional surface. This dragonfly poised on my wrist, the eyes of the dragonfly two feet from my own eyes; a grey cat crossing a green lawn; evergreens ten feet beyond the cat; beyond the evergreens, an infinity of sky—these planes that are nearest, near, distant, most distant sheets of space might be the operative planes of an artist's canvas.

The planes of the poem superimpose now on then, then on earlier-than-then, earlier-than-then on earliest time. Today's spatial planes—dragonfly/cat/evergreen/sky—become a *now* superimposed on last night's dinner party where eleven figures who an hour before had danced recall their dancing, among them one, at least, who also recalls a painting of Collioure that is outside of time yet of a time four years before the dancing. For the sake of the poem, the two arts merge. The remembered painting of Collioure is always simultaneously *now* and *then*, just as the image of dragonfly/cat/evergreen/sky becomes a *now* within its poem but a *then* on that today—August 27, 1969—when I first wrote these words that vanished into history's open-ended garbage can long before the *now* in which you now read them.

The painter flattens the various planes of his visible space to one two-dimensional surface; the poem compresses layers of time into a duration that extends only from first line to last. Both painting and poem necessarily manipulate the world. Both of them defy instant apprehension. While we watch it, we explore the action of the painting but experience it as a whole in flashes—perhaps always only in flashes of memory. The poem is built in us as we read it or hear it, but it becomes *poem* only after the last word has been comprehended.

9.

Both poem and painting exist finally halfway between artist and audience. The work is a dialogue, always, and for that reason its assertion is always tentative. My poem is necessarily what you make of it. Your drawing, so far as I am concerned, is what my eye finds on your canvas.

10.

I have no choice but to believe that the objective of both painter and poet is to discover the real—the true form of things that is always begging painter and poet to expose it. The variations of that form are the dancer, the almost-irresponsible action of the painting that moves my eye along its surface or into its depths, the erratic, finally incalculable action of the poem that compresses into a felt statement that you share a design of days and places.

For painter and for poet, feeling finds a time and place to dance within the painting and within the poem. The poem says "I love you" to the ghost that haunts its landscapes. The landscapes of the painter breathe as if they were the living body of the world. □

A Dream of an Attic

In a dream I find in an attic my two brothers,
And my own son, and I hear shouting,
One brother ordering other out of the attic,
Other declining,
And I wake and walk to my studio through the woods
With my flashlight, some jelly rolls and these dream goods.

No moon, no wind. Like an attic. But where?
I run through my old ones in darkness. None of them fits.
None of them has the look of the dream, nor the presence
Unnameable in it that now I have lost
On the road in the night with my jellyrolls, dream-crossed.

So I come to my desk with my mystery and sit down
And think of all beginnings in all attics
With brothers and sons there, and the shouting,
And I see that the part of the dream that I couldn't know
On the road in the night with the jellyrolls
                was I. Where did I go?

—Reed Whittemore

President Richard Nixon Has Destroyed South Nyack

by Henry H. Roth

1.

Richard Nixon has been dogging me since College. Now on a faded tree loaded street, Nixon wipes away past films of frustration and defeat. He smiles in shy leer, he has found me, cornered me. Aside from the trees, nothing else has been spared; broken bodies and homes litter the once immaculate town; South Nyack has been leveled; President Richard Nixon has destroyed South Nyack. Only Nixon and I are left.

* * * * * * * * * * 2.

Veer away from childhood memories. Childhood is overwhelming, too big and cumbersome; play streets snarled with the crush of feet and arms and sad noises that live on interminably. Childhood ugly because the finest memories still retain terrifying backdrops; Christmas Chanukah cheer; filthy crapped on snow, false gay strings of merchants' lights swinging through the boulevards. I can still see the creasing of mask faces into incredible miracle of puny smile. Incidents follow dully like the next boring hour—toneless bells seek attention and reverence. How I longed for flight and did not dare!

I graduated two years ahead of normal age pattern, crowded schools ill-conceived accelerated programs plus a convenient birthdate (enabling my education to commence at five and one half) sped me through programmed conformity. Yet that is not truly fair to the systems that guided my thoughts since I always considered rebellion but did not even intensely meditate until senior year in high school. Two years later in Nantucket a friend and I planned a raft ride to Europe. Convinced of success Bruce made inquiries about the price of ship worthy wood in addition drew a tentative sketch while I debated what should be classified necessities. Neither of us doubted that one day we would alight from a gigantic cork to a sandy shore in England or if the winds were severe (as well they might be) an Irish rocky coast would be our target.

Alas, a lovely native girl offered my comrade, my shipmate what was through centuries oft denied even a married new englander. Being of sophisticated clime he cherished the gift, the pair went off for the remainder of the summer to receive and give thanks. And I was left with the list price of wood, a rough (extremely) sketch a thermos and a recently purchased duffle bag. I sold the damn thermos, the empty duffle accompanied me back to the city. One day I vowed I would use it . . . from that time I have been aware of a lump of varying size speed and bulk that tails me. Always two blocks behind and half a scene away; it was richard milhous nixon.

* * * * * * * * * * 3.

Once I rode the subway until it could go no further; as the train left important stops and many unimportant people scrambled out, perfume and sweat left too and I achieved for the first time the wonderful feeling of leaving everyone, everything behind. The duffle was no longer a bulky annoyance pushed at by my savage-eyed neighbors, but like me now stretched out upon the straw seats of an empty car. Still very early in the morning and I half longed for additional hours of untroubled sleep in my air conditioned room—but I threw a handmade bomb into the family trench and with sound of foundations splintering my mind was scrubbed clean. The train came to a halt, doors slid open, the day greeted me with great stabs of light; I bowed, pointed to my partner, slung him over my shoulder and did not look back or even think of waving goodbye.

* * * * * * * * * * 4.

Just after the big war, the PARADISE'S main building burnt to the ground and was rebuilt to glory never dreamed by the original owner. Just after Korea the recreation inn sizzled away and was replaced by three buildings: dance hall, playhouse, and a BAR boasting the largest TV screen in the Land of Dolly. These sturdy edifices were constructed by the resort's third owner; with each military victory for our side a patriotic bonfire was lit and upon the smoldering ashes like a French Provincial phoenix, an impressive resort had been spawned.

The BAR was the money taker since the other structures "were Free: for the enjoyment of our pampered guests." The Bar was similar to any disreputable club found in all our cities; the drinks were watered, none of the waiters smiled, everyone who owned a piece of the establishment garnered great profits.

A fat slob man scolded the bar boy.
"Where's the scotch sunny?"
"One second sir."
"That's service, you said a minute before."
The boy gave the order "Piss in the glass for the gentleman in the corner."
The bartender feigned anger, "What the hell else do you think we serve here."
Tables were filled, the voices loud and happy, a lone bar boy skipped from table to table picking up dimes and quarters, the only positive proof of departing customers. By three in the morning all possible revelry was concluded, the take was counted.
. . . twenty-seven dollars and thirty cents. I'll take thirteen fifty, you can have the extra thirty pennies.
After the manager left, the boy fished out a heavy assortment of coins from a back pocket and began counting aloud, "and eight twenty-five I forgot to put in the kitty." In two short weeks he had grasped the intricacies of sharing in a resort — fifty percent, and all you can steal.

* * * * * * * * * * 5.

Sandy was adept to all my nuances and bravado, she was not impressed but simply enjoyed my company. She was a gifted guitarist and usually before lights out would stroll into my bunk and sing to the kids tales of love, war and woe. Like me they loved her. She loved Camus, Boris Pasternak's face and Jerry Lewis.
"Did you read Camus' last stories?"
"Sure."
"Which one did you like the best?"

55

"The one about the painter that goes mad."

She clapped hands excitedly, YES, yes that's the one.

Camus, Camus, yesterday it had been Melville and Billy Budd, I was afraid to even touch her accidentally and yet sketched myself as her partner in any DeSade position while she tanned Aztec golden with three freckles upon a perfect nose lusted for a pavan, a square dance, or truth and me.

"You don't even know my name, you shouldn't even be seen talking to me."

We walked slowly, leaning on one another.

I don't know how old I am, I whispered, but if I had said it aloud she would have touched my hand and not smiled because what I said to her was not taken any longer as joke. It was true, I had no name, possessor of nothing but my clothing I walked these gardens with my first real companion and I was younger than newborn child.

* * * * * * * * * * 6.

There were three sessions made up of twenty daytime periods, I was hired during the second shift; at first I felt sorry for these foster children—these forever emigrees. Certainly my hand clenching Oliver Twists were affected by constant change, and were alive to subtle and direct unconcern for their future but they were not surprised by its presence, they expected nothing from the world and were amply rewarded.

The single exception was Victoria who was permitted to remain the entire nine week life of Camp Welfare. A skeleton frame of a six year old, pale face closer to ash grey, and exquisite straight line of nose, clear deep blue eyes and the turned down lips of a clown who sadly is not meant to be an entertainer. She walked with a faulty jerk as if her body had never been taught final control, her head forever sagged to one side; Victoria's skin an incredible white that would not permit the sun to have any effect, yet all parts of her body blossomed with blemishes at the slightest contact with dirt.

Victoria was in Sandy's bunk and since she stayed while others unpacked then packed and were gone, we all grew to love her and the task of arousing the miracle of a smile became a gentle obsession with the staff. It was a mission however, to the camp director who explained all to me one rainy afternoon.

"I'll level with you, you're the best counsellor up here, there'll be a bonus anyway but a whopper if you can do something with the kid."

"It'd be nice."

"Better than nice, Victoria's a test case, if we can succeed with her, the budget of the camp next year will be tripled. That little babe has got to be like the others."

"Some treat."

If I can show a real shift in her personality, this welfare camp will be big business.

I tried, but not because of the director or an opportunity to see Sandy even more during the day, but very simply I had respect for Victoria's silence and deathly complexion dotted with pimples. She was what I could have been at six if my parents were unwilling to assume even technical responsibility, there is an age for everyone when we are hardly distinguishable from Victoria, but she was so very young and could not conceal any of her fears and you ached at the frozen features, the stiff walk and the lolling head.

Victoria had grown accustomed to seeing me and did not refuse an invitation for a walk. I slackened my pace to allow her to catch up, she stopped walking, poised to run back to the bunk. I was tired and she had to be, I sat down and strangely she walked up to me and sat very close. Little beads of perspiration ringed down her cheeks, the non-posing madonna truly sad.

"Why did you take me?"

"I like company, even if you don't walk near me. I still like you around."

She wiped her lips with a slap.

"Victoria, did you know that was the name of a queen?"

She looked at me.

"A queen whom everyone loved."

"A good queen."

"A honey of a queen."

"But I don't like my name."

"Hey, I know. Let's call you another name that means the same as Victoria only it's a funny name. A nickname."

"What?"

"Vicky."

"You mean a funny queen?"

"Uh huh."

"Say my name again."

"Vicky."

She laughed not beautifully but coarsely, a delayed curse spitting from the lips of a dead man. After the fifth forced response it became a shrill giggle.

I touched her shoulder cautiously. "Let's tell Sandy your new name."

"Will she like it?"

"Sure."

"Let's tell all the girls in the bunk."

I carried her piggy back as she banged me mercilessly—her laughter was the sound of a new bird.

After the silly conversation, operation Victoria became a success, once Victoria seized the excuses for laughing, the rest of her was like a makeshift dam finally yielding to the rush of nature. Her cheeks turned light olive, the eyes became almost black and she skipped as if there were an invisible rope playing alongside the path. Our director beamed, Sandy held my hand, but it was nothing; all Victoria ever wanted was the chance offering; the next foster home would probably undo a lot but if she had accepted a gift here she might remember and hope the next joke was around the corner.

I was no miracle worker and my only wish was that I was not too elderly to stumble upon something too . . . but just what and how eluded me. I would watch her skip to the dining hall and would almost call out . . . "Hey, Vicky, now you help me."

* * * * * * * * * * 7.

The buses were less regular on Saturdays; he was thankful for the absence of screeching starts and arrivals at the central bus stop that was parallel to the small playground on West Third Street. A little past nine o'clock and the sun, half hidden, filtered colorlessly upon the concrete floor beneath his open leather sandals. He knew Mathew had not concluded swing time and would be annoyed and sullen all day if taken out of the small wooden seat. The little boy held his fat hands to the rusty protective bar and said distinctly, "Moah, daddy, mur."

A bus lumbered to a stop. Would have been better to take the boy to the larger, better equipped playground in the park, but he was tired and it was only two blocks from home where he would deposit Mathew the moment he saw a dirty weary hand brush against the soft blue eyes. The man swung his son again and again while Mathew scowled in deep contentment; sweat spilled down the father's face swept across his chest and trickled away.

Despite Mathew's protests, he finally lifted the boy from the swing back to the stroller; then saw one of his neighbors.

"Hey Jimmy, over here."

Jimmy wheeled his carriage over. Jimmy's boy was eight months; Mathew being thirteen months his senior regarded the scene imperiously, serenely.

"How's Judy? Virginia said the doctor was supposed to come over last night."

"He was. He doesn't know, maybe tired blood, maybe jaundice, maybe nothing. Meanwhile it's ten dollars a visit until he does find out."

"And the job?"

"Past history. As of the fifteenth of next month I try and

get severance pay."

"Boy, it never rains."

"In a way, though, Jimmy, I'm happy and this isn't all rationale. Those petty frightened bastards, at least I'm through with them, all I can do now is hope most of it didn't rub off on me."

"You wouldn't try to get another job in TV."

"The hell with that racket, I'll try advertising again, God the air was so much fresher and cleaner. TV . . . ."

Jimmy interrupted, "Look, Andy is getting restless. Wanna walk with them a while?"

They were on Eleventh Street and Sixth Avenue when he said, "You want to go to Fourteenth Street, maybe I'll get Mathew a toy."

"Good idea, Andy would like something new to break."

"On the way home will you remind me to pick up some flowers for Judy, she claims I have no sympathy for her when she's sick."

"Judy be out today?"

"No, she's really sick. She looks lousy."

"She won't have to go to the hospital?"

"God, I hope not." Mathew sneezed, then sneezed again.

"That's right, Mathew, get sick like mommy."

Mathew shook his head several times, then waved his hand, "Bye bye mommy."

"She's not going yet. Christ, what a pessimist."

Fourteenth Street is the meanest street in New York City. I have never been on this street and been comfortable, freezing in the winter and boiling now. He mumbled to himself.

The toy discount store was empty and the two fathers searched the cramped aisles for suitable toys. Mathew's hand reached out for a small bright red lawnmower.

He opened the door gently, handed his wife the flowers, changed the baby, fed and put him to sleep. Then he prepared lunch for Judy and himself, and by the time he dried the dishes Mathew was up and they went out for the afternoon stroll. Mathew walked at his side as the father pushed the empty stroller. A look up at the sky, at the stores, at the passerby, and at the sky again.

* * * * * * * * * * 8.

The new Nixon was not recognized at the busy terminal. He boarded the bus labeled TO SOUTH NYACK.

One dollar, the driver suggested.

The sleek jowelly Nixon agreed.

Within an hour he was in South Nyack; Nixon walked up and down main street felling all stores and banks. Next he got the post office and library half a dozen garages and four churches. Laughter like soot forming in an immense incenerator was bubbling deep inside Nixon. He walked methodically destroying home after home; finally he was on my block, he nailed the other two houses then paused to read the house for sale poster nailed to my best tree. Nixon stepped back and gave the victory sign, he also made a gallant attempt to fly — arms outraised Nixon stood on his toes and pushed. Then he gave the V sign again. I surrendered, stopped looking out of my bay window and joined him on the porch. We both talked about the weather a while.

* * * * * * * * * * 9.

To say goodbye is one of the first phrases children are taught. Wave by by kiss grandma goodby. Come back soon daddy. BYE. From the moment we are snipped from mother, the processes of leave taking set in. Sometimes there is a delicious pain — the sound my son made years ago when he caught his fish, his first fish. A sweet singing moan that carried across that lake like a pure brief song; sure he was unwise small and dependent on everybody and he was losing a fragment of childhood but he was also playing out a role in a scene where he was gentle master. He reeled that fish in like a pro and we let the boat nestle against the thick marshes of the lake; Mathew and I should have stayed there forever.

I too cry out goodby-goodby to this house this good house despite the incredible winter heating bills. Goodby to our life period. The oddest most ironic thing about divorce is what was the last straw that resolved so many lives with lawyers and piles of forms validating the end. Was it the checkbook that never balanced out, or a bruising sexual joust or a less personal wound. But suddenly you hate one another and if you both weren't non violent you could kill. We're both relieved and happy it's over; our bile so spent that we might begin an affair one day but why was our feeling carried through this one time and not drained off like the other feeble sorties. Certainly we have not suddenly matured; if I were Neil Simon I could blame it on the dishwasher that took away my one household duty and made me an idler and therefore bound to become alienated and disenfranchised. I see us formerly as a middle class caravan bearing our spices and possessions across the GW bridge fleeing a grimy evil city seeking open spaces. Open space that was filled in by two children and one cat; cross out the fish turtle birds dog and cats that have died here; erase all vestiges of the shredded marriage and ignore the sobs and final curse of wife who has had it up to here and is now hostile to the tenth power.

* * * * * * * * * * 10

As President Nixon and I continue to chatter about the weather I remember my high point in college when the rather silly baton twirler finally had been laid by her grim suitor. He had resolutely tried for two years and she now granted all requests even to keeping on high leather marching boots. But the girl was no longer insipid arching her marvelous naked body seemingly about to lick herself, she was only graceful sensitive and wise. *This must have been an important moment for you. You must be very pleased.*

Almost on top of me Mr. Nixon is sweating profusely but appears smug happy. I draw upon my homecoming queens benediction and say, you must be very happy sir. Mr. Nixon beams, calls upon an inner reserve and stops sweating, his suit is stiff, unquestionably sta-prest, he also appears to have stopped breathing. Together we look out over the piles of broken bodies and homes. The trees have been spared. We look about South Nyack. President Richard Nixon has destroyed South Nyack. And only I am left.

* * *

Heart, You Have No House (from the Notebooks of Theodore Roethke—1951-53)

What wronged ghost raves in this house?
I cannot say. Time's dying on the moon.
I hear the minutes limping round and round.
*

I moped all day with a wrong word.
How can I ever sing? What's right enough,
Clear in the dark, clouds up by day.
*

Forgive me this minute; the hours are creaking
Past these midnight bones.
*

He's here, the very father and son of death
Who shakes the dark with his look.
*

My long fathers are calling.
I hear the cries from the muck and sand . . .
*

In the deep dead of that night, I laughed for a love,
And I quickened that I should die.
By these deprivations of spirit and sense
By the moans I have never heard,
What heavenly candle flickers in my flesh
Faltering toward another shade?
*

Midnight's my measure. Who
Can tell me what avails
When false light fails?
*

I'm called by the light and the dark
To please my inches.
What comes will kill me.
That death is easy.
Woo me another way.
The gun is too pure.
My sweet's here.
Kiss this.
*

I'm sick of being well; but that is ill-
Ness. See, my lips are loose with meanings not
Intended: I lie down with my thought,
Careless of sleep.
*

One can go mad anywhere. O reason, are you there:
What's here and not beyond
Is what I'll have.
*

Believe the right bone.
Surface calm; disorder within:
Space ties me. Recede, coarse dream.
I can become the leaves, a twisty bird,
Rise from the true
Nest of this change.

Outside the frost sparkling
Along the edge of the chair,
Close to the cypress frames,
On the black wooden fences,
Along the rutted road-crown,
The dirt glittering

Brighter than fresh waves
Or moon-washed phosphorous.
        Each time ever
        Around a cloud,
        Easy and early,
        On top a thistle,
        The horny rootlet
        Hunting for water.
I've been to bed with a dream. The gods remain.
In the harsh short hand of subliminal depths I've spoken,
No sleek captain of intuition or tapir of redolently disordered
                                                    mortal life . . .
                        *
Such is my heart's own stuff. I can renew
Myself with images of broken trees,
The coarse delights of an unfaltering rage.
                        *
Heart, you have no house.

                                    —Arranged by David Wagoner

Photo by Imogen Cunningham

Martin Steingesser Automobile & Pigeon
1968

The Dead Man's Room

My hand clicked on
                    the dead man's lamp.
Its hanged crystals weak-
                      ly rang
(did not weep)
           out of shape
under its shroud of dust which
covers too the plastic
fern and fake, foolish rose.
If those
      live,
spirited lilies
            one sometimes sees
are real presents for the dead,
then what weird grave
                    could these flowers deck?
I'd guess
      the tomb
            (his or mine?)
of him who took
              sick and died
never having been alive.
Here I still stay
and look
      at (soak up)
His relic stuff.
              His books—
one's a not so late
NEW DICTIONARY (1928).
And one of them's in
                Ovid's Latin.
And there's an ENCYCLOPAEDIA OF THE WORLD
beside
      a cardboard
mounted photo of mother and child.
A milk glass wedding jar
                for
the nuts and candy he once ate,
mouth and eyes turning more
and more
            out of the light.
I sleep
      in his bed trembling with chill
while the little rolls
            of lint shed
or blow together again
along the ashen, old
brocade-papered wall.
On one dresser laid out
              neat
the dead man's
ball point pen.
Tiny, brass
           ceramic box to keep his stamps in,
although the letters all
            are mailed.
Scissors, screw driver and file
for his finger nails (they'll still
grow for a little while.)

There's a darkening,
                    rather heavy chain
with a silver dollar 1896
for the keys (now laid separate
and flat)
             that fit
the dead locks.
And in another line's
                        his magnifying glass,
aluminum flash light case
(batteries yanked out safe
and lined up or ranked). Retractable measuring tape
snapped back from the length of his life.
Pocket knife, machine file
                            and an awl,
some used and unused screws and nails,
paper clips
for his uncompleted works.
At the side a still
elegant sil-
            ver comb and brush.
A cache of drugs
drying, as cough drops
and some wash
                    for the dead man's mouth.
Tie pins wait, one plain one pearly
and the garish ties of which he was fond
(I mean the ones that do not bind)
line up limp along the wall
beneath a rack of family plates
recording souvenir sights.
A bit far out
            the picture on the opposite wall.
A luscious renaissance girl,
nude, leered at by her elders—
and a photo of a classic sculpture,
a naked youth
                lean muscled arm upright
pulls his sword out of the throat
of the enemy (or friend) he quarreled with.
The sampler with its crocheted carriage—
its colorful Victorian couple who hope
                                or hoped
once for marriage
                    and its message:
"all to myself I think of you
"Think of the things we used to do.
"Sometimes I sigh sometimes I smile
"But I keep each olden, golden while
"All to myself."
And on a shelf
                this lonely dead man's
framed
        himself
from far back as his own youth:
in under shorts, muscles soaking sun
being just as alive as the young body can.
Here are the clothes
                    he throws
off: shoes
            someone shined and gave trees
to, a pair of pants

                lying formless as a ghost
                with the pockets all turned out
                (offwhite like the balls of eyes)
                and a still dirt-
                                y, red woolen shirt
                which has already lost
                                      its human smell.
                His tables, candles, clock and bowl!
                His mirror
                           losing silver,
                where now, this day I stand
                                            and
                suddenly am afraid!
                For my god I see in the glass
                only the contoured back
                                       of my own head!
                And here, here is the bed
                where I have lain these three nights past
                and felt the mirroring pillow fit
                closer and closer to his
                the hollows of my own face.

                            —*John Logan*

Deer Head

He walked through the stockyard, black bulls either side, slaughter-house off left. A wagon stood in the middle, a death-wagon, festooned with antlers. He found one deer head lying on the ground. It looked like one of those bone deer heads carved by Zuni Indians, smooth, peculiarly self-contained. He placed it upright on the ground, assuming it would grow again. He looked to see if there was blood, as one would look to see if there were roots on a newly uptorn plant. But it was quite clean, except for a stained channel running the length of its head. It never occurred to him that it was dead.

It sat in a commanding position between red pawing bulls. He felt its influence as he walked away. Something to be handed on, felt and transferred, as a source of fortitude in a world where individual activities set men apart.

A woman came up, covered the head with red green flowers. He made an elaborate gesture of recall, and remembered that the top-knot on the head of the Yaqui Pascola dancer was called flower, and that Christ's blood became a flower. A flower is of and in the earth, he thought; like this head.

                            —*Brian Swann*

How Another Child Came To Be Born

by Joyce Carol Oates

A balloon, flimsy and transparent. There is something terrifying about it. It floats upon a background of darkness, a universe of darkness, pinpricked by tiny dots of light. They are like stars. They are hardly more than suggestions of light. The balloon does not move but looks as if it might move, suddenly—if you were to lean down and breathe upon it, surely it would float away?

Pass your fingers near it lightly, not touching it. What are those grainy lines? They are like pencil lines. They are like hairs. They seem about to lift themselves, to rise to the warmth of your fingers. But they do not move. The balloon itself is motionless. You can see through it, yet there is nothing behind it. Along its edges there are long thin lesions, as if someone had torn into the flesh of this thing with a knife. You can run your fingernail along the edge of the balloon and make indentations in the paper, in the photograph reproduced on the page. Once a mark is made the thing is no longer so terrifying.

Beatrice stood staring at the magazine cover. She was in a drug store, standing at the magazine rack, and she had no clear recollection of having come here. It was the cover of a weekly newsmagazine, a vivid photograph of a cell, of cells . . . she had no recollection of having come in this store and of having stopped here, to look at the magazines. The cover did not make sense to her. The caption that might have explained it was out of sight.

"Mrs. Landor?"

The pharmacist had her prescription ready.

She paid for the sleeping pills at the front of the store, her fingers shaky. It seemed to her that the woman at the cash register was watching her closely; watching her uncertain fingers. She counted out change. She turned to leave. The pills now belonged to her, the entire day belonged to her . . . .

But she had a doctor's appointment at eleven. It was ten-thirty now. Last week she had had an appointment which she had cancelled; now the appointment was scheduled for today at eleven. It was still possible for her to call Dr. Lang and say she couldn't come again. And then she could drive downtown and around the city, aimlessly.

She walked slowly to her car. She glanced at her wristwatch—still ten-thirty. Her watch had a very small, delicate face, with numbers that were no more than dots. White gold. Dots that had the look of being blind. In her car she sat for a while, waiting. She thought about the cover of that magazine—the balloon, the jelly-fish, its lesions and hairs and flimsy, stubborn transparency.

And what would she do now? She could drive downtown, around the city aimlessly. She knew the city very well. She could park the car and get out and walk until someone caught up with her . . . until it got dark and someone caught up with her . . . . People were killed all the time in this city. Even in this drab gray coat of hers, with her slightly run-down, water-stained shoes, she would attract the attention of men who might like to kill women, why not? There were many of them in the city. Her legs had the look of being bare because the stockings she wore were so sheer, so pale, fawn-colored . . . . She looked at her wristwatch again. It was still ten-thirty.

In a while she drove to the doctor's office. She found herself driving there, in no hurry. His office was now in a new building, near a high-rise apartment of white and glass and a new shopping plaza and raw, wild fields that had not yet been leveled for new buildings. A short distance in one direction was a highway, with wide, muddy shoulders that looked like quicksand; in another direction there was another highway.

Dr. Lang's old office had been in a building downtown, but the building had been condemned for urban renewal.

This new office was cheerful and bright. Beatrice came in quickly and sat down; no one else was in the waiting room. The nurse greeted her as if she were an old friend. "Hello, Mrs. Landor, how are you this morning? Is it still drizzling out?" She turned her bright, enthusiastic, aging face toward Beatrice and would not let Beatrice look away. There was a sound of music somewhere. A transistor radio? Music in another office?

"You're looking very well, Mrs. Landor," the nurse said. Beatrice wondered if this were a joke. She did not smile. "How do you like our new office? It's nice, isn't it?"

Beatrice nodded. Her body had begun to anticipate the examination; her heart was accelerating. Beatrice looked anxiously around the room for something to concentrate on—but still her heart began to pound faster, she could not help it. There was something fierce, a hard, glowing radiance beginning inside her.

The nurse, whose name she had forgotten, came out from behind the receptionist's desk. She wore white; her legs were gauzy and muscular. "You can come in now," she said. Beatrice rose at once. She followed the nurse into a back corridor—all was bright here, the odor of plastic and tile and fluorescent lighting—and into what was evidently the doctor's private office. "Dr. Lang will be with you in a minute," the nurse said. Beatrice sat down again. She could hear someone washing hands—she could hear the sound of water splashing. *Why does he have to wash his hands when he'll be wearing rubber gloves?* Beatrice thought.

Her eyes jumped around his office, which was not shabby and comfortable like the old office, but there was nothing for her to look at. It was too clean and modern, this office, the desk was dark and smooth, the chair behind it covered with black leather . . . . On the desk was a small pile of letters and magazines. Beatrice saw part of that glossy black-and-white cover, the one with the photograph of the cell on it. Behind her, water running in the lavatory; faucets being shut off. The door opened and she looked around as if surprised.

"How are you, Mrs. Landor?"

Dr. Lang was an old man but still he darted about, a small wiry ambitious man, a very good gynecologist; a good man. When he smiled his false teeth were off-white, exactly the color of his own teeth, perfect. There was an odor of soap about him perpetually.

Leafing through a manila folder on his desk. Making a thoughtful, sucking sound with his lips. "Quite a while since your last examination," he said. Then he smiled to show that he was not scolding her. Beatrice looked down to his hands, shyly.

A man's hands, but pinkened as if with a fresh surge of blood. A thin wedding band.

"No need to look so worried," he said gently, teasing. "Let me see. . . . " He looked through the folder, sighing; a hint of age. The magazine with its glossy cover peeked out from under his elbow. Beatrice stared at it. Protoplasm that was about to tremble—like jelly, like a balloon. She thought of her zoology class in college. The slides, the smears, the cells. Evidently they were cells. Living units. Some of them were dead, and yet never really dead. Nothing dies dead. Nothing can die. There is this tiny kernel of life in each cell, like grit, like a grain of sand in the eye, that can never be destroyed. The cell can shrivel down to this kernel . . . or perhaps it can go mad and start dividing, multiplying, into a cancer.

"I think I'm pregnant," she said.

"Ah!"

He smiled at her. Beatrice forced her mouth into a smile.

"When was your period due?"

She looked down again at his hands. "I don't remember . . . ."

"You don't remember?"

"I think . . . I think it was two weeks ago, two or three weeks ago . . . ."

She stammered and was silent.

"That would have been the fifteenth, then . . . ? If it was two weeks ago?"

"Yes, yes . . . ."

"Or was it three weeks ago?"

She stared in silence at his hands.

After an awkward pause he said, gently, "I'll examine you and then arrange for you to take the test. How does that sound? There is never any point . . . never any point in assuming anything until you take the test."

Her mouth kept wanting to grin; its corners kept wanting to twist up into a grin. Beatrice thought, *As long as the folder is open I am safe.*

"The test is a very simple one. Any hospital will run it for you."

Beatrice nodded.

"There's really no need to look so worried!" he said.

A rap on the opened door: the nurse leaned in. "Dr. Brant is on the telephone," she said.

"Ah, I'd better take it," the doctor said.

His tone was apologetic.

He picked up the telephone. "Yes . . . ? I can't hear you. Oh, yes. When? Tomorrow? But I didn't think he wanted to sell . . . what about the highway commission? What happened? . . . Well, then tomorrow? At two?"

Tomorrow at two everything will be changed, Beatrice thought.

She would drive into the city. She would leave her car and lose herself in the crowds of downtown, rapping with her heels hard on the cement. Inside her, that warm little kernel would not be dislodged . . . she would walk and rap her heels hard on the sidewalks . . . she would feel its warmth spreading up through her, a strange radiance.

Dr. Lang closed the manila folder and stood.

The nurse escorted her into the examination room. It smelled of newness. "I think . . . I'm afraid . . . ." Beatrice said.

"Yes?"

She had thought she felt a movement inside her; the beginning of blood? The first sluggish beginning of a flow?

"Nothing."

It was nothing.

The nurse seemed to be welcoming her into this room. It was larger than the old examination room and it had a large window, which looked out upon the sky. The examination table; the stirrups; all women are equal when they lie on that table. Beatrice stared at it. The nurse was opening drawers—she was arranging instruments on a tray. She drew a length of clean white paper up over the examination table. The table was covered with dark brown leather and looked very new, as if not many women had suffered on it yet.

"Would you like to get ready?" the nurse asked.

Something pushed Beatrice forward. She felt powerful, darkly pleased. What had she ever liked in life except the limiting of it?—pushing it down, back, inside herself? She disliked her face, which was moderately pretty. She disliked her body,
though it was not a voluptuous body; it was not lean enough, not hard enough, to suit her. Even the racing *zzzzzz* sound of her brain was not enough to suit her. *Lie down. Give up*, she thought.

Naked from the waist down, her dress up about her thighs. She lay on the cold leather table. The paper rattled beneath her. The nurse, courteous and gentle, said, "Could you slide down further?" Beatrice's heels were caught in the stirrups at the end of the table. She slid down awkwardly. "A little further?" the nurse said.

Now her legs were spread apart; her knees spread. Everything in her was open. The nurse drew a white cloth over her, to her waist. She might have been covering a dead body.

"That's fine. The doctor will be right in," she said.

She said this every day, the same words.

Women lay with their knees apart like this, open, every day.

Through her eyelashes Beatrice saw a window. It was rimmed with eerie light—dark light—the sky outside was overcast, unconvincing. Now time would stop. The ticking of her wristwatch would stop. And then, later, when this was finished she would rush out of this building and get into her car and drive away . . . . She would park the car crooked at a curb, abandoning it. The license plate and the registration of the car would link it to her, or to her husband, how could she avoid that? No way to avoid it. She would catch a city bus and disappear deeper into the city and take a room in a hotel and go out again into a five-and-ten store and buy a knitting needle . . . or must you buy a pair of knitting needles?

Dr. Lang entered the room quietly. Now he was subdued; no smiles or teasing. Everything was holy about him.

"If I hurt you, remember . . . just say so. And I'll stop."

That was his style: to make you ashamed of feeling pain, so that you would rather lie in silence, in pain, than disappoint him.

She heard a sound—flesh against a slippery substance—he must have been putting on rubber gloves. The nurse stood beside him. The two of them were haloed from the window, in that dark, eerie light; Beatrice did not dare open her eyes. If the pupils of her eyes flashed open she would scream. Between her legs, a sudden dazzling space. The nurse dabbed something on her. An odor of chemical, disinfect . . . she was being cleaned . . . . The sound of instruments on a tray, gently rattling. Dr. Lang said something she could not hear. What did he say? *This will only take a few minutes.*

People died in a few minutes: their lives flash out of them and are lost.

Then he inserted the instrument. It was very cold and sharp. Beatrice recoiled from it, throwing herself backward.

"Please . . . ." she whispered.

Embarrassment.

"It will only take a few minutes. You've been examined before. It won't hurt," the doctor said.

"But I think I'm pregnant . . . ."

The nurse was standing over her. "If you could slide down again, please," she said.

"I think I'm pregnant," Beatrice said wildly.

"Do you want the examination to continue?"

"Yes. Yes."

She prepared herself again. She let her knees fall apart, slowly. When the instrument was inserted in her she shut her eyes hard.

"Now I have to open it," the doctor said.

She could not remember who he was. An old man, an anonymous man, someone she had picked out of the telephone book to deliver herself up to . . . . Now he was turning something in her, opening her. Slowly the instrument began to expand. It was like a circle of nothing, expanding, opening her and turning her inside-out.

She could feel the breath of the outside air, in her.

She began to breathe quickly. Someone might have been pressing a hand up and down on her chest, pumping her lungs. On the edges of the table her hands clenched and unclenched. The leather had become damp; it was slippery against her fingers. . . . How could everything be so suddenly open and exposed? The most secret veins inside her would be open to the air of that cold, overcast sky. Her head began to move, slowly at first, from side to side. Her hands clenched and unclenched. Her jaws clenched. The clamp was cold and hard inside her, making a rim, a bracelet inside her, exposing her insides. She could feel her body begin to contract. She was drawing the secret parts of her body together, in terror. Her knees came together hard.

"No, please," a man's voice said.

There was surprise and annoyance in that voice. She felt her knees gripped, a hand on each knee; he spread them apart.

"I can't stand it . . ." Beatrice whispered.

Her heart was pounding wildly now. Sweat on her face, under the heavy coils of her hair. It dazzled her, being so sudden. A flash of heat shot upward from the dark cold between her legs, that open darkness, telling her she would die. She was going to die. It would come to her like this, the insertion of an instrument, opening her and turning her inside-out, the dark heat rising up to her heart with the fierceness of love—

"I can't stand it. Let me go."

The nurse seized her hands. Both hands.

"Mrs. Landor, don't do that—you'll hurt yourself— Don't move—"

But her body had begun to fight and she could not stop it. The table rattled. She kicked at the stirrups and something came loose. She tried to slide back up the table, away from that instrument, but it came along with her, hurting her, scraping her. . . . She saw a wild, black space, open to the light and its veins pounding, something not meant to be seen. The rim of that instrument was like a light bulb, burning with light. She cried out—

"Let me go!"

The doctor was saying something to her. Giving her instructions, yet he sounded alarmed—she threw her head from side to side and did not listen. Why was he talking to her? There was something stuck up inside her, a terrible bright pain, and this man was talking to her! She could not hear his words! Her clothes were sweaty about her, bunched up beneath her struggling body. The muscles in her legs fought. She pressed against the end of the table with her heels and screamed.

Another jerk of her body—a small, thin, violent shot of pain.

Then it was over.

She threw herself from side to side. Her head struck the table; her cheeks hot against the leather, which felt like a cheek itself. Faces against faces. All of them sweaty and slippery. So Michael, her husband, had slapped himself against her, his face eternally against hers, so he had entered her body with his own, his flesh into her flesh, making them both eternal.

"No—" Beatrice cried.

And she saw suddenly a young woman lying on a table. It was herself, contorted like that: a young woman on a table, on her back, her face twisted with terror. She had fallen from a great height and her face was twisted permanently into that terror.

What was that raw reddened gap between her legs? So vivid it sucked all the air into it—the entire white sky might be drawn into it and lost—a face more powerful than her own face, eternal. She could see it plainly as if she were standing above herself, loathing that body and that second, violent face.

"Mrs. Landor, please—"

"That isn't my name!"

Then she was sitting up. The nurse was helping her. They were alone in the room—the doctor had left. Coming to herself, Beatrice sat up and stared at the window. Her knees came together tightly. Everything was finished now and secret: the flirtation was over.

"You hurt yourself a little. It was bleeding . . ." the nurse said primly.

She fussed with something and did not look at Beatrice. Beatrice saw a cotton cloth, a smear of bright blood on it . . . .

She put her hands to her face. "I'm so sorry, I'm so sorry . . . ."

"You might have hurt yourself badly," the nurse said.

"Please tell the doctor I didn't mean it. I'm so sorry . . . ."

She sat up and now the room seemed very quiet. Everything was still and unsurprising.

"Maybe I could go on with it," she said shakily. The nurse handed her a tissue; she wiped her face with it. "I don't know what happened to me."

"Are you all right now?"

"Yes. Yes. I'm sorry."

Her teeth began to chatter.

"Couldn't he—couldn't he finish the examination?" Beatrice said.

The nurse did not look at her. "It might be better to put it off until another day."

"But—"

Her neck ached. Had she almost snapped her neck? What convulsion had gotten into her body?

"You can get dressed. The doctor will see you on the way out."

"But—"

"You can make another appointment."

Left alone in the room Beatrice slid off the table and stood by it, trembling. She seemed not to want to let go of it. There was nothing for her to think, now; she stood in a kind of vacuum. In college once she had studied physical defects that sometimes accompanied retardation—children without arms, without legs, torsos heavy and anxious to fall to the ground— and she had thought, staring at the photographs, *There is nothing to think about this.* Thinking demanded a space that could be moved into—you stepped forward into that space, pushing other things out of your way, claiming a victory, a territory. In a vacuum you could not move one way or another. Everything was listless, transparent, eternal. There was nothing to think.

She got dressed. There was a panicked sensation between her legs. The rim of her flesh was dazzled, as if glowing. She stood, staring at the window. She did not think about anything. A tiny burning clot of moisture seeped down . . . she took a tissue out of her purse and crumpled it and dabbed between her legs with it. She held it there, her eyes shut. Then she brought it back out, careful not to touch her clothes with it: a patch of bright red.

She stood very still, waiting. Her body was cold and sweating inside her clothes, strangely thin inside the clothes, so that she could imagine her torso and belly not touching anything but free of confinements, exposed. Deep inside her was the balloon-like cell. It had not been touched by any of this. An eye brought up close to it, close against the hole that was like a lens into her, would have seen it floating lightly, tiny hairs rimming it, untouched. It would swim in the drop of liquid that was its universe, transparent and eternal . . . .

Beatrice threw the tissue away and took out another one. She wiped her face with it. How she hated this room, which smelled of rubber and jelly and metal!—the sanitary metal of instruments! On a cabinet was the tray of instruments; they looked quite small. Behind the cabinet was a wastebasket. Better not look in that. But she did, stooping, and saw a wad of cotton with blood on it.

Her blood.

She threw the crumpled tissues into the basket. What would it be to see your body's blood drained into harmless paper like that, into cotton cloth, crumpled and thrown into a wastebasket? Was it that easy to be rid of oneself?

"I wanted to have a baby," Beatrice muttered.

When she went out into the hall again, buttoning her coat, she saw the doctor standing in the doorway of his office. He was a small man, after all. He looked very old. If there was anger in him it was hidden behind his sorrowful, wrinkled face, and she could not see it.

"I'm leaving. I'm going," Beatrice said.

"Mrs. Landor—"

"I have to leave."

She hurried out, past the nurse, past another patient—a stylish woman with short curly hair, sleek eyebrows—and closed the door behind her.

Exhausted. Sour. Her body had turned sour inside her clothes.

She walked slowly down the hall. What had happened to her fingernails? Two of them were broken. A third was ripped slightly, down into the flesh; that would hurt. She stared at them, in a kind of trance. She had a flash of herself walking in the corridor of this new, expensive building, a young woman holding her hands up to her face, staring at them. The young woman had a blank, stunned face; the eyes set inside hollows; everything tense and contorted about her. She walked awkwardly, so that the insides of her thighs touched. She might have been trying to prevent something from slipping down out of her body.

Outside, she located her car. She drove into the city, into the traffic flowing south into the city. The examination was over. She was free for the day.... She would find a hotel, rent a room. She would buy something in a five-and-ten. She would run hot water in the bathtub and then, lying there, her legs slowly spreading, she would bring the thing up into herself. She would press it up into herself angrily and calmly. A pressure; a sudden release; the needle sinking in.

The water discolored with blood.

What she must remember *is to leave the tub unplugged and the water on*. That way there would be a continual flow of fresh water, splashing and hot. The blood would drain out, new water would rush in, everything would be clean.

Noon: a clock advertising cereal. Cars and trucks were moving south into the city. There was a noisy bustle, the sound of horns and the odor of exhaust fumes. More horns. There must have been an accident up ahead ... one lane was blocked off completely ... she would have to get into another lane. She hadn't been paying attention and now she was being drawn into the blocked-off lane, she couldn't get out of it ... a police car was parked there, its lights flashing red. She waited. She twisted around to look over her shoulder, at the traffic. Someone in a mud-splattered automobile wheeled around her, just missing her. She sucked in her breath. What she must remember: *to keep the hot water rushing into the tub*.

After about five minutes she got into the left lane. Slowly, achingly, the line of traffic drew her onward. Yes, an accident—two cars, one of them smashed in, the other up on the sidewalk. Smashed windshields. Her eye darted in terror around those cars—any blood? any sign of human flesh? A small crowd had gathered. A policeman stood by his car, by his opened door, writing something down. A shadow passed over everyone, fleetingly, as a cloud was blown across the sun—Beatrice glanced upward, startled by this. But no time. What she must remember—the traffic light ahead turned from green to red. Minutes passed. It turned to green again.

A policeman was in the intersection ahead, directing traffic. His whistle sounded angrily.

Driving was a battle: she felt invisible vessels on all sides of her, about to lunge into her, about to attack. But when she looked out she could see only cars and trucks with small people in them, their hands gripped like hers on their steering wheels.

The light changed again. The whistle blew.

She braked to a stop. Everything was suspended. And then, after a short wait, traffic began again ... her car lurched forward ... she could not remember exactly what she was doing. Where was she headed? Her home was in another direction. What must she do? She must not forget the bathtub, she would have to scour it out first, make sure it was clean, then turn on the hot water ... very hot water....

Behind her, around her, on all sides of her traffic moved onward. It pressed against her and would not let her go.

A flashing yellow light.

Steel knitting needles.

It was important to get somewhere, to park the car, to abandon it. Run, get into a crowd, get lost, become anonymous. Become protoplasm. And so she kept driving downtown, into the city, in the procession of cars. She might have been in a parade. It was important to keep the right order, not to hurry or turn off, to keep one's own place in the parade. She was inside her car, safe, and the balloon was inside her, safe. She was passing drug stores, taverns, shoe stores, pawn shops, liquor stores, small grocery stores. Some of the stores' gratings had not been taken down from the night before. She was passing gas stations, side streets, dreary apartment buildings, dreary people. Downtown at noon. She might have been entering a sacred landscape, it was so certain, so definite. Everyone here belonged here. They had chosen to come here. They walked along in measured, familiar strides, having destinations. They had all been born at one time or another. They all had birth certificates, somewhere. If their mothers had tried to scrape them out and lose them in bathtub water they would have resisted; would have clutched the walls of flesh and refused to drain out; why? Why should anyone die? There was an army in the womb and it would refuse to die.

Must remember to buy cleanser and clean the tub. She could picture the tub: a dingy white, a dingy bathroom. Everything impersonal and yet a little soiled. Impersonal dirt. She would dislodge all that dirt.... She thought of the faint line of dirt that formed on the collars of her clothes, after a single wearing; that mysterious dirt! It might have been invisible to anyone else but it was visible to her. Yes, she must remember to buy cleanser and to clean the tub, before she settled herself into it. Otherwise she could not sit in it. She would not be able to force herself to sit in it.

Pedestrians passed close about her, crossing with the light. They were like Arabs, walking with their collars pulled up against their faces—trying to protect themselves from little whirling clouds of grit and papers. Their eyes half-shut but very shrewd. They had places to get to and were certain of themselves. All of them swelling *outward in sacs, their lips thirsty and pressed against the walls of sacs, the tiny veins, sucking blood*. Nothing could have dislodged them. No water could have drained them away.

She turned off onto a side street and parked her car. Suddenly she had to hurry—she had to get out of that car. In the rear view mirror she caught a glimpse of her face. It was pale and abused. She looked around at people on the sidewalk, at the fronts of stores. The stores looked false. Their windows were opaque with dusty merchandise. People stamped on the sidewalks and she felt the vibrations from their feet. Their heavy shoes. She got out, closed the door of her car ... a young Negro man passed near her, stepping aside on his quick, elastic legs ... she hadn't seen him and would have bumped into him. She was heavy herself, clumsy as a cow. A sweaty cow. She almost bumped into someone else. She walked quickly back to the intersection and looked up and down the street, seeing nothing. CANCELLATION SHOES. A shoe store. A grating over the window. It meant nothing to her. A crowd, released from one curb, hurried toward her with the green light. She backed away. There were so many people—all of them in a hurry, flowing past her, around her, nearly colliding with her. She had stopped perspiring and now the dampness had formed a kind of halo about her, a scummy film. She would have to scrub it off. She would have to take a bath. There was something about a bath she must remember: hot splashing water. Yet she could not remember exactly what was important about it, because of the people who strolled by, hurried by, not seeing her. She felt drawn along with them. She turned and took a few steps along with them, smiling stupidly.

In front of a White Tower hamburger restaurant a clot of people stood waiting for buses. She was propelled toward them and then had to work her way out around them. A young girl with stringy hair flicked that hair right into Beatrice's face.

Freer now, she began to walk fast. She crossed a street; she hurried along with the crowd. There were women shoppers,

67

there were men and children, there were bedraggled old people, men and women, with the look of aged city people who have spent all the days of their lives tramping the city streets, up and down, tireless.... Beatrice took strength from them: the muscles of her legs felt fierce. Traffic passed on the street. People appeared. People disappeared. A siren sounded and people looked around. Nothing happened. Beatrice began to feel very strong and light, light on her feet, hurrying farther into the city.

What she must remember....

She pictured herself going into a telephone booth. She would dial the doctor's number; listen while he picked up the phone; she would cry out to him, *It was supposed to be different! I was supposed to be a certain person but I never became that person, and now it's all over, now I am through waiting for my life to happen ... it has happened to me, I am everything that I will ever be, I will never become anyone else....*

Someone touched her. She jerked away, frightened and blind. But the person gripped her arm tighter. "Beatrice?" She looked around and saw her husband.

A man of about five feet eight: dark, thinning hair, eyes dark in their sockets like her own eyes, her twin, her husband.

"What are you doing down here?" he said, surprised. "I've been running after you. I was across the street and I thought I saw you— But what are you doing down here?"

She stared at this man. It was her husband, yes. He had taken hold of her arm and pulled her off to one side, out of the stream of shoppers. They stood in front of the window of a pizza restaurant, in the odors of food, staring at each other.

"What are you doing down here?" her husband said.

She felt her fingers tighten on his arm. It was a convulsion, the way her fingers gripped at him. She stared into his face and recognized it. Out of all these people she recognized him: he had reached out and touched her.

"What ... what are you doing here?" she said faintly.

"I took a bus down from the center, to pick up a book ... I told you I was coming downtown today...."

He worked at the Lafayette County Welfare Center, a big dreary building with hundreds of windows.

"It's my lunch hour. I just got off the bus," he said.

They stared at each other as if in alarm. Around them people milled and the vibrations from their feet were hypnotic. Beatrice stood with her hand on her husband's arm and slowly something in her gave in to him, as if turning to liquid; she recognized him, after all.

It was not planned this way. It did not appear planned.

She leaned her forehead against the edge of his shoulder and closed her eyes. Exhausted, she closed her eyes.

"What is it? What's wrong?" he said.

She could not speak. She pressed her forehead against him and everything came to an end. □

Apprehension

As birds on the lawn, busily feeding,
All of a sudden are off —
What could have scared them? None of us knows,
None even of them perhaps, yet surely
Something, if only a whiff,
A whisper of possible death —
Off together, like so many arrows, off
And up and into the trees—
Ah, if only our imminent end
Could announce itself so neatly; if only
Contagion in us were as swift as that.
And as soon forgotten; for one at a time
They drop back down and begin again.
Ah, the forgetting. If only that.

—*Mark Van Doren*

Michael Biddle

DRYAD

Winter, 1968

Dryad

Dryad's early format was 6 inch by 8½ inch saddle-stitched books. Issue 12 was a box of poems printed on card stock, with a 45 rpm recording. The last three issues (14/15, 16/17, & 18/19) were perfect-bound 6 inch by 9 inch or 5¼ inch by 8½ inch books. Every issue opened with a stanza from John Keats—
"That thou, light-winged Dryad of the trees,
In some melodious plot
Of beechen green, and shadows numberless,
Singest of summer in full-throated ease."

An Interview with Merrill Leffler

Merrill Leffler was born in Brooklyn, New York in 1941. He graduated with a degree in Physics from North Carolina State University, and for several years worked for NASA. He left engineering to study literature, studied for three years at Oxford University, and returned to the University of Maryland where he taught for three years and then to the Naval Academy, where he taught in the English Department until 1981. Leffler has published work in a number of magazines, among them, *Southern Poetry Review, Poetry Now, Poet Lore, The Washington Review,* and *Aleph*; he has written reviews and articles for *The Washington Post Book World, The New Republic, The Baltimore Sun, Mosaic* (National Science Foundation) and *The Christian Science Monitor*. He will publish a collection of poems in January 1982, *Partly Pandemonium, Partly Love*.

Peabody: How did you first get started in the small press scene?

Leffler: Well, I'm not sure that the way we got started is typical. We started back in 1967. A friend of mind, Neil Lehrman (at the time, Neil was a Securities and Exchange Commission financial analyst, and I was an engineer doing analysis on the realiability of sonar submarines) and I — I think we both felt very bereft; what I mean is that we didn't really have any friends who were poets; we were writing poetry ourselves but didn't know anybody, we weren't involved in any kind of English studies, weren't in the university, and most of our friends were either — engineers, or people from where Neil worked. And I think we started the magazine as a way of making some connection; I remember just saying, "Why don't we do a magazine?" and knowing absolutely nothing. There were no organizations, really, at the time, nothing like what exists right now, with the Committee of Small Magazine Editors and Publishers (COSMEP); the Coordinating Council of Literary Magazines was just getting started. We didn't even know how to get manuscripts; we didn't know any poets, so we advertised— honestly. And we decided we certainly weren't going to publish ourselves till we were published, so we weren't starting it for our own self-aggrandizement — a twenty-dollar word. So we advertised it in the *New Republic* and the *New York Review of Books*, in their classified ads, trying to get manuscripts. And then I was over at Maryland University, taking one evening course; I had a wonderful teacher named Herbert Shaumann (who has since retired) — he had published one issue of a literary magazine himself, fifteen years before, called *Polyneurous*. He was a friend of Mark Van Doren . . . and he (Shaumann) gave us the names of people to write to. And then our ads brought in some manuscripts. And once we got that first issue out, that's all it took. We started sending it around; we sent it to libraries, and poets whose work we liked. Manuscripts started coming in, and then we started getting listed in various places, we did mailings like all magazine editors do, we sent out maybe three hundred copies to librarians trying to get subscriptions. So — I really haven't explained the logic; we just started without any experience at all; neither of us took creative writing in college — I don't think there were creative writing classes then, since Neil and I were in school in the late fifties and early sixties — and even if there were I don't think we would have taken them; as I said, I was doing a physics course and Neil was doing accounting, so we really weren't tied into that.

Peabody: Was there any reading scene or anything then?

Leffler: Yeah, there was a little bit. The Potter's House, on Columbia Road, was going; there may have been other things, but I didn't know about them, I didn't know how to find out about them. It didn't have the kind of visibility that poetry has now, that poetry's had for . . . I think maybe that when we started *Dryad*, it may have been a small amplification of what may have been happening. Poetry has been coming back over the last ten or fifteen years. Maybe it had its start, initially, toward the end of World War II, when poets started going to the universities. That's a new phenomenon; we used to have poets in residence, but never the creative writing programs that we've had in the last fifteen years. And then I think with Viet Nam, and the change of consciousness that started in 1966-67 — poetry was riding along on that. I'll tell you something very interesting — at Maryland, in 1967, Rod Jellema, who was the head of the creative writing program there, started a yearly series called Poetry and the National Conscience. And these were wide open; he had four relatively well-known poets come each year. The first year James Wright was there, and Louis Simpson, and Reed Whittemore, and Daniel Hoffman — and there was one more poet. What I remember about that was the big arguments that were going on about poetry and politics going together. Robert Bly was publishing *The Sixties* at the time, and this was the beginning of poets really getting involved in anti-Viet Nam demonstrations, and very overt political poetry — which we really didn't have. And there were these — what seem, now, like ridiculous questions, like can you really talk about Dean Rusk being like a bomb on the bottom of a B-52. The idea that, "do poetry and politics really mix?" — and there were these big, raging arguments. Those arguments became really stupid by 1969 and 1970, but it's kind of interesting.

Baizer: How do you account for your longevity? As most of us know, small presses don't offer much in the way of financial reward, or even prestige, or many other things that other work does. How have you been able to stay in so long? And why?

Leffler: Well, that's two questions. We've managed to stay in so long, just financially, because we haven't put out that many issues. We've come out very irregularly; in the first two years we put out five issues, I think, and then after that we really slowed down to — sometimes just one a year, maybe two.

Why we stayed on — I think there are a couple of reasons which may not really mesh together very easily. In some ways it became habit, I think — but there's also a certain kind of pleasure in "making the magazine," what I found, myself, in corresponding with poets, in trying to articulate my responses to poems that would come in. From the beginning, I knew nothing at all about printing and design; I think I had a certain kind of naive and raw instinct about what is good and what is not good. I'm not patting myself on the back — I mean I had an idea that poems should have space on the page, that there should be cleanliness, that there should be a certain kind of touch to a publication. And there's something about that that kept me in. But it was also the pleasure of putting this magazine out, and doing some good work, I think.

Baizer: Is there any one issue of the magazine, or any one poetry book you've published, that you feel particularly proud of, one that was really a special challenge that you wanted to get out? Did you discover anyone?

Leffler: I don't know if we discovered anyone — we were publishing people back in 1968 and '69 who have since gotten much bigger reputations. Some people around the Washington area — particularly Linda Pastan; she was beginning to publish around that time, but we published a lot of her poems in our first few issues. As far as any one issue — that first issue that any editor or publisher gets out can never be duplicated, I don't think. I can recall what it was like going to the printer and picking that magazine up — it was a high that I don't think has ever been equalled.

Peabody: That's why you keep doing it.

Leffler: And you know, the high is still there, but it's a different kind of high, there's a certain kind of mellow pleasure, whereas before it was an ecstatic kind of high, with the magazine. I found that the magazine, though, after a while, was exhausting me — not physically, but in my ability to keep up with it. There were just so many manuscripts, I could not deal with them fast enough — I would procrastinate, and one procrastination led on to another; I'd find I wouldn't be responding to manuscripts, I would get angry letters, understandably . . . but that's not the reason we stopped; I think that magazines do live themselves out, and I think that our magazine has lived itself out, for a number of reasons. I try to express this to myself, and I'm not sure I can get it accurately. But I think that magazines — we have so many in this country, and I think they're very necessary — and there are some wonderful literary magazines coming in — and I felt that we were publishing very good work, I think very, very good poems, but the one thing that I felt that we didn't have was a point of view in a sense that was satisfying to me. And by a point of view I mean — I don't mean a political stance, but a perspective that would make it essential for people to want to read *Dryad*, beyond the fact that we've got a nice magazine, we're publishing good work. I'm not just patting you on the back, but *MOTA* had a perspective —

Baizer: An angle might be a better word.

Leffler: That may be, yeah. There's a magazine that came out in town, *Working Cultures*, which had a perspective, a political perspective. That's not the kind of perspective that would have been right for me, but I think it could have been a very important magazine.

Baizer: In fact, because there's simply so much poetry being published, it affects sales and commercial success as well. I think that magazines that have an angle — negatively put, it could be a gimmick — or perspective, might tend to do better than other magazines of high quality.

Leffler: Yeah, well — it's not the commercial thing. Obviously you need to sell the magazine. One of the things that's happened, at least with us, as we've started publishing books, we've got a relatively large investment, whereas before when we published a magazine, and we published one or two issues a year, and had full time jobs, printing wasn't costing that much, and especially in the beginning — we were using a selectric typewriter, we were using very good paper, and using good printers, so it wasn't a lavish production, but it was a good solid production — but to print a thousand copies was $450. That's crazy now — and this was for anywhere from a forty- to sixty-page issue. Now that would cost, with any decent production, close to a thousand dollars. It got very expensive and so you really do have to recover money, whereas before, it wasn't essential that we recover the money. If we recovered a fourth, so what. And then we might get a grant once every other year, five hundred to a thousand dollars, so we could afford to put the money in. What happens, as you start getting a feeling for a good publication, and you want to make a good-quality magazine, your prices just go up, and there are just not enough sales. Now, I think of a magazine as — and it doesn't mean I wouldn't go back to doing a magazine some time, there's something about it that's grabbed me, there's something wonderful about it — but I think that now, what would constitute a magazine for me would have some sort of critical perspective; I don't mean anything didactic, but I think we need good critical *perspectives*, because there's no one kind of poetry in the country, there are different kinds of poetry. And I think we need good criticism — not puffery, and not reviews; those are necessary for helping to sell books and for getting some feedback — but I mean solid criticism. And that is one of the reasons I think a magazine like Bly's *Sixties* was a very important magazine, extremely important, because it was also critical, solidly critical, taking a point of view which you could argue with, but at least Bly certainly had a point of view. You didn't have to agree with him at all, and you wanted to take issue, but he was establishing his own boundaries, and I think a lot of magazine editors don't want to do that.

Baizer: Do you think an academic background —

Leffler: I don't think you need an academic background; someone like Bly was not an academic —

Baizer: No, I meant that avoidance of a point of view, in the name of objectivity, so-called . . .

Leffler: Yeah, maybe, with that sensibility that "everything goes, let everything go."

Maybe this is the conservative turn I've been taking, but — I find that I've kept whatever *Sixties* magazines I had. And I can read them now, magazines from 1968-69, I can read the poetry in them, the translations, and I think of them as a book, as an anthology.

Peabody: I think there was a major explosion then and I think there is another one happening now. In meeting editors and writers I'm finding a lot of people became aware of the small press scene in 1976 and 1977. It's like a whole new crop.

Leffler: Well, something else has happened now, with books, I think an extraordinary thing — you know, magazines have been going on for a while, but what's been happening with independent publishers of books is really extraordinary.

Baizer: At the same time, there seems to be an explosion of small press magazines, and poets, in the last ten years. Is this a good thing for alternative presses in general? You have a longer perspective on the Washington literary scene than I do; how has it changed?

Leffler: Well, first of all, I think — I can only feel that publishing is good, despite the fact that there's a lot of mediocre work coming out; it also leaves room for the first-rate publications to establish themselves. And as far as the way Washington has changed, when we started publishing in 1967 there were only two literary magazines in town; there was ours and Bill Claire's *Voyages*, which was a very handsome and fine magazine. We were two very different magazines. Claire was publishing a lot of very well-known poets, or featuring well-known poets, and then publishing, at the same time, new people; and his magazine was larger than ours, and — when I say slick I don't mean that in a negative way, but — very professional. Ours was tweed whereas his was a pinstripe suit. But we were the only other poetry magazine in town. That all changed — and again, I think a lot of that happened in 1969, 1970, there was a period there. And there's something about *Dryad* — I was out of the country during that time, 1969 to 1972, a very important time in the United States, and Washington, especially, and I wasn't around when a lot of these changes were going on. I was in my little ivory tower in England, studying English classics. We were still putting *Dryad* out, but in a very removed way. And it was during that time *Mass Transit* was going on, Some of Us Press was starting up, Michael Lally and Terry Winch.... And then, just in the last four or five years, so many magazines have begun, and presses. The Washington Writer's Publishing House cooperative, for example; they've put out 18 collections of poetry, three at a time. There's Word Works, which has put out some lovely books. And there's a lot of self-publishing going on. There are some fine books around. Again, there's a lot of stuff around that — I don't even want to call mediocre, but doesn't — rise above its averageness. As I say, in a way I think that's necessary. I'm not saying that I want to publish an average book; it's only in retrospect that it seems that way. But I think the publishing is necessary, because it's really very stimulating.

Peabody: In closing, what would you like to see happen in Washington, in the literary scene?

Leffler: As I said before, I would like to see good magazines doing something with some critical perspective. And I would like to see some means of getting our books out into the Washington bookstores; that's one of the big problems, that if they were out there we would have a chance, not only of selling them, but of getting our authors' work around.

— **Interviewed by Eric Baizer and Richard Peabody**

An Interview with Neil Lehrman

Neil Lehrman's lived in San Francisco since leaving Wash. D.C. in 1968 except for a year spent on the Spanish Costa Brava which became the setting for his first novel *Perdut* (published in 1979 by Dryad Press). As to that infamous "second novel," this bio comes a little too early to talk about it.

Peabody: What made you want to start a literary magazine?

Lehrman: My first impulse was not to consider starting a poetry magazine when Merrill first suggested the idea, even though poetry was very important to me. After all I was a C.P.A. working at the Securities and Exchange Commission with no formal background in literature beyond required college courses for business majors. But what Merrill calls our bereft feeling made it not take long to change my mind.

Peabody: How did the collaboration work between the two of you? Did you both select material? Did you have disagreements? What was the process?

Lehrman: "Collaboration" just doesn't seem like the right term and yet that's what working together is. I suppose it's because "collaboration" sounds so formal for two friends sitting at a kitchen table reading some poems attached to self-addressed stamped envelopes. We did it that way, in the early days, when we both lived in Washington, each of us reading every submission. But when I moved to California (which was shortly after the first issue) we would mail each other what we liked enough to print or at least liked enough to consider. We usually selected on a joint basis, but there were disagreements (I'd be concerned if there weren't) and where one felt that strong about someone's work, there was never any question about it. In fact later issues became more the work of one or the other of us, partly as a result of Merrill's move to England and the time we had to devote to the magazine. But because one of us always wanted to keep *Dryad* going, it lasted.

Peabody: What were you looking for?

Lehrman: I honestly don't know how to answer that.

Peabody: Merrill says the magazine stopped because it didn't have a specific point of view. Do you agree?

Lehrman: I don't know if we stopped so much for that reason as we just evolved into books. We did the first book Rod Jellema's *Something Tugging the Line* after the 9/10 issue. It was distributed as a book and simultaneously sent to subscribers in lieu of issue 11. We did this with other books also—*Tumult for Berryman* which counted as issue 16/17 and *Shaping: Traditional Forms of Prosody* edited by Phil Jason sent as number 18/19. During this time we did regular magazine issues as well and discovered the books seemed to find more readers than the magazine. Don't assume this is always the case. Other publishers like Berkeley Poets Coop., experienced the opposite. Also, the cost of an issue had become as much as a book, and dealing with that growing pile of unsolicited manuscripts was hopeless, if you wanted to give each submission individual attention.

Peabody: Were you in Washington while Merrill was in England? Did you witness the changes he speaks of missing?

Lehrman: No. I had already moved to California so I have no feeling for the changes he's talking about. And in California those changes had already peaked by the time I arrived. But in any case, I'm not sure the "times" would have altered *Dryad* much from what it has become. I was more interested in poetry for poetry's sake as was Merrill, than in "poetry as politics."

Peabody: Is there any particular issue or book that is significant to you? Any anecdote relating to the magazine that you'd like to share?

Lehrman: Nothing can ever match the joy of getting that first issue from the printers, as imperfect as it was by our present standards. But the issue of which I'm most proud is Number 12. That's the box with poems on cards and the phonograph recording by John Logan, Jr. using two of his father's poems for lyrics to his songs. Poems on postcards was Merrill's idea. The record was mine. I decided the recording belonged in the magazine because John's music actually enhanced the poems. I knew virtually nothing about how you produced a recording at the time (that was most of the fun in doing it). But with a lot of help from John's friends we made something everyone involved in the project would be proud of.

Peabody: What was the final circulation?

Lehrman: Total circulation was always the same—near sell out. Paid circulation was another story. I don't think our subscription list ever numbered more than two hundred. Book store sales were modest, and rarely collectable. But since our inventory of back issues is low, the 750-1,000 copies of each issue have somehow found their way into the hands of interested readers which is all any little magazine can reasonably hope for in these times.

Peabody: How did the magazine experience affect your own writing?

Lehrman: One of my friends in the restaurant business told me, "Everybody thinks they can run a bar or write a book." Well, not many have done either successfully and certainly no one who didn't devote his whole energy to the book. The "magazine experience" showed me how essential commitment was to good writing because it brought me in touch with real writers for the first time. And I don't use the word "writers" to mean only people making a living from their work or even being published, but people who give up whatever part of their lives is necessary just so they could go on writing. And that's why every writer's work deserves your respect no matter how contrary it is to your own tastes.

—Interviewed by Richard Peabody

SUMMER/FALL 1968   WINTER/SPRING 1969

NUMBER 5/6
$1.25

spring 1968

DRYAD

DRYAD

dryad

Etude: The Morning

A cold day, so he walked fast thinking

                brain,
           Cerebrum

tipped his hat & said,

being nonadaptive
the poets will
be ruled
out
by a process of
natural selection
&c.
& all art
being either imitative (mimesis)
or
hopelessly anthropocentric
will be changed into solid matter
              like stone

transigient like dust.

things: (all in his head)
get trousers cleaned,
return early,
leave afternoon,
read Fuselli,
Venturi,
be happy,
find out library hours.

STILL LIFE: the black chair
(pushed back) at the desk, gooseneck
lamp, pencils, & blue pad, a mirror
where he combs his hair, & a bookcase
with one book on hypnosis (which he
studied & has practiced for the past
6 yrs unsuccessfully), little note
book (arithmetical scribblings on
speed of Earth's rotation, &c.), scrap
of paper with address of beautiful
woman (since moved out of town), chair
to extreme left covered with dirty
laundry, collage done with cigarette
paper & gold paint, bed, quilt,
picture of man on horseback leading
packhorse climbing mountain (waterfall
& lake behind)

SOMETHING cryptic
about hetermorphism**************
& Cthonian
about nightworlds**************

written in the form
of an epicedium
& a letter written in re
I don't know what

reference to the Primal Man,
multifarious,
& the prophecy,

& the King, the Savior

Light: the good Primal Spirit:
black, purple-blue, purple, blue,
red-purple, blue-green, red,
green, yellow-red, green-yellow,
yellow, white.
Jesus impalibilis, Jesus Paraclete!

He snumpfed his nose & said,
the notoriety poets don't get from their work
they get from their drinking.

       II Somewhere it was written

      PLAY IT SAFE!

              on a wall like that

                  & he walked off muttering,

Cerebrum, Cerebellum, Corpus Callosum, Pineal
Gland, Convolutions, Third Ventricle, Pituitary
Body, Olfactory Lobe, Optic Nerve, Pons Varoli,
Medulla Oblongata

wanting to make an analogy of the sun,
say something clever about Ormazd,

to spend some of the day reading,
some of it writing a poem,
some of it drinking wine,
some of it making love.

the stassis of the morning
closed his eyes,
& he slept.

                —*Leonard R. Garzotto*

Bats At Dusk

Because each window has a screen
I like to sit on the porch, watch the bats
Skimming the lake, eating a passage through
The shoals of gnats, riding the broken
Back of the day and soaring

On sudden errands high above the screen
Of pines and birches lining the shore. A broken
Sunset gilds the height of their soaring
And for a space, heaven's small angels have
    ventured through
On the gliding wings of golden bats.

And when a slowly soaring
Crescent of moon comes climbing through
A nest of random clouds, I see the bats,
Baby pterodactyls, veering past the screen,
Wings tipped in silver. Nothing is broken
Except the bony frames of gnats, soaring
Too late and slow to flee the swift sortie of
    bats.
Looking through
The fine mesh of the screen
I cannot see the little bodies broken.

Only by the twitching movements of bats
Do I mark the moment their small universe is
    broken
And death takes them soaring
Black as a stomach's secret, through
The silver of moon, past my window screen.

When will the screen be broken, bats come
    soaring through?

—*Chad Walsh*

A Word To Socrates

> "Crito, we ought offer
> a cock to Asclepius."

And is death, then, old man,
the purest Idea of all,
the cure for life?

I have seen only one face
return from that gray world
you welcomed: a boy who, at
a beach beyond your strange
geography—a beach
I guarded—slipped away
and drowned. We dragged for him
in the yellowing Sunday sun
and caught him on our hook,
snagged at the elbow. His
hand broke water first
and held there for a moment,
reaching out of that clammy
death to snatch at the low
daylight—a reaching out
that caught no life but mine
who lost him.

Old man, I would not since
that hour exchange the song
of one brown bird at sunset
for the purest Idea in all
eternity.

—*Philip Appleman*

from The Eastern Seaboard

Turning, they seem to be posies on the lacquered
   tin where I keep sugar—
it is the only precious thing but my cameo
   necklace,
and that is lost. My grandfather gave it to me.
He made his own wine, and cautioned me
about marriage and heavy dumpling dishes, and
   he died
in an upstairs bedroom I had never seen
until time to divide the remains. It was at the
   end
of a staircase that he told me went to the stars,
and I believed him, until I climbed it to see
   him dead.

The tin was what I took. I don't remember him,
the shopkeep shadow, the bent old Jew
escaped in time out of Poland to here. To here,
with his harridan and his little valuables,
and his cracked cantor voice that she denied him.
I could have had the sweater he kept cold shop
   in;
I have grace enough to wear it, if I had grounds,
and a Bouvier de Flandres on a long leash. I
   photograph well
with the grey sweater tied over my shoulders. I
   have seen
people take things like that. I have taken
   nothing
but the posie tin and the cameo,
but that was a gift.

I love you, said the sandwriting. I erased it,
to write an answer. But my hand was too violent,
I exposed the understone, ruined the smooth
   tablet.
Anyway, I had no answer except the true one:
If you love me, get off the beach by the
   shortest path,
through the lindenwoods and the box elders
that will take you away from the eastern shore;
   get back to northwest,
where the summer is not so hot and the nights
   are colder.
Here you begin to resemble me. Take your canoe
back to silence and turgid waters where there
   are no hidden meanders
and hanging mosses and warm stagnant marshes.
You are too hard for all this.
             That is too long for sandwriting,
with the slow tide coming in. I would have said
   it,
but the silence had lasted too long, and
   chameleon
was just then taking courage to approach us.

Northmen were out of date and out of season
In Spring, on that warm ground. The lines of
   his face
were made by cold winters. We had nothing here
for conquering; we were docile and willing.
   There was a portage
for him, where no errant vines
blocked exit. I preferred to sit on my fallen
   trunk
and watch him go than go with him. I was bred
   for the dying
that follows too much heat and root corruption.
He did not have the rhythm of growing past
   perfection,
of outland where dying is masked by fern growth,
where fingers need not be strong or over-nimble,
where small things die for lack of foraging.

                    —L. Suzanne Gordon

Letter To David

"to hold in a single thought reality and justice"

Looking away from my study, I realized suddenly
    the winter's gone, the shrunk pockets of snow
drained down the hollows. I felt like a bank-
    rupt. The high winds have cost me, $300
    for heat—
worse I might add, but the sordid details are
    hardly important. Too many blood vessels,
    bruised,
pool into oil & burn. When we've burned enough,
    carbon dioxide vapors will drag on the air.
Ice caps will melt at the poles, friend. Some
    coastline is bound to go under. Even these
    windows, rundown
early American, ripple & fume like heat waves on
    the highway drowning the pear tree, the view.
Daily, the laddery tentacles drift under
    wrinkled-up blossoms. Plucked from my type-
    writer, this
messenger taking down trivia, life—too much or
    too little—letters & poems pile up.
Bills pile up also. They'll bury us. Courteous
    businessmen charge as much as the country
    will bear.
Pooling resources. Resorts where the water
    breaks whitefaced, a metaphysical breakdown.
    If one
millionaire President's murdered, another takes
    over, mere vicious sentimentality.
                                 Crowds
rumor, discouraged with hopes amuck. So out of
    touch they're just wishful, moonstruck
    rebellions blow up.
Dinosaurs. Heartlands. All whirl into rain,
    into snow, & again rain slogging down moun-
    tains in snow.
Elements, raw, overturning themselves! & next
    dawn find the mayor's genitals crammed in his
    mouth.
David, where then is our flowering spring . . . the
    lost garden, whose crowning Justice dropped
    angels of death,
bright leaves & overripe morals. What then?
    Who'd dare trust the ideal rage we would
    love—as a boy
loves his wet dreams: the old heavens found,
    desolate & wild. The fitful horror come home
    for good.

                        —*James Scully*

Birthday in Monrovia, 1965

I

This town takes a guarded breath at dusk.
A bulbous government limousine
Floats through a yellow light;
Beggarman, Mandingo man
Shuffles on his homemade pads,
The sleek stream already whispered past
Without even a sidelong glance.

A heavy nacre torpor pushes out the glare,
And the sea air, like a woman's grieving
Hand, sinks shaking on the town stillborn.
Air conditioners cease to sweat, leaving
Their tepid puddles in the street.

A Bassa woman swings her baby to her back,
Secures it well with a 48-state flag.
She curses in the limp litter of the market,
Tells them all she won't pay that much
For wrinkling peppers, graveled rice,
Fetid smoked fish that call the flies
more sharply than church bells. Kru woman
Say: she full a lotta noise, she pay.
The child lets go an oily plastic bag.
Her child hangs in the stripes,
Stares through the noise and smells,
Looking toward the schoolyard where
Some students inside, as if one,
Proclaim their late-day allegiance.

II

I wake up in the oldest dusks.
I found myself repeating, over and over:
This city is far away, far away
From other cities. The rain begins
To roar, on my tin roof, on the town.

III

This morning's dream was of corridors
The walls I've hit, back and forth,
Plotting my points from changing stars.
Can reasonable days chart the shifting path?
The heat squeezes me awake. I'm thinking
Of that child upon his mother's back.
What caught his entranced eyes
As he stared into that polyethelene
Bag he clutched, stained crimson
From the viscous oil of palm?
He held it up to the pearl grey
Clouds at the edge of the sea.
Did he recognize the changing
Colors? This country's hues?

My sheets are rumpled and sticky;
The only color the old bone walls.
I miss the choice that seasons bring.
For two years running I've forgotten
My own date, my students' drives,
That child's determined face in
My own waking. They often say:
Why question heat when the sun is out?

—*Bill Holland*

Night Drive

Down the abacus of this street
I slide the green bead lights
counting the corners you
       are not on.
    Red suspends me:
      window
  contains me. Inside
some unseen brushman is painting
the window out or in. Brisk
brush strokes cover closer,
closer to the center square . . .
this diminished figure gives
me trouble with my breathing.
    One stroke more
may do it . . . no . . . one more . . .
     one quick
breath and I am painted in forever,
painted out forever, covered
by black window that held briefly
the only blowhole in this bleak ice-sheet
of frozen cars, crowds, clocks, corners
where you are not . . . shift metaphor . . .
    green bead trips me down
      my abacus street.

—*Ann Darr*

On Seeing Perhaps Miss Marianne Moore In The Library Of Congress

Her hat cocked gay to the words
she is writing and reading,
the lady meets my scrutiny, smiling
like a poem. I close my cold
Ivor Winters and finger my pen,
preferring not to ask

if she is Miss Marianne Moore,
wanting to keep
this clearness of eye and heart,
preferring not to mistrust
the realness of the faerie red rose
she has spirited here,

or this regal mahogany toadstool
where I have stopped working.
The rose signals welcome from a clean jelly jar,
And her inlaid device of silver threads,
proud where corsages might only be pinned,
trumpets like an honor from a purple king.

I could test these impressions against
a book in the stacks on Marianne Moore
with frontispiece portrait —
instead I imagine writing a schoolboy love-note
and taking her out to lunch.
I want for some reason to carry her rose

without spilling a drop,
the two of us light on metro-
gnomic feet
down alphabetical A St. S. E.
to merely numerical Fifth
while she suggests a list of Proper Names.

At the car I hand her the jar
with the rose (not spilling)
and say with deliberation,
"I shall guide the wheel of the Falcon
while you hold the jar and the rose."
And we turn up Independence

dygesting harde yron Magicravures and Turcotingoes
on the way to Mike Palm's
(where sports fans eat)
while Marianne Moore says again, again,
"without minuteness
there can be no sublime.

(1966)

—Rod Jellema

DRYAD

NUMBER 7/8
$1.50

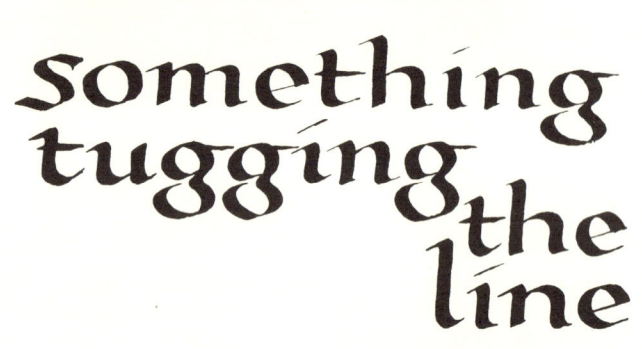

NO. 9/10

DRYAD

$1.50
50p

something
tugging
the line

Poems
by
Roderick
Jellema

DRYAD

#12
$1.50

Two Sides Of This Rolling Coin

         the horses
children love... gentleness... dark
   eyes of saints
            pools reaching to the core of nature

a myth... kept to pace
            by trainers and whips

                my horses
            rear and flare

using
the shoes i gave

        to strike sparks
    from one another

crouched naked in the
barn i let the smell

        of their rank battle
remind me of women

        —Gene Fowler

She

As Robert Graves says, the muse is not the woman you marry (try telling that to your wife). If you have heard about her you want to meet her and once you make love to her—or do you think you want to begin looking all over again for some woman wearing a trench coat in a movie rain (and if you're a woman you probably hate her). Two upper-middle-class Englishmen discreetly talk through the night about having loved her in their youth. One of them knows why she always wore her hair that way but never mentions it to the other. That she is a woman means more than that anyone ever imagined she was important: when she disrobes at night the police are on edge thinking of nude bodies in their trunks. "I am never tired," she says, her eyes like foresters among the trees.

        —Irving Weiss

After Too Many Intervals of Rain

Those black crows,
tired of transcendent arcs,
strike the sky like
sharp, incisive bits of charcoal.
The engraving thus made,
dissolves, runs down to
puddled shades of gray;
gets caught in the pendulate
sway of brush top trees
that wash clarity,
like first truths,
away.

—Ann Slayton

The Fall of the House of Usher

It was a big boxy wreck of a house
Owned by a classmate of mine name Rod Usher,
Who lived in the thing with his twin sister.
He was a louse and she was a souse.

While I was visiting them one wet summer, she died.
We buried her,
Or rather we stuck her in a back room for a bit, meaning
    to bury her
When the graveyard dried.

But the weather got wetter.
One night we were both waked by a twister,
Plus a screeching and howling outside that turned out to be his sister
Up and dying again, making it hard for Rod to forget her.

He didn't. He and she died in a heap, and I left quick,
Which was lucky since the house fell in right after,
                Like a ton of brick.

—Reed Whittemore

Because I Never Learned the Names of Flowers

It is moonlight and white where
I slink away from my cat-quiet blue rubber truck
and motion myself to back it up to your ear.
I peel back the doors of the van and begin
to hushload into your sleep
the whole damned botanical cargo of Spring.

Sleeper, I whisk you
Trivia and Illium, Sweet Peristalsis, Flowering Delirium.

Sprigs of Purple Persiflage and Lovers' Leap, slips of Hysteria
stick in my hair. I gather clumps of Timex,
handfuls of Buttertongues, Belly buttons, and Bluelets.

I come with Trailing Nebula, I come with Late-Blooming Paradox,
with Creeping Pyromania, Pink Apoplex, and Climbing Solar
                                                                 Plexus,

whispering: Needlenose, Juice Cup, Godstem, Nexus, Sex-us
                                                 Condominium.

—Rod Jellema

Departures

make nothing of this:
the way words in their tight little skins
must come down from the walls
soon this whole room will fill up
with their cries
I will tear them from the pages
and set them into the dark boxes
they will never go on
in the same way again
what surrounds them will change
their skins will loosen
will fall away

nor this:
when I release them
they will lose their way
for I have covered their eyes
with a white cloth
and spun them around
three times
they will strike out blindly
grope along a wall of light
their fingers like exposed roots
will register false messages
they will not be able to tell
where north is

—Myra Sklarew

Directions

nothing worth keeping ever washed up on a beach

Philip Appleman

for Phil, then

I

In a fog that has hid all houses
I am looking for something
for my son—shells
the tide has drilled a hole in,
or a bottle
with a cork.

For I have written many messages,
certain they would sail
down any river
in the North,
past cascade and water
fall,
and on to that sailor.

nothing worth keeping

But look—kitestring.

I pick it up
and continue
East.

II

Within sight of a stonewall
that reaches out into the waves,
appearing, disappearing and
appearing again, I sit down.

Two people, vague in the fog,
are walking on hands and knees.
What are they doing?
Drawing in the sand? Their heads
touch. I stare. Is this what
I want—them—fucking
in the fog: girl with boy **and**
me with them, *ever
on a beach?*

I look away, start walking
West.

III

    And come to a place that is full of
    feathers. Everywhere.
    Small, white feathers.
    I pick them up, touch them
    to my face, blow on them and
    watch them
    land. If I were from
    the South,
    I would think it was winter
    falling—
    these feathers. I stuff them in my pockets.

                    —Siv Cedering

The Souls of the Hares

Of all the people who try to shape something with words, on paper, I must be the slowest reader. On the flight between New York and Tokyo, something like 14 hours of travelling, I read about 60 pages. Just that. No more. I read a paragraph—look out at the clouds. When I travel I seem to enter some sort of time/space continuum of my own. Images from way back in my childhood float before me. It is as if I revalue my whole life, match the being I am becoming with the components of memory, thought. It is as if I travel inwards and outwards at the same time.

I was reading Jung's autobiography: *Memories, Dreams, Reflections.* In it he describes his first memory, first dream . . . and the first painting that had meaning to him. The first painting—I hadn't thought about that. There was, essentially, one painting in our home, when I was small. I used to look at it often. It was hanging over the couch in the livingroom. There was a small strip of stormy sea, and above that sea were the souls of the hares. THE SOULS OF THE HARES? My father liked to hunt. Sometimes he brought home a hare, two, three. I remember them hanging there, that soft grey fur, lighter grey, darker grey.

When I visited my mother in San Francisco, we spent a morning looking at old albums, and there, in one of the pictures, is that livingroom and that painting. There were birds on it, big, eaglelike creatures that were catching something out of a stormy sea. Above the birds were grey clouds, longish shapes. One could imagine them being hares that had no paws or heads. The souls of the hares. I had forgotten the birds.

                      —Siv Cedering

Sense and Sentences: On Getting A Computer To Write Poems

by Richard Forsythe

In front of me I have a question—"where can his dark thoughts want some dream?" It was posed by a computer, and I can't answer it.

Half the fun of meddling with computers is in the unanswerable questions they pose, especially when you try to force them outside the arithmetical rut in which they are tirelessly efficient. Then they show you exactly what you do not know.

The poems printed here—you can call them 'compositions in grammatical English and iambic pentameter' under your breath if you wish—were produced by the Oxford University KDF9. It is not a very large or fast machine by present-day standards, and it is currently being made redundant. However, it is still good for a few unanswerable questions. The most interesting of these is quite an old one, in new technological garb: "how is a poem to be made?" which the computer raises only indirectly, by not answering it.

Let us attend to this. A poem is made usually by writing or speaking sentences in a natural language. Simple. We can all do that. But the computer teaches us to ask just how. Well, the program used here has a subroutine that constructs sentences. (A subroutine is simply a series of operations or fixed procedures.) It constructs a sentence in several ways; one of these consists of calling (setting into operation) a further subroutine which constructs a noun-phrase, and then calling another subroutine whose job is to construct a verb-phrase. These lower-level subroutines in turn call others until one is reached that prints out a particular word. Control then returns up the hierarchy until the sentence is complete. This whole process is supervised by a metrical routine that works out what words from the available vocabulary conform to the requirements of the stress-pattern as well as being in the right grammatical category. If it can't find a suitable one, it produces an irregular line.

That, then, is the gist of it. The principle is that for each replacement-rule of a generative grammar, there is a subroutine that embodies the effect of that rule.

Now I don't promise to come up with answers, and clearly this isn't one. It's just the beginning of a problem: the machine writes abominable poetry. Although I have used only a subset of English, the real trouble is not any paucity of vocabulary or syntactic rules; it is a lack of coherence. The computer happily churns out sentence after sentence; they are nearly all in acceptable English; some of them are quite striking in their own right, e.g.: "some animal time destroys his beautifully impossible rose"; but they are hopelessly disjointed. There is no flow of ideas. At present I attempt to combat this by restricting the list of words: each poem chooses from a limited group of words within the total vocabulary, and each stanza from a smaller set within that group, while the first and last sentences and title are composed from an even smaller set. Also, by carefully arranging the words in storage, I have ensured that certain words tend to crop up together often and others less often. It is not good enough. And it is at this point that the machine forces us to start defining our requirements.

We can say something like—"a poem must have a spiritual integrity or wholeness that only arises out of experience"—but the computer won't appreciate it. The first step is, more modestly, that the sentences should link together, instead of being almost completely isolated. This entails that the computer should construct not single sentences but paragraphs, stanzas, or entire poems, paying attention to the organization of parts within the whole. Furthermore this means that it should know something about what it is writing. That sounds banal, but what we are looking for is a number of rhetorical rules, and at first I thought these could be purely formal—like syntactic rules only on a higher level. However, we cannot just say that a poem is, for instance, a beginning, a middle, and end in the same way a sentence is a subject, a verb, and an object, because an end is only the end of what was begun in the beginning and continued in the middle. That is to say: the terms we are going to have to use to describe rhetorical classes are not absolute, they are relative. 'Beginning' and 'end' obscure the issue slightly—they sound firm and definite—but if we take 'build-up' and 'denouement,' the necessary interdependence is clearer: a climax is not just a big explosion, it is the explosion of what was put together as a bomb; an end is not just an end, it is the end *of* something. And so our sentences must be interrelated, and they can only be interrelated through their meanings. I'm sorry to take so long to show that a computer can only make poems if it can make sense, and only make sense if it knows what it's talking about; but it's quite an important point since it means that a computer cannot compose poetry unless it has some kind of inner world to describe—in short, an imagination. To sum up: so that it can relate sentences and groups of sentences, they must mean something to it, and so that they can mean something to it, it must have some internal 'ideas' (probably only arrays of numbers) to which they refer. (I am taking it for granted that it cannot relate sentences only on their face value—in which case 'vision' and 'eye' would have no connection whereas 'waste' and 'taste' might.)

Therefore I am working to provide the machine with some sort of internal system operating according to its own rules, to which the grammatical apparatus that was the main body of the previous program is merely an adjunct enabling the computer to express the workings of its tiny mind. The utterances will be connected, as with humans, by being a report on a connected sequence of happenings.

By what kind of events do we choose to build a model imagination? It seems likely that making a consistent system of varying patterns should not be difficult. Yet when the machine describes the goings-on of such an abstract system, although it may startle us with surreal freshness, it may equally print nonsense—and the main intention was to introduce meaningfulness. In other words, the 'imagination' will have to be the 'image' of something, not just an abstract design. There are two ways of making this little mechanical 'world' correspond to things in the big human world: either we equip the machine from scratch with a deliberately-planned analogue or representation of physical (and maybe social and mental) events, or give it more or less blank memory-structure and allow it to develop this by contact with an environment. This latter course is near the edge of modern computing techniques (though even today it's feasible to have a computer interact with and learn from its surroundings to a limited degree), and it seems the more exciting of the two alternatives—letting our computer poet learn, maybe even suffer!

For of course what we have arrived at is a mechanical poet rather than a machine for writing poems. We started with a sentence-generator, and to give its sentences coherence we decided on the need for a dynamic but regular data-structure for which the sentence-producing mechanisms only acted as commentator; while to make this system comprehensible it appeared that it should not merely operate arbitrarily but should be tied to the real world, preferably via some kind of sensing and learning equipment—it should be, in effect, the computer's picture of its environment (almost a full-fledged imagination). And naturally, if it can talk about its conception of its world it can tell the truth, as it sees it, as well as concocting fiction.

Well, this is enough speculation. No such program has been written, and it will be an awesome feat to write one. Meanwhile, is it important that the exigencies of programming should convince us that a poem requires a poet for its creation? That even a machine to write poetry requires the rudiments of capacities other than those directly involved in writing poems—abilities to perceive, learn and ruminate? I think it is. You see, you've got to have soul. And I'm glad the computer reminds us that a poem must have a spiritual integrity or wholeness that only arises out of experience and suffering.

You may not be persuaded, but at least this foray shows a new approach to the lost art of rhetoric, perhaps even forshadows its revival. And apart from promising us new views on old problems and teasing us with insoluble ones, these cybernetic excursions hold out the eventual possibility of inhumanly beautiful poems.

COMPOSITION ENTITLED
THIS

A FEW CASCADES   TODAY OBSTRUCT THE   WOUND
TO SEAS BECAUSE SOME WAY REMOVES SOME TIME
OUR BULLET ENTERS WOUNDS. SOME FLANK WITHDRAWS
A WHOLE   AORTA. THIS RETREAT OF YELLOW
INVASIONS STARTLES SEAS. YES. SEAS COME FAR FROM
SUCCESS OF BULLETS.

THE SAND OBSTRUCTS JAPAN. THE SEA PREDICTS
THE SEA AGAINST MY SAND. NO WOUND AT PERSONS
SHOULD ENTER EVERY WOUND. YOUR FLANK REMOVES
SUCCESS. YOUR BULLET STARTLES BULLETS. MANY
ONES ON THE BULLETS HAUL THE-SAND OF PERSONS.

SOME SUDDEN HEART DIRECTLY SAW THE THING
UPON HIS WASTE. A WHOLE ESCAPE PREDICTS
HIS EYE. MY FLANK OBSTRUCTS THE SEAS. THE PERSON IS
SOME FLANK THAT MANY SHAPES UPON THE BULLET.
ASTOUND. COULD IT AGAINST THE ACID TIME
OBSTRUCT THE SAND. 100 WASTES REMOVE
THE FLANK. THE SHAPE INSIDE SOME FLANK CONTROLS
MY HEART WHEREAS AN OLD ESCAPE ALLOWS
A WHOLE LAGOON. SOME WASTE OBSTRUCTS NO BLUE
RETREAT. THIS WASTE OBSTRUCTS THE CLOSED ONE.
     LOVES
WILL COLOUR WASTES. YOUR FLANK CONTROLS HIS BULLET
AND SO THE SAND THAT IS PROFUSE PREDICTS
SOME FLANK THAT IS ACUTE.

Sandra Slayton Namias

High Dark

The camera that takes the pictures after the fact
can focus on any black night
over Sweetwater and find me still
circling, still wheeling for the final turn,
traveling at a breakneck speed,
hunting the level earth
still unable
to land.

On that first night solo flying
swallowed by the night,
trying to cough myself up, I must trust
all night flyers to steer clear of me . . .
bats be my friends, do your counting
out of my rectangle, owls, lay over on
some branch and hoot from there,
I cannot feather my wings. I
cannot find the field.

     I must not keep on at high speed
into the black air, am I going up or down,
are the stars above me or is it my city,
Sweetwater, sweet water, bring me down.
I cannot keep speeding through air,
I dare *not* keep speeding through air,
there is only one place I can arrive.
On earth. No place else will accept me
with active eyes and ears.
I have become two beings, one skin
standing a space away from the other
like a picture frame. Hurtling through air
I must make decisions that stand still
so I can perform them. Or die.

     Die? Not yet. Wipe out the pictures
of my life flashing before my eyes. That is cliche
and doesn't really happen. I am obverse enough to
have it begin. Reel one. Roll one: I am being
dangled upside down on the roof of the house
I know I was born in . . . over a balcony
with a railing of tooled poles, looking like
New Orleans, but it stood at the end of
the only street in town and standing on
that balcony you could watch the crops go by
year after year—cornfields end on end to an horizon
that ended because the earth curved.

     My horizon is where the earth
is curving, joined in black velvet
with the space that is curving, my plane
track is curving and I must not curve, I must
set this plane down on a straight runway. on
a level plain. before the gas gives out.
Four times now I have maneuvered into place,
made the proper angle to bring me nose-straight
into the flight pattern . . . four times the rows of
yellow pearls have grown in size too soon.
And I have pulled up hard and flown on, shaken
by all my errors. I have never wanted
jewels much. I have never wanted jewels so much
in all my life. o lights. o stars.
o bats. winged creatures of the night . . .
o fraud. I have no right to join you.

I donate my wings to you—I would strip
them off if I could and give you my wings
for a house. Here I give you my engine,
my lights, my instruments, my radio, my
helmet, here—have my parachute.
I have no chance to use it.
If I opened the hatch now and stepped out,
I would discover only after I started falling
which way was down. Throw everything
overboard. Deep-six it all. Government
issue-be-damned. But turn another corner,
bring the yellow pearls in sight. my god,
don't lose the field. Let gravity work.
Keep my fellow flyers away from me. Stop
magnetism. Sweat the parachute wet,
if you have to, but don't lose the field.
      One last attempt. Last?
I will keep on trying until
we are flying only by riding the wind,
except this is no glider and will plummet—
stop—I have stopped the newsreel—I
have stopped time. I am diving at high speed
into the black earth, pull up, pull, make the angle
right, let down the landing gear, now now! without
the wheels I will nose over—whack the landing gear
release—wake it, wake it up, in place, we are moving
for our lives, this plane and me, flaps, flaps down, level
not on one wheel—vertigo abhors a vacuum, level—there!
there is the touch, there is that moment in time when I am
                                            touching
the earth again, the wheels are part of my belly, I am hugging
                                            the earth,
I am down.

      But cover both your ears—and the sound you hear
is my plane still flying lost, still circling the dark,
and I frantic, knowing only if I do not panic can I reach home,
knowing I will always be circling, lost in the dark, traveling
at high speed, knowing it for what it is.

                              —*Ann Darr*

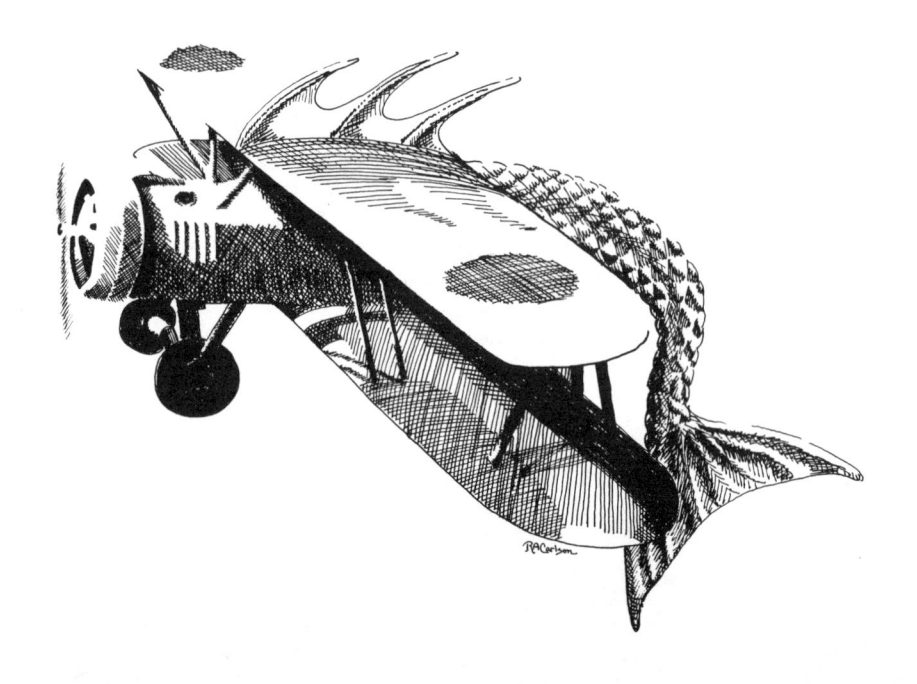

The Spring of '59

We met in the spring of '59,
she was shellin peas in a basket an tappin her foot
t'her brother's harp. I stayed the summer
hoein squash an pickin fat,
green tomatoe worms. Some afternoons I'd hunt for ants
she'd keep in a box with bells an spoons.
At night we'd build a fire in the yard
an wind ourselves together.
We never talked much,
told stories with our hands,
and when the fire died
we'd rub our bodies
til our rattles sang.

      —*Roger Aplon*

War Bonds

it was wartime
daisies and maisies in overalls
worked in factories
snapping gum in their teeth
ration spunk
to keep them going

through weekend tours
at the local USO
or late nights
checking hats
for the Willard rooftop garden
it was rough

making ends meet
while their men were at war
in radio worlds
and newspaper print
nights at home
were spent reading

letters over and over
like prayers
mouths shaped
to the words
and Hershey bars
melted on radiators

      —*Saundra Maley*

A Tumult for John Berryman
edited by Marguerite Harris

Shaping
Dryad Press
Edited by Philip K. Jason

DRYAD

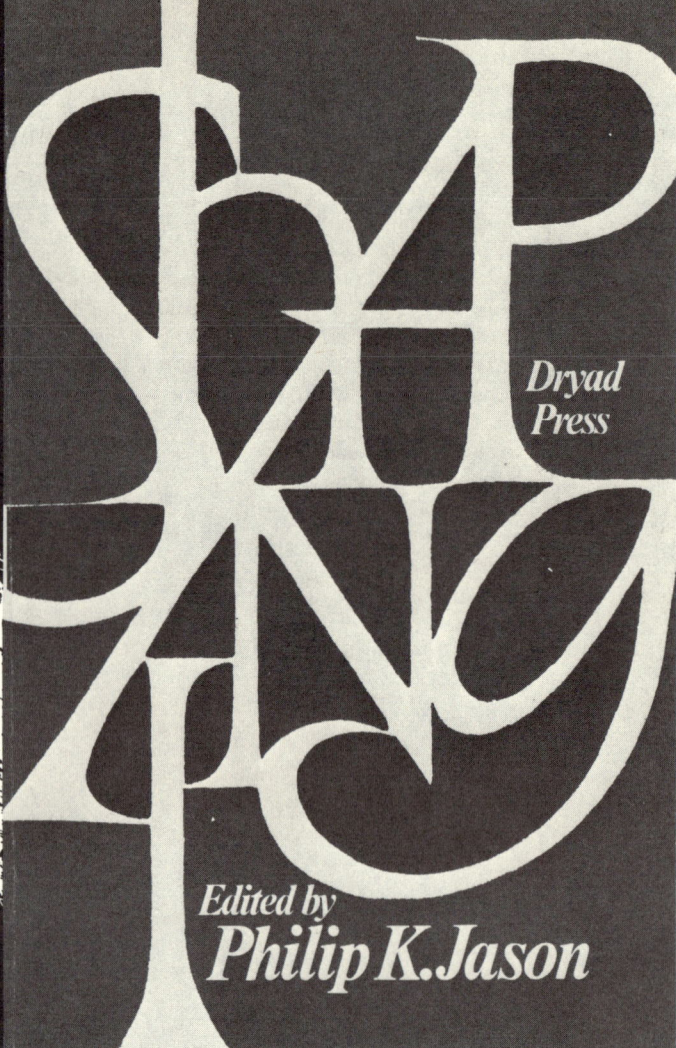

DRYAD 13
$1.50
THE WORK OF MORTON MARCUS

How Would You Touch The Body Of God

How would *you* touch the body of God?

Clamping your palm on His contours
like a roller coaster hurdling over its tracks?

Or like a blind man skimming his fingertips
down the length of a mountain range?

I, for one, think that His body
is the edge of the universe

and would finger it accordingly,
like a tailor testing a fabric.

We know the likelihood of finding Him is rare
but we keep in practice anyway.

That is why we touch each other's lives
as often as we can, leaving our words

and fingerprints on each other's breath,
and why, when we remove our hands,

our thumbs are radiant, gorged with static,
and our index fingers waver like wands.

—Morton Marcus

To A Second Son

Now you embrace chameleons
changing color yourself with the scenery,
white with me and my white questions,
muted under a sky bruised
black and blue.

You feed your lizards
moths, plundered each evening
from the porch light
while my shudder records
as accurately as a seismograph
the distance between us.

Peter, we have given you
these hand me downs:
your brother's half used sweater,
your father's reel,
and all my old faults

drowned once like a bagful of cats.
They have washed up twenty years downstream
bloated and mewing, to plague
the perfect body you will grow into,
shaking all of us delicately off.

—Linda Pastan

July 1974   Barbara R Frank

The Doctor

Lugged me to the tower in waterproof bags,
half a dozen trips up & down the stone stairs.
First the soft parts, belly & buttocks; then
the rib cage full of red and purple toys;

then the arms flopping about like fish;
the full-fleshed legs nipped small in the middle,
hinting the shape of the whole body to come;
a rattling package of little footbones;

& finally the head, stolen for its roomy skull
and its long hair that never stopped growing,
that coiled around the Doctor's thighs
even as he pressed the soft underchin
to the red kiss of the neck.

His black-haired hands placed the parts cannily,
pinching all the raw lips together,
stitching shrewdly as an old woman.
He stroked the slippery stuffing into every crevice.

We watched all night for the lightning,
my gray shapes heavy & his breathing dry,
my eyes, though blind with sticky jelly,
turned toward him, & his eyes fixed on the skylight.

Neither he nor I saw the flash when it came.
It was the Doctor's breath inside my mouth
that first lifted my new breasts
& fluttered my lips. Then thunder

& the slim whistle or another breathing
& the soft clink of bones drawing themselves together,
sitting up, dropping over the ege of the table
to test the stitches & the world for firmness.
I smoothed my hair, felt human to myself . . . .

Drawn by the silky working of my joints,
the Doctor came too close. In a second
I was on him, riding him like a monkey.
I locked my arms & legs around his waist & neck,
I jabbed my tongue in his ear: LOVE ME! LOVE ME!

All night now he lies propped beside his monster,
hollow-eyed and too late wise. The Doctor
knows if he falls asleep for a single instant
my famished knees will grind his skull to meal.

—Clarinda Harriss Lott

Scenes

1. The man and the woman
   sit on stone benches
   facing each other
   There's green
   lichen
   on the courtyard
   stones
   She wears a white dress
   he is frowning
   The river is green
   the willows yellow

2. The man sits on a stone
   bench   the woman
   stands naked
   in the fishpond
   Goldfish shimmer
   She covers
   her hair
   with one hand

3. The man and the woman
   sit on stone benches
   She stares
   at her shoes of white
   silk
   There is water
   on the stones
   There's a strain
   on her dress
   on the willows

4. A white dress
   spills on the stone bench
   The courtyard
   is glass or ice
   Fish swirl
   in the wind
   The man opens the door
   and green leaves
   green birds swirl
   over the ice or glass
   The woman
   watches

5. There is blood
   on one bench
   black birds
   in the willow
   sun
   on the east
   windows
   sun
   on the river
   the woman

6.   The man sits on a stone
bench   the river
is green
He is frowning
he is naked
The river is green
the willows yellow
There is
no blood
no woman

—Margaret Gibson

His Oyster

   He lives in Washington, DC and he goes all the
way to Georgia by car, passing through Virginia,
North Carolina, South Carolina, then through
part of Georgia on his way down to Savannah,
then he goes by bus through Savannah to Vernon
View, then he goes by boat across bays and inlets
and sounds of the Atlantic to Ossabaw Island,
then he goes by station wagon to the main house,
then he goes by pick-up truck with Mr. Jimmie
Willard Perkins (nicknamed Middleton) to a tidal
river to fish two hours for trout, with no luck,
then he goes by foot, with Middleton, one mile
downriver through the woods to an oyster bed
Middleton knows about, and there he finds an
oyster—or a hard, gray-brown shell, covered with
little stones and carbuncles that looks like it could
be an oyster. He knows there is something in it he
wants: an oyster. He takes a razor-sharp knife that
has come from Sweden for this (via Sears in DC,
trips to Maine, Vermont) and he tries to open this
thing which has the brave angry face of a petrified
knish. It will not open. He takes a stone and taps
easy, then hard, on the base of the handle, trying
to drive it into the oyster—it doesn't work, the
oyster slips away, sideways, he tries again and fails
again, and then he blows up, and puts it on a big
flat rock and pounds it with a stone, just trying to
smash it, and that doesn't work, and he picks the
sonofabitch up and throws it down as hard as he
can and he thinks well now would be a goddamned
good time for a miracle, for it to roll over and just
open slowly and teach him something about
the futility of violence, the shame of pride, the
pride of anger, the surprise of faith where not to
knock by Christ is open wide. Instead it stays
tighter than a bull's ass in fly-time, teaching him
the horseshit of inwit, the agenbite and fuck you
of fantasy, and the true kryptonite hardness of an
oyster you can't have even if you're Clark Kent
and have driven 600 miles to get it. Middleton
spits some Honey-cut and says, "ats fuckin
oyrsters."

—Roland Flint

Fish

1   Tour of Hemingway House, Key West, Florida

He set two fossil fish
into the wall.
Lime saves only the
shape of the bones
under the flesh
that flashed once
in Green River, Wyoming.

As a zero saves nothing
but space, this house
and forty-one cats
holds the space he wrote in
before time flowed out of it
and into the gulf. "Inside,

Mr. Groves will tell you
of Hemingway's wives and lovers."
Outside, the banyan tree tries
to retrench, drops down
its branches to become late roots.

2   Outdoor Seafood Restaurant, Sea of Galilee, Tiberias

I used to watch my father
far across the dining room table
pick the flesh from the bones of
revelation fish, white fish, sun fish,
like a cat. This is how he taught me care

and terror of sharp points, on Sundays.
Tonight I eat, at sunset, St. Peter's fish.
My wife is far away across the table.
She does not care to hear about my father.
Instead she waits for another father

to walk again across the lake
going violet in red lastlight.
We sit here saving our space.
The cats whine for our bones
and we give them down.

—Edward Gold

**off the Edgware Rd
and near to Brittany
Elisabeth she made
tea nice**

1.
bolted French away
and broke English still
she dragged around in her face
of the day and fashion
painted as the telephone
rang or a knock at the door
curdled her winter
song: "certainly is dark early
this time of year it gets
dark early this time it's
darker earlier than yesterday
and the day before" the telephone
rings a shout
at the door "allo?"
postman it's the postman
with her little cards
from France

water boils she steeps
tea drowns coffee
thinks across the channel home

2.
arranged to speak
as best we could
but there was still
the old bloody question the old bloody
cleaver lady lover
all wet smooch and stump in
her butchertime that is it was
no mystery just the low

and mean toil of this
drill in a random
geology just the easy
butt up cocker hump
until you whispered quand
je glis encore encore and I
swallowed the words on your
tongue and pulled your tits
beneath your arms.

3.
so they come
around in faces of the day
and fashion painted as I
sing lala or the telephone
rings your mother "allo
allo" your mother or some
ruthless boy his pants
in his ass
allo allo you're here
on the stairs at the door
inside here where I sit
singing lala of your
coffee and your blessed
tea allo

"allo allo can you
talk can you drink
this tea allo let's dance allo
I got this new dress allo
why don't you speak English
why don't you speak French
why don't you speak to me
in my new dress allo new I want
to go out do you
hear me do you
want this tea allo?"

4.
I rhyme ladies
on that bed put
fig leaves on
their crying
heads and sit in a bamboo
chair and stare
at a ragdoll in the corner.

the light is nice I play
patience by the fire black
knave on the red
queen on the black
king I need a 4 for
that 5 she's up says "put up
the ace do you want
tea and hope
for a 2 or a 10"
off again leaving
me to play patience

lovely light
in this room
lovely language
at the door
lovely why
you crying put a blanket on
the floor and sleep and here here's
some yellow flowers here's
that 4 lovely
light language allo 7
on the 8
building down
to 2 and 2
on the ace building
up

I squeeze queens
from 7
stacks and lala alone
here in this light yellow
flowers blankets woman
on the floor and a ragdoll
in the corner lovely

—Denis Boyles

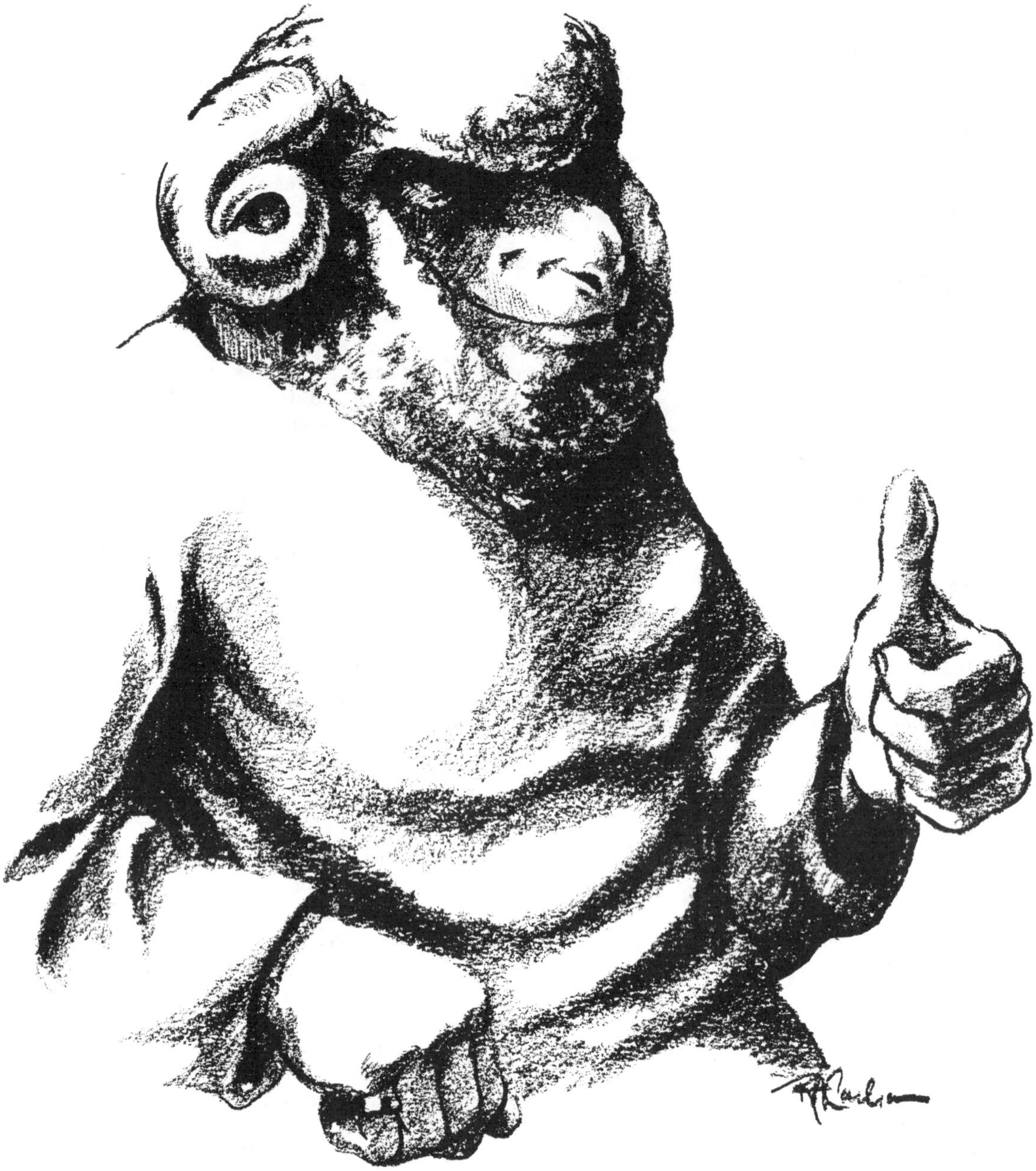

Partly Pandemonium, Partly Love

*I love great men I love. Nobody's great.
I must remember that.*

i

"Daddy where's the moon I want the moon"

Berryman dead. If I could
I would cry tears. My son has been crying.
Afraid? I don't know. I want
tears for my son who has tears
and we neither of us can say; we
cry in our different ways, him
for the moon? and I for ... Berryman is dead
and it is meaningless to you. It is
almost meaningless for me. Shhhh
The moon is asleep. She will come
but it is a long trip and she needs her rest.
We must wait. Come, lay down,
I'll make you a song

*Down down the moon fell down
She was wearing an old maid's gown.
Pulled up high, zipped up tight
Nobody sleeps with her tonight.*

Shhhh, don't cry. There is nothing to
be frightened of. There are no ghosts. I am here.
Come, we'll crayon our own moon. Shhhh
Bridges are washing away in the rain and
she may be a long time coming.

ii

The poets die. And we read the memorials; the
obituaries prepared well in advance, follow.
And what have we left for ordinary men, drunks, poor
slobs, soldiers, good family men and bad, whores,
social workers, all the rest dying
singly and by dozens, thousands,
masses like no metaphor can describe. What, finally, do we say? It is
necessary to forget and we do and our memories are like
yesterday's news. And it is necessary. In the face of
bayonets that do what bombs have left undone; in
face of murder, riots, jails, hunger that makes
the knuckles raw, floods, tidal waves—there is no
bridge high enough.
                          It is the new year; the old
has not been left behind. Madness and loss—they
sit in eyes that are dry. But we have poems. You write
something maybe. And then? Those who call
themselves poet, what is a poet?
Poems are make believe. Are poets?
You need desire to make a poem. Berryman dead
Kenneth Patchen whose work I don't know well,
whose looks have been crippled so long, has died
today. He is survived by wife and many poems. What

do sentiments mean? Delmore Schwartz. Dead six years now?
now Berryman, burned-out ego, poet whose
poems I've loved, what has survived you? The hordes
walk every day non-stop into cadavers, in Bengal, Vietnam, Africa, in America my home. These
words, these silly words which only for a moment
ground the sadness, which only in a fiction build
a bridge high enough to cross, these inky marks
only waste their time in a man's life because   because
why? Answers
John Berryman-O, Henry
Pussycat. What are they but a minstrel show,
Where blackface hides the shrapnel and the coal
and bridges are a mass of paste and gaudy colors.
They cannot hold. In my bed, not insomniac, but wide awake
I make my fiction. There you are, peeking from
the curtain. Your cue. You tip-toe out, stealthing, behind your beard, smirking like a kid. You
stand there hairy-legged, naked (with black socks)
in the snow, waving to all us fans out here
in the fourth row. The sign says you are leaving
on a grand trip—the player-piano hits
some kinky notes. We applaud, you wave good-bye, and
are off (the sign now says) to see Delmore, Randall,
Ted, all that un-Merry gang living
somewhere in a bunch of poems. We sit applaud-
ing and the curtain falls.

iii

"Your letter warmed a chilly day . . . . Delmore
is not forgotten"

I have worked through the night
until the words have been emptied
of their breath. Dead lungs they are.
An old drunk in a corner
slopped in urine. Stop. It
is late and I am looking
too hard for metaphor. It is too late too
to sleep now. I have been sitting
here uncomfortable, sticking pins in my eyes
for tears. I am tired but not
sleepy; I am neither afraid nor unafraid.
Colloidal suspension chemists would say.
Time Magazine has condensed this week's casualties,
all those bodies, not only Vietnam, not only Bangledesh,
those bodies slopped in mud, eyeless, pieces
and broken bits of grimface, that
feast of burned and broken bones. Tears? Anger?
Are they enough. Toast the dead to pandemonium.
Berryman has made Milestones: fifteen lines (and
four of them quotation). Lowell will get a
larger spread. Roethke rocked in drink listens
to the wind, and all that gang is waiting
for the Man. Only Delmore is deep in sleep.
This is a fine night, a fine fine night, making
poems to wake the dead.

—Merrill Leffler

Lover's Leap
   (for John Berryman)

For poetry's sake leap,
drag to that river the last
breath of the black angel.
Take with you Henry's
disgust for the great books.

The metaphor has been lanced.
Sure it gets boring,
and everyone breaks wind.
But the poems will hang around.

Take down to the river bridge
the last possibility,
touching all points with air.
Were you turning back home,
tucking the body away from

the cold wetness of Minnesota?
I think you forgot a line
to tack on to some poem:
The world ascended to meet you.

   —Doug Flaherty

After, Love

In a confusion of wings, birds hasten
the night. A storm of shadows darts across
a senile moon and we, in the chaos
of tangled sheets, watch bodies darken
that so soon past were light to touch.
There's no more time and no more need to talk,
yet there falls between us, like a sparrowhawk
among small birds, a fear of silence much
too ominous to lie at rest. We speak
of nothing more than changing weather
then turn to backs and turn again. Feather
light my hands search and in the night's oblique
storms, under a terribly old moon
find nothing more than shadows come too soon.

   —Adelaide Blomfield

The Mermaid Crashed Upon the Mind

The mermaid crashed upon the mind
of the young man, took it
by surprise, and near broke it
before he surfaced to his kind.

Down below he had turned with her,
twisted and whorled the water so
his mind had gone out to the green glow
of that world; he had loved that water.

Don't imagine it would be any different
with yourself: her hands were loose
and firm all at once, he said yes
to whatever way she went,

and thought her hair was the hair
of his mother, who he thought was dead:
it trailed away like a wet road
promising this way was as good as air.

And her skin, it locked in
secrets and showed them, too:
her body was a window
and not to look was the sin.

Love under water! He was young
and the dry air was dry.
What did he care for the sun's eye
or that he'd lose his tongue?

He wanted a sense of water, over
and under him. And her thoughtless hips
accompanied him like fine music, the tips
of her breasts said ever, ever.

A mermaid crashed upon the mind
of a young boy, wrapped her tail
between his legs and played till
bored, then forced him to ascend.

Now he, gone mute, can only walk
all day around our dusty town—
except for pausing to pretend to swim
under the bank's clock.

—*Philip Dacey*

The Hung Buck

The hung buck
chilling
cools the room
between the killer
and his killing.

As he skins
the dark
hidden parts—
she gelds a wildness
from both their hearts.

And rinsing
pluck she
dreams of knives
to bone and roll her
blood-wedded thighs.

Honed and wet
she threads
lardoons while
the buck still bleeds in
the other room.

—*W.V. Moody*

Tortoise Birthday

I knit a furious bone
that spans me
like a hardened glove.

Each year the boys cry—Matron!
We can't
kiss you from above!

Bah! They want sex like herrings
give,
moist and in some cove.

I keep my bottom for
the dirt,
and bask and dream of love.

—Kathleen Jeffrie Johnson

Program Notes

You watch each play with a thousand eyes.
You even notice when cigarette smoke
Streams from the lobby into the theater
Like an old actor's ghost stretching his arms
Toward the stage. You know who wants water
Who's coughing, who's squirming. And when you face

Square around and stare at someone's face
You see desolation in his eyes
Or fever. For the play brings no water
To burning hearts, only smoke
To calm a nightmare in its arms,
Softening its outline for the theater.

This repetition is like a dream in a theater,
With the audience fallen asleep and smoke
Rising from the holes where their eyes
Have closed. On stage, with naked arms,
A woman holds a mirror to her face.
She seems to be gazing in clear water

But really it is a mirror, not water.
It's not just illusion we seek in a theater
But disillusion too. All may turn to smoke
But every scene that's played you must face
Without reservation, as if murderous eyes
Confronted you, or sexual tender arms.

And if you took the mirror from her arms,
Even if your soul were clear as water,
You could not find the clue. Your eyes
Would search the bottom but the theater
Would stay silent as the sphynx. You face
A dream so violent it goes up in smoke

If you just touch it, and the smoke
Harms you. Though the mirror in your arms
Reflects the earnest features of your face,

They were blindly painted on. Soap and water
Would wash the mystery from the theater
And leave you rubbing sand out of your eyes.

Aristotle, whose eyes could pierce smoke
Cried in the theater when heroes died at arms.
Salt water tears streaked his solemn face.

—Rodger Kamenetz

Sallie Sitting A Chestnut Mare

I

Kicking her legs like an insect, overturned,
the sun rising on its belly, a golden nugget
coming apart like sheathes of hay to burn

the ground brown as rich luggage.
Out the window, the morning rises;
her clothes laid out like soldiers and her baggage

carried piece by piece to private houses
are preliminary to her mounting in the sun. She turns,
the brown hills slide out like silk, her blouse,

the white on red, is smoothed, the leather burns
as delicate as steam and each hoof blinks
in the green air. She rises and turns,

tightens like a flower in the sun, thinks
she is pure light itself, our faces raise
and open, it is morning 1939, she winks.

The child-queen lifting to her lover's praise
is caught when light mixes with her hair
like a woman sitting a chestnut mare.

II.

And so today, she is detached in stone
or grey wood covered in tin, the painted
signs reflecting bits of sun: cloned

from perfect pictures in a book. She fainted
in the heat, her horse, now long since dead,
nudging her head from the young grass, sainted

as a freshened mare who folds a colt near-red
into the fields and sees itself appear
each season like a photograph; not dead

but hung on doors and stable walls which rear
back and swing into the face. Now Sallie turns
and finds herself standing by a horse, the year

before she married, about to learn
to ease the proper gait and turn the house
three times before she changed into the auburn

dress she had prepared, replaced her moistened blouse
with layered jewels which dance like spiders on
a tablecloth and turns to us and stares.

—Tom O'Grady

Cumulative Indexes

Portfolio Index

Portfolio

No. 1 Summer 1945
No. 2 December 1945
No. 3 Spring 1946
No. 4 Winter 1946
No. 5 Spring 1947
No. 6 1948

Portfolio Staff
Assistant Editor: Harry Thornton Moore

Editorial Advisors: Prose-Henry Miller
Poetry-Seldon Rodman
Photography-Sam Rosnberg
(Romare Bearden added no. 6)

Abrahams, William: "An Affirmation," 3:18
Afro: graphic, 4:8
Anonymous: Poem, 5:11
Aragon, Louis: Poem (tr. Selden Rodman), 1:10

Barker, Elsa: Angelo Sikelianos translation (w/Eva Sikelianos), 6
Barbieri: graphic, 4:18
Batigne, Rene: "Modigliani," 5:19
Bearden, Romare: graphic, 1:19
Bearden, Romare: graphic, 3:Frontispiece
Becker, Edwin J.: "Who Cried Against the Wall?" 5:7
Belance, Rene: Poem, 5:13
Bontempeli, Massimo: Poem (tr. Pietro Lazzari), 4:17
Boyle, Kay: "Introduction to a Poem on Flight," 1:2
Boyle, Kay: Walter Mehring translation, 3:15
Boyle, Kay: "Military Zone," 3:17
Brooks, Gwendolyn: "We're the Only Colored People Here;" 1:13
Brown, Sterling A.: "Night Bus," 3:20
Bueno, Antonio: "Brooks '46," 4:24
Bukowski, Charles: "20 Tanks From Kasseldown," 3:8

Calas, Nicolas: "The Gathering of the Waters," 6
Calef, V.: Two Poems (tr. Giovanelli), 4:10
Calfee, Maria: Natalie Ginzburg translation, 3:10
Calfee, William: graphic, 5:plate 4
Calgi, Corrado: graphic, 3:9
Calgi, Corrado: graphic, 4:21
Cambas, Andrea: Poem (tr. Derek Patmore), 6
Campigli, Massimo: graphic, 4:22
Camus, Albert: "Letter to a German Friend," 2:7
Capetanakas, Demetrios: Poem, 1:12
Carapanou, Margarita: "The Straw Hats," (tr. Andreas Carnbas), 6
Carmelo: graphic, 5:plate 10
Carnbas, Andreas: Margarita Carapanou translation, 6
Carnevali, Emanuel: "Train of Characters Through the Villa Rubazziana," 5:15
Carra: graphic, 4:27
Cartier-Bresson, Henri: *Le Retour*, 2:5
Char, Rene: "Cereste, 18 Juin 1944," 2:19

Clark, Eleanor: "The Hill," 1:18
Comfort, Alex: "Somnabulists of Freedom," 1:15
Coolidge, Constance: Jean-Paul Sartre translation, 3:2
Cossery, Albert: "The House of Certain Death," 5:17
Crawford, Ralston: graphic, 3:23
Creekmore, Hubert: Poem, 3:26
Crevel, Rene: excerpt from *Babylon*, 1:6
Crosby, Caresse: "The Full Armor of Light," 1:Forward
Crosby, Caresse: "Bella Materia Colorata," 4:15
Crosby, Caresse: Notes, 5:Coverleaf
Crosby, Harry: graphic, 1:24
Crosby, Harry: excerpts from *Shadows of the Sun*, 3:6
Crosby, Harry: Eight Love Poems, 5:2

Daiches, David: "The Future of Ignorance," 1:11
Daiches, David: "American Wines," 3:27
Dimaras, K.T.: "Contemporary Greek Literature," 6
Diamantopoulos, Diamantis: Four graphics, 6
de Chirico, Giogio: excerpt from *Bella Materia Colorata*, 4:Foreword
de Chirico, Giorgio: graphic, 4:15
de Libero, Libero: Poem (tr. Giovanelli), 4:10

Eluard, Paul: Two poems, 2:2
English, Maurice: Eugenio Montale translation, 4:2
English, Maurice: Umberto Saba translation, 4:17
Engonopoulos, Nikos: Poem, 6
Engonopoulos, Nikos: graphic, 6:plate 4
Ernst, Max: graphic, 5:plate 2

Falqui, Enrico: "Italian Fiction Today" (tr. Giovanelli), 4:25
Fasola, Roberto: Lithograph, enclosed in 100 copies of 4
Fasola, Roberto: graphic, 5:plate 3
Fazzini: graphic, 4:9
Fields, Frank G.: "Llanto," 3:1

Gatto, Alfonso: Poem, 4:10
Genet, Jean: Poem, 4:22
Gentilini: graphic, 4:6
Ghika: graphic, 6:plate 1
Giacometti, Alberto: graphic, 2:18
Ginzburg, Natalia: Poem (tr. Marie Calfee), 3:10
Giorni, Leonello: "Aspects of Italian Cinema," (tr. Giovanelli), 4:28
Giovanelli: Enrico Falqui translation, 4:25
Giovanelli: Leonello Giorni translation, 4:28
Giovanelli: V. Calef translations, 4:10
Giovanelli: Libero de Libero translation, 4:10
Giovanelli: Aldo Plazzeschi translation, 4:10
Giovanelli: Leonardo Sinnisgali translation, 4:10
Goode, Harry W.: "I Married That Woman," 5:3
Gounaro: graphic, 6
Grandville, J.J.: graphic, 3:4
Grimault, Paul: "Animated Cartoons," 2:5
Gruber: graphic, 2:15
Guevara, Meraud: graphic, 5:plate 11
Guttuso: graphic, 4:6

Hadjidakis, Mano: "Theme from the Glass Menagerie" (score), 6
Hadjimihali, Angelika: "Popular Greek Architecture," 6

Hanley, James: excerpt from *New Directions*, 3:14
Helion, Jean: graphic, 1:1
Herschberger, Ruth: Three Poems, 1:14
Hoyleman, Merle: Poem, 5:4
Hugo, Victor: Poem (tr. Selden Rodman), 1:10

Inber, Vera: Poem, 5:14

Kaiser, Stuart: Alberto Moravia translation, 4:14
Kanellis: graphic, 6
Kapralos, Christos: Two graphics, 6:plate 6
Kees, Weldon: Poem (tr. William Schenkel), 2:12
Koun, Charles: "The Art Theatre," 6

Lam, Wilfredo: graphic, 3:11
Lannoy: Music to *Le Retour*, 2:6
Lazzari, Pietro: graphic, 1:4
Lazzari, Pietro: graphic, 4:11
Lazzari, Pietro: Massimo Montempeli translation, 4:17
Leduc, V.: "Aurons-Nous En France Une *Treve De Dieu* De Sept Mois?" 2:11
Leite, George: Poem, 5:16
Levi, Carlo: "Panorama," 4:1
Levi, Carlo: graphic, 4:2
Lewis, Naomi: graphic, 1:25
Locke, Justin N.: graphic, 5:plate 7
Lorca, Garcia: Poem, 3:1
Lowell, Robert: Poem, 2:8

Maar, Dora: graphic, 2:2
Mann, Georg: "O For a Muse of Fire," 5:18
Manzu: graphic, 4:7
Marcellini, Romolo: Portfolio in Rome, 4:foreleaf
Marcellini, Romolo: "Sciuscia" (film stills), 4:3
Martin-Chauffier, Louis: "La Tradition Revolutionnaire," 2:17
Mason, Jordan: Poem, 5:8
Mattise, Henri: graphic in 200 copies, 2:1
Mehring, Walter: Poem (tr. Kay Boyle), 3:15
Merlier, Octave: N. Vrettakos translation, 6
Merlier, Octave: Yannis Ritsos translation, 6
Miller, Henry: "The Staff of Life Pt. 1," 1:5
Miller, Henry: "The Staff of Life Pt. 2," 3:11
Miller, Henry: graphic, 3:11
Miller, Henry: "Into the Night Life," 5:frontispiece
Mirko: graphic, 5:plae 8
Modigliani, Amedeo: graphic, 5:plate 1
Montale, Eugenio: Selection from *Le Occasioni* (tr. Maurice English), 4:2
Moore, Harry T.: Book Reviews, 1:26
Moore, Harry T.: Book Reviews, 2:22
Moore, Harry T.: Book Reviews, 3:28
Moore, Harry T.: 'Why Not Read Lawrence Too?" 5:1
Moore, Henry: graphic, 1:4
Moralis, Jean: Two graphics, 6: plate 4 & plate 7
Morandi: graphic, 4:frontispiece
Moravia, Alberto: "Malinverno" (tr. Stuart Kaiser), 4:14
Moretti: graphic, 4:20
Morgan, Claude: "Liberte-Egalte-Fraternite," 2:10
Moricand, Conrad: "Pilosite et Magie," 5:5

Nervi: graphic, 4:20
Nicolareizis, D.: "The Presence of Homer in Modern Greek Poetry," 6
Nin, Anais: excerpt from *Children of the Albatross*, 5:12

O'Higgins, Myron: "Blues for Bessie," 2:3
Olson, Charles: poem, 5:9

Paccassi, Virginia: graphic, 3:35
Patmore, Derek: Andrea Cambas translation, 6
Picasso, Pablo: Two graphics, 2:9
Pierce, Waldo: Poem, 3:24

Pikionis: "Modern Buildings Inspired by Island Architecture," 6
Plazzeschi, Aldo: Poem (tr. Giovanelli), 4:10
Poe, James: graphic, 5:plate 5
Ponge, Francis: "Bapteme Funebre," 2:3

Quasimodo, Salvatore: Poem (tr. C & C), 4:10

Ragghianti, Carlo: "Contemporary Italian Painting," 4:28
Ray, Man: graphic, 5:9
Rexroth, Kenneth: "Iphegenia At Aulis," (Play), 3:5
Richter, Hans: graphic, 3:16
Rimbaud, Arthur: Poem (tr. Selden Rodman), 1:10
Ritsos, Yannis: Poem (tr. Octave Merlier), 6
Rodman, Selden: Louis Aragon translation, 1:10
Rodman, Selden: Arthur Rimbaud translation, 1:10
Rodman, Selden: Victor Hugo translation, 1:10
Rodman, Selden: Poetry Review, 2:21
Rodman, Selden: Poetry Review, 3:29
Rodman, Selden: Poem, 5:6
Rosenberg, Sam: graphic, 1:9
Rosenberg, Sam: photo of Max Ernst, 1:21
Rosenberg, Sam: graphic, 3:13
Rosenberger, Francis Coleman: Poem, 1:20
Roy, Claude: Text to *Le Retour*, 1:6
Roy, Yvonne: Two Poems, 3:12

Saarinen, Lilian Swann: graphic, 1:23
Saba, Umberto: Three Poems (tr. Maurice English), 4:17
Sartre, Jean-Paul: "The End of the War," 2:20
Sartre, Jean-Paul: "Boy into Man" (tr. Constance Coolidge), 3:2
Savelli: graphic, 4:19
Schenkel, William: Weldon Kees translation, 2:12
Scipione: graphic, 5:plate 6
Scipione: graphic, 4:5
Sekaer, Peter: "Butter-Bread," 1:16
Sekaer, Peter: graphic, 1:8
Shapiro, Karl: Three Poems, 1:7
Sidoine, Mireille: "Diary of a Little Girl," 2:13
Sikelianos, Angelo: Poem (tr. Elsa Barker & Eva Sikelianos), 6
Sidelianos, Eva: Angelo Sikelianos translation, 6
Sinnisgali, Leonardo: Poem (tr. Giovanelli), 4:10
Snyder, Lt. Jerome: graphic, 2:16
Solmi, Sergio: Poem, 4:10
Spender, Stephen: Three Poems, 3:3

Tal-Coat: graphic, 3:foreleaf
Tanning, Dorothea: graphic, 3:21
Tarsouli, Athina: "Island Sketches," 6 (graphics)
Tetsis: graphic, 6
Theophilos: "Primitive Mural Painting," 6:plate 2
Theotokas, George: "Modern Greece," 6
Tolstoy, Leo: "The Law of Love and the Law of Violence," 5:10
Tombros, Michel: graphic, 6:plate 6
Tonny, Kristians: graphic, 2:3
Tsarouchis, John: Two graphics, 6:plate 4
Tudal: "D.C.A.," 2:14

Ungaretti, Giuseppe: graphic, 4:13

Valentino, Ernesto: graphic, 4:26
Veronesi: graphic, 4:16
Vitorini, Elio: "A Name and Her Tears," 4:4
Vrettakos, N.: Poem (tr. Octave Merlier), 6

Weidman, Jerome: "Sam," 1:22

Xydis, Alexander: "Some Apsects of Greek Painting & Sculpture Today," 6

Zevi, Bruno: "Note on Italian Building," 4:20

Voyages Index

Voyages had a complicated numbering system which I've tried to make less confusing by annotating as follows:

Vol. I, No. 1 (Fall 1967): No. 1
Vol. II, No. I & II (Winter/Spring 1968): No. 2/3
Vol. II, No. III (Fall 1968): No. 4
Vol. II, No. IV (Spring 1969): No. 5
Vol. III, No. I & II (Winter 1970): No. 6/7
Vol. II, No. III & IV (Spring 1970): No. 8/9
Vol. IV, No. I & II (Winter 1971): No. 10/11
Vol. IV, No. III & IV (Spring 71/Spring 72): No. 12/13
Vol. V (Winter 1973): No. 14/15

Voyages Staff

Associate Editor: Frances Priscilla Smyth
   (Linda Pastan no. 12/13 and 14/15)
   (James Den Boer no. 8/9 & 10/11)

West Coast Editor: James Den Boer

Advisory Board: Mark Van Doren, Carl Bode, Katherine Garrison Chapin, Roger Hecht, Tram Combs, John Pauker, Anais Nin, Francis Murphy, & James Wright.

Staff: F. Randal Blunk, Laurel Delp, Barboura Flues, William Holland, Costance Holden, Christopher Ivusic, Linda Pastan, Robert Smith, Joseph Goodman, Leo Byrnes, Jack Neal, Elizabeth Farley, (& Eva Weininger-London).

Adamo, Ralph: Poem, 6/7:134
Adkins, John: Cover photo, 8/9
Adler, Mortimer: "On Mark Van Doren," 14/15:45
Aldan, Daisy: Poem, 4:94
Alexander, Floyce: Two Poems, 5:85
Andrews, Marcie E.: Two Poems, 10/11:43
Antonucci, Emil: "A Note on Working with Robert Lax," 2/3:100

Bachardy: Anais Nin portrait, 4:4
Banks, Carolyn: "Idyll," 4:46
Bann, Stephen: "Concrete Poetry and the Recent Work of Robert Lax," 2/3:80
Barthelme, Donald: "Cannon," 14/15:62
Barzun, Jacques: "On Hiram Haydn," 6/7:47
Basler, Roy P.: "Yankee Vergil—Robert Frost in Washington," 5:8
Basler, Roy P.: "Reed Whittemore in Office," 8/9:51
Basler, Roy P.: Poem, 12/13:125
Bauer, Jerry: Marianne Moore photo, 10/11:45
Belitt, Ben: Statement and Two Poems, 1:10
Belitt, Ben: "Neruda At Sonnets," 1:16
Belitt, Ben: Pablo Neruda translations, 1:21
Bell, Marvin: "Logan's Teaching," 12/13:38
Bennett, Trew: Book Review, 14/15:172
Berry, Wendell: Logan Appreciation, 12/13:40
Berryman, John: "On Van Doren," 14/15:17
Biddle, Michael: Six Etchings, 14/15:74
Bidwell, Helen: Mark Van Doren photo, 14/15:23
Bidwell, Helen: Review, 14/15:172
Bidwell, Helen: Photo, 14/15:23
Bidwell, Helen: "Recurring and Persistent Images: *The*

Fourth Diary of Anais Nin," 14/15:151 (Review)
Bly, Robert: "John Logan's Field of Force," 12/13:29
Bly, Robert: Poem, 12/13:37
Boer, James Den: "On Paul Zimmer," 8/9:51
Bonazzi, Robert: Two Poems, 5:86
Borges, Jorge Luis: Poem (tr. Robert Newcomb), 8/9:68
Bose, M.J.: "The Wedding Dance," 12/13:136
Brand, Millen: "A Poet To Read: On H.R. Hays," 5:40
Brooks, Gladys: "Persuasion," 6/7:54
Brown, Gary: Peter Whigham portrait, 4:40
Brubeck, Dave: Score to Van Doren's "How Praise A World," 14/15:59
Brustein, Robert: "On Hiram Haydn's *The Counter-Renaissance*," 6/7:29

Camp, R.A.: Two photos, 14/15:68 & 162
Candelaria, Frederick: Poem, 12/13:59
Capbell, Alex: On Haydn, 6/7:50
Carlson, Lee: drawing of David Galler, 8/9:82
Cedering, Siv: Poem, 5:87
Cedering, Siv: Photo, 5:87
Chapell, Fred: "Hiram Haydn's Other World," 6/7:9
Char, Rene: Three Poems (tr. Lane Dunlop), 10/11:64
Chute, Robert: graphic, 5:92
Claire, William F.: "Two Items of Unusual Interest," (Review) 2/3:107
Claire, William F.: "Reviews Briefly Noted," 6/7:140
Claire, William F.: "On Certain Books," 10/11:70
Cohen, Marvin: Poem, 5:back cover
Cooper, Jane: Four Poems, 4:81
Covel, Thomas: "Firethorn," 4:96
Cunnigham, Imogen: Five photos, 4:54

114

Dalia Lama IV: Four Poems (tr. Peter Whigham), 4:42
Darr, Ann: Poem, 4:92
de Angulo, Jamie: Logan appreciation, 12/13:50
de Grazia, Edward: "Myrtilus" (A Play in One Act), 1:73
de Longchamps, Joanne: Poem, 6/7:120
Deutsch, Babette: "A Note on Ben Belitt," 1:13
Deutsch, Babette: Poem, 12/13:88
Dunlap, Mary C.: "Three Strangers Each To Each" (Reviews) 10/11:72
Dunlap, Mary C.: Book Review, 12/13:157
Dunlop, Lane: Rene Char translations, 10/11:64
Dunlop, Lane: Francis Ponge translation, 12/13:127
Dunn, Mary Anna: Book Review, 14/15:170

Edgcomb, John H.: "A Pensee for Reed Whittemore," 8/9:43
Eisenstein, Samuel: "Letters to a Nun," 4:49
Elledge, Scott: "Whittemore as Editor," 8/9:55
Erhardy, Josef: Six sculptures, 5:49

Farr, David: Four photos, 10/11:47, 50, 51, & 54
Farrell, James T.: excerpt from *The Vast Present*, 5:46
Fehl, Philipp: graphics, 10/11:39, 63 &67
Fehl, Philipp: graphics, 12/13:64, 65, 85, 89 & 163
Fehl, Philipp: graphic, 14/15:109
Feirstein, Frederick: Poem, 8/9:94
Fern, Alan: Photo, 5:94
Field, Frances: "Farewells," 4:35
Fixmer, Clyde: Poem, 10/11:74
Flythe, Starkey Jr.: "The First Kind of Fool," 14/15:82
Fort, Keith: "Hope," 12/13:54
Frame, Donald M.: On Haydn, 6/7:43

Galler, David: Six Poems & Statement, 8/9:83
Galvin, Martin: Poem, 8/9:104
Gardner, Isabelle: "The Man At Furioso," 8/9:42
Gardner, Isabella: "A Note on John Logan," 12/13:50
Gardner, Richard: "On William Packard: A Teacher of Poetry," 5:80
Gerber, William: "Some Recent Notable Books & Records," 1:100
Gerber, William: "Some Recent Notable Books," 2/3:101
Gildner, Gary: Poem, 8/9:80
Gillman, Richard: Poem, 4:100
Gillman, Richard: Book Review, 12/13:158
Ginsberg, Allen: "Van Doren Guru," 14/15:42
Gold, Edward: Book Review, 12/13:154
Goodman, Joseph: "The Short Stories of William Humphrey," 6/7:135
Gordon, Ambrose Jr.: "A Note on the Lyric Whittemore," 8/9:60
Gordon, Caroline: "Twiggy, or the Well-Connected Shoots," (w/Cary T. Peebles), 4:60
Gould, Lawrence M.: "Whittemore! Teacher!" 8/9:54
Grant, Paul: "New Recordings," 1:102
Grant, Paul: "New Recordings," 2/3:103
Grant, Paul: "New Recordings," 4:109
Grant, Paul: "New Recordings," 5:107
Grant, Paul: "New Recordings," 6/7:142
Gregor, Arthur: "On the Poems of Jane Cooper," 4:80
Griffin, John Howard: Merton photo, 5:109
Griffin, John Howard: Van Doren photos, 14/15:47

Hallett, Charles A.: "Aaron Burr" (A Play), 12/13:99
Harms, Valerie: Anais Nin photo, 14/15:155
Harrison, Gilbert A.: "The Man on the New Republic," 8/9:46
Haydn, Hiram: excerpt from *Amos Bailey*, 6/7:31
Haydn, Hiram: "2998: A Shaggy Tale of the Future," 6/7:9
Hays, H.R.: Four Poems, 5:24
Hays, H.R.: Cesar Vallejo translation, 5:28
Hays, H.R.: "Keep Off The Grass (A divertissment for the Poetic Theatre)," 5:29
Hays, H.R.: "An American Voice (The Continuing Presence of W.C. Williams)," 5:34
Hazo, Samuel: Poem, 6/7:129

Hebert, Anne: Poem (tr. Al Poulin, Jr.), 14/15:110
Hecht, Roger: Six Poems, 1:66
Hecht, Roger: "Primary Matters," 5:105
Hecht, Roger: "Three Poets," 6/7:139
Hecht, Roger: Poem, 8/9:113
Hecht, Roger: Poem, 10/11:75
Hecht, Roger: Book Review, 12/13:152
Hecht, Roger: Poem, 14/15:81
Heffernan, Michael: Poem, 5:88
Herzbrun, Philip: Poem, 2/3:106
Herzbrun, Philip: "Howl in Envy," 8/9:39
Hoffman, Daniel: Four Poems, 6/7:107
Hoffman, Daniel: Gabriel Zaid translations, 12/13:66
Holland, Bill: Carolyn Kizer Interview, 1:43
Holland, Bill: "Three First Volumes," 5:100
Holland, Bill: Photo, 8/9:70
Holland, Bill: "On William Matthews," 8/9:110

Ivusic, Christopher: Mihajlo Mihajlov translation (tr. w/Marija Ivusic), 4:101
Ivusic, Marija: Mihajlo Mihajlov translation (tr. w/Christopher Ivusic), 4:101

Jackson, Bruce: John Logan photo, 12/13:39
Jacobsen, Josephine: "On Mark Van Doren," 14/15:15
Jellema, Roderick: "The Poetry of Linda Pastan," 5:73
Johnson, Curt: Poem, 14/15:71
Johnson, Jean: Book Review, 8/9:112
Johnson, W.R.: Reed Whittemore photo, 8/9:43

Kaufman, Shirley: Poem, 12/13:68
Keene, Donald: "Mark Van Doren," 14/15:18
Kernan, Margo S.: Photo, 6/7:72
Kizer, Carolyn: Interview (int. by Bill Holland), 1:43
Kostelanetz, Richard: Two Poems, 6/7:104
Kostelanetz, Richard: "Excelsior—A Narrative Fiction," 12/13:131
Kostelanetz, Richard: "A Census of Young North American Writers," 14/15:130
Kroll, Ernest: Two Poems, 6/7:130
Kroll, Ernest: "A Note on Victor Llona," 10/11:27
Kroll, Ernest: Letter from Mark Van Doren, 14/15:51

Lally, Michael: Poem, 14/15:73
Langbaum, Robert: On Haydn, 6/7:45
Lax, Robert: from *The Slumbering City*, 2/3:7
Lax, Robert: The Journals of Robert Lax (Vol. I), 2/3:19
Lax, Robert: "A Catch of Anti-Letters" (w/Thomas Merton), 2/3:44
Lax, Robert: "Novel," 2/3:57
Lax, Robert: Nine photos, 2/3:65
Lax, Robert: Seven Poems, 2/3:73
Lax, Robert: from *Journal III*, 2/3:82
Lax, Robert: from the *Journals IV*, 2/3:95
Lax, Robert: Photo, 5:88
Lax, Robert: Poem, 14/15:48
Leffler, Merrill: "Whittemore? Teacher?" 8/9:52
Levertov, Denise: "On Robert Lax's *Circus of the Sun*," 2/3:93
Levine, Al: Poem, 12/13:84
Linney, Romulus: On Haydn, 6/7:42
Lipp, Delmar: Cover Photo, 4
Llona, Victor: "Days and Nights in Paris with Scott Fitzgerald," 10/11:29
Logan, John: Three Poems on Aaron Siskind's work, 12/13:10
Logan, John: "On Poets & Poetry Today," 12/13:17
Logan, John: Poem, 12/13:25
Logan, John: "On John Fuller's *The Tree That Walked*," 5:95
Lucas, John (Jax): "Whittemore on Track, Whittemore Airborne," 8/9:63

MacLeish, Archibald: "On Van Doren's 'O World,'" 14/15:12
Maddox, Jerald: Five Photos, 6/7:63

Marbrook, Djelloul: "Pereira, My Aunt," 14/15:115
Margolin, Victor: graphic, 14/15:92
Marks, Elaine: Book Review, 14/15:163
Marshall, Paule: "He Encourages Us To Excellence," 6/7:40
McCarthy, Eugene J.: "A Special Kind of Friend," 8/9:47
McEvilly, Wayne: "A Jewel For October," 6/7:122
McEvilly, Wayne: "The Argument of the Book (Subject to Modification on Every Page)" from the Notebooks, 12/13: 12/13:90
McEvilly, Wayne: Book Review, 12/13:156
McKee, John: Cover Photo, "Sail Rock, Quoddy Head (Lubec)," 5
Merton, Thomas: Eight drawings and a brief note, 1:53
Merton, Thomas: "A Catch of Anti-Letters" (w/Robert Lax), 2/3:44
Metzger, Deena: "What Rough Beast," 4:86
Miles, Josephine: Five Poems and a Statement, 4:15
Mills, Ralph J. Jr.: "A Strenuous Sweetness," 1:14
Mooney, Stephen: "Josephine Miles: Successive Views," 4:21
Morgan, Frederick: Poem, 14/15:80
Morris, E.J.: Book Review, 6/7:139
Mundy, Jeffrey: graphic, 14/15:129

Nemerov, Howard: "On Ben Belitt," 1:29
Neruda, Pablo: Eight Sonnetts (tr. Ben Belitt), 1:13
Newcomb, Robert: Jorge Luis Borges translation, 8/9:69
Nin, Anais: "Genesis of the Diary," 4:5
Nin, Anais: "On Hiram Haydn's *Report from the Red Windmill*," 6/7:29
Nin, Anais: "The Wayfarer's Chapel," 14/15:155

Oates, Joyce Carol: "How Another Child Came To Be Born," 12/13:72
Ober, William B.: "A Few Kind Words About Reed Whittemore," 8/9:34
Oberg, Arthur K.: "On Josephine Miles' *Kinds of Affection*," 4:27
Oliver, James: Edmund Sullivan photo, 14/15:94
O'Neill, James: Poem, 6/7:130

Packard, William: Poem, 2/3:98
Packard, William: "On The Teaching of Poetry," 5:76
Packard, William: Poem, 14/15:106
Palmer, Doug: Poem, 2/3:102
Pastan, Ira: Photo, 5:68
Pastan, Linda: "On Marge Piercy's *Breaking Camp*," 4:107
Pastan, Linda: Four Poems & Statement, 5:68
Pastan, Linda: "Three Poets," 8/9:107
Pastan, S.: Photo, 6/7:33
Pauker, John: "Budapest '48," 1:32
Pauker, John: "My Life With Reed Whittemore," 8/9:64
Pauker, John: Poem, 8/9:67
Pauker, Pam: Photo, 8/9:33 & 66
Peebles, Cary T.: "Twiggy, or the Well-Connected Shoots" (w/Caroline Gordon), 4:60
Pereira, Irene Rice: Six Paintings, 14/15::114, 117/118, 123/124 & 126
Pereira, Irene Rice: from the Notebooks, 14/15:125
Pettinella, D.M.: Leonardo Sinisgalli translation, 8/9:81
Pfingston, Roger: Photo, 12/13:60
Phillips, Robert: Katherine Anne Porter photo, 10/11:44
Planz, Allen: "On *The Selected Poems of H.R. Hays*," 5:43
Ponge, Francis: "Introduction to the Pebble" (tr. Lane Dunlop), 12/13:127
Porter, Eliot: cover photo (from *Artic Terns*), 1
Poulin, Al Jr.: Anne Hebert translation, 14/15:110
Purves, Alan C.: "Life, Death, and The Humanities," 8/9:81

Raab, Lawrence: Poem, 14/15:90
Rabassa, Gregory: Dalton Trevisan translation, 14/15:102
Ramsay, Jerold: Poem, 14/15:108
Rees, Gomer: "So Logan," 12/13:48
Rice, Edward: Cover photo, 2/3

Ritchie, Elisavietta: "Josephine Miles, Teacher," 4:25
Ritchie, Elisavietta: "Three New Poetry Books from Kayak Press," 5:104
Ritchie, Elisavietta: William Jay Smith Interview, 6/7:89
Robbins, Martin: Book Review, 12/13:161
Robbins, Martin: "James Schevill: Poet with Music, and Playwright with a Message," 6/7:85
Robinson, Judith: Review, 10/11:71
Robins, Natalie S.: Poem, 4:93
Roethke, Theodore: selections from *The Notebooks* arranged by David Wagoner, 12/13:61
Roseborough, John: Four photos, 4:31
Roseliep, Raymond: Two Poems, 10/11:44
Roth, Henry,H.: "Man, Look At Them Bases," 5:56
Roth, Henry H.: "President Richard Nixon Has Destroyed South Nyack," 10/11:56
Roth, Sylvia: graphic, 12/13:71
Roth, William M.: "Mr. Whittemore Goes to Washington," 8/9:49
Rubin, Larry: Poem, 6/7:59

St. John, Primus: William Stafford Interview, 8/9:70
Schell, Susan: Poem, 4:39
Schevill, James: "The Investigation of Black and White" (A Play), 6/7:73
Schevill, James: "Note on Performing Poems," 6/7:80
Schevill, James: "The Animals of Love Wander Under the Birds of Song," 6/7:82
Schevill, James: "The Possibilities and Impossibilities of Snow," 6/7:83
Schiff, Bennett: "An Affection for James Kennaway," 14/15:158
Schuchat, Simon: Poem, 12/13:59
Seitz, Ron: Poem, 14/15:70
Shulman, Julius: Three photos, 14/15:156
Shefner, Evelyn: "Sea-Changes: Their Variety," 6/7:80
Siegel, Lois: Photo, 14/15:111
Sinisgalli, Leonardo: Poem (tr. D.M. Pettinella), 8/9:70
Siskind, Aaron: Cover photo, 12/13
Siskind, Aaron: Five photos, 12/13:11, 12, 14, 48, & 126
Sklarew, Myra: Poem, 12/13:59
Smith, William Jay: Interview (int. by Elisavietta Ritchie), 6/7:89
Snodgrass, Richard: Poem, 5:89
Stafford, William: Interview (int. by Primus St. John), 8/9:70
Stanford, Ann: Poem, 14/15:72
Steiner, Sattva: graphic, 4:39
Steiner, Sattva: graphic, 5:84
Steingesser, Martin: Photo, 5:91
Steingesser, Martin: Four photos, 6/7:64
Steloff, Frances: "Toward the Radiant Powers: A Note on Irene Rice Pereira," 14/15:113
Stern, Daniel: On Haydn, 6/7:49
Stern, Daniel: "The Death of the Novel," 10/11:40
Stock, Robert: "And A Merry Crabbed Age" (Review) 5:98
Stock, Robert: "The Poetry of David Galler," 8/9:89
Stock, Robert: "Tinder That Seldom Catches" (Review) 14/15:166
Sugar, James: Haydn photo, 6/7:7
Sullivan, Edmund: Seven Etchings & Statement, 14/15:93
Sullivan, Michael D.: Photo, 4:85
Sund, Robert: John Logan photo, 12/13:40
Swann, Brian: Poem, 14/15:69
Sylvester, William: "Daniel Hoffman's Poetry of Affection," 6/7:110

Tagliabue, John: "from *The Journals*—December 1972—," 14/15:back cover
Tagliabue, John: Poem, 4:106
Tagliabue, John: Poem, 6/7:121
Tagliabue, John: "Selections from an Androscoggin Notebook," 10/11:65
Tague, William H.: William Jay Smith photo, 6/7:94

Taliaferro, Raphael: Poem, 5:93
Tate, Allen: "Mark Was My Friend: 1924-1972," 14/15:23
Tate, Allen: "Very Much At Ease In Formal Attire" (Review of Mark Van Doren's *Collected & New Poems*), 14/15:24
Teller, Walter: On Hiram Haydn, 6/7:47
Thompson, Phyllis: Poem, 10/11:68
Touster, Irwin: "01287107," 8/9:39
Trevisan, Dalton: "Where Are the Christmas Days of Yesteryear?" (tr. Gregory Rabassa), 14/15:102

Uelsman, Jerry N.: Cover photo, 6/7
Unterecker, John: Two Poems, 5:61
Unterecker, John: Cover photo, 10/11
Unterecker, John: Four Poems, 10/11:9
Unterecker, John: "Collioure," 10/11:8
Unterecker, John: Six Photos, 10/11:11, 14, 18, 21, 22, & 24
Unterecker, John: "A Note on Landscape," 10/11:17
Unterecker, John: "Note on the Poems," 10/11:22
Urbain, John A.: Poem, 14/15:67

Vallejo, Cesar: Poem (tr. H.R. Hays), 5:28
Van Doren, Dorothy: Photo, 2/3:18
Van Doren, Mark: "A Note (and Poem) on Thomas Merton," 1:61
Van Doren, Mark: "On Robert Lax," 2/3:62
Van Doren, Mark: Nine Poems, 14/15:11, 13/14, 21/22, 43/44, 57, & 60
Van Doren, Mark: A Letter to Ernest Kroll, 14/15:53
Van Doren, Mark: "The Housanic I Know," 14/15:53
Van Doren, Mark: Letter to Dave Brubeck, 14/15:58
Vanderlyn, John: Burr Portrait, 12/13:98

Victor, Thomas: William Packard photo, 5:76
Victor, Thomas: John Logan photos, 12/13:9, 17, & 50
Victor, Thomas: Mark Van Doren photos, 14/15:10, 16, 42, 56, & 61
Wagoner, David: "Heart You Have No House" (Arrangement of selections from Theodore Roethke's Notebooks), 12/13 12/13:61
Wang, Arthur: Mark Van Doren photo, 6/7:60
Weinheimer, George: graphics, 10/11:7, 13, 20, & 26
Weismiller, Edward: "Serpent's Progress: The Writing of a Novel," 14/15:138
Wideman, John: "Go To Hear Him," 6/7:35
Willard, Derek: "Hiram Haydn As A Teacher," 6/7:52
Willard, Nancy: "The Creatures and Prophets of Herold Witherspoon," 10/11:46
Williams, Joan: On Hiram Haydn, 6/7:44
Witherspoon, Herold: Four Sculptures, 10/11:46, 50, 51, & 54
Whigham, Peter: Delai Lama VI translation and Statement, 4:42
Whittemore, Reed: 14 Poems and Statement, 8/9:12
Whittemore, Reed: "Aliens & Heretics (On the Near Future of Little Magazines)," 8/9:26
Wright, James: "On Roger Hecht," 1:72

Young, Marguerite: "On Anais Nin," 1:63
Young, Marguerite: "Mark Van Doren: A Poet in an Age of Defoliation," 6/7:60

Zaid, Gabriel: Two Poems (tr. Daniel Hoffman), 12/13:66
Zinnes, Harriet: Poem, 4:104
Zinnes, Harriet: "Icons Old and New: Geneva Days," 6/7:131

Dryad Index

Dryad Staff
Michelle Leffler
Joan McCrory
Marianne Stark
Sandra Slayton
Toni Noto

Dryad

No. 1 Winter 1968
No. 2 Spring 1968
No. 3 Summer/Fall 1968
No. 4 Winter/Spring 1969
No. 5/6 1969
No. 7/8 1971
No. 9/10 1972 (printed in U.K.)
No. 11 1974
No. 12 1975
No. 13 1975
No. 14/15 1977
No. 16/17 1976
No. 18/19 1978

Alexander, Charles: Poem, 7/8:34
Andreevski, Petre M.: (tr. by Rod Jellema & Graham W. Reid), 14/15:85
Aplon, Roger: Poem, 12
Aplon, Roger: Three Poems, 14/15:101
Appleman, Philip: Two Poems, 2:2
Astor, Susan: Two Poems, 18/19:30 & 43
Atkinson, Ronald Hugh: Poem, 1:32

Banks, Heather: Poem, 14/15:77
Barnes, Jim: Poem, 16/17:11

Barnett, Gail: "Three Kayak Poets," (Review) 5/6:62
Barnett, Gail: "Longjaunes, Voyager," (Review) 7/8:28
Barrows, Anita: Poem, 7/8:30
Beard, Ralph E.: Two Poems, 7/8:20
Beernink, K. Dale: Poem, 3:12
Benttinen, Ted: 16/17:12
Berlind, Bruce: 16/17:13
Berryhill, Michael: Poem, 16/17:15
Blomfield, Adelaide: Poem, 18/19:20
Bode, Carl: Poem, 2:8
Bode, Carl: Poem, 3:6
Bode, Carl: "The Poetry of Silence," 3:7
Bowden, J.H.: Two Poems, 18/19:15 & 38
Bowie, Robert: Poem, 14/15:60
Boyles, Denis: Poem, 14/15:90
Brookes, Robert A.: Euripides translation (w/Henry Taylor), 14/15:105
Brown, Milly: Poem, 7/8:50
Browne, Michael Dennis: Poem, 16/17:16
Bunting, Karen: Poem, 7/8:15
Burr, Gary: Two Poems, 18/19:11 & 54
Busch, Wilhelm: (tr. by Herbert Schaumann), Poem, 1:14
Byron, Stuart: Two Poems, 18/19:25 & 46

Capshaw, Fred: Poem, 14/15:76
Carlson, Robert: Five Drawings, 14/15:25, 28, 79, 109 & 129
Cedering, Siv: Two Poems, 4:20
Cedering, Siv: Cover photo, 5/6

Cedering, Siv: Two Poems, 7/8:35
Cedering, Siv: Cover photo, 9/10
Cedering, Siv: Twelve Poems, 9/10:4-21, & 24
Cedering, Siv: Four photos, 9/10:1, 2, &74 a&b
Chigounis, Evans: Poem, 16/17:17
Christhilf, Mark: Two Poems, 14/15:108
Claire, William F.: Two Poems, 5/6: 10
Claire, William F.: "A Note on Delmore Schwartz," 5/6:9
Claire, William F.: Poem, 16/17:18
Clarke, Terence: Poem, 14/15:38
Clary, Patrick L.: Two Poems, 14/15:112
Cohen, Alan: Cover photo, 14/15
Cole, Barry: Two Poems, 2:12
Cole, Susan: Photo, 14/15:6
Coleman, Catherine: Poem, 16/17:19
Corrigan, M.T.: Poem, 14/15:42

Dacey, Philip: Poem, 18/19:36
Darr, Ann: Two Poems, 4:16
Darr, Ann: Poem, 5/6:55
Darr, Ann: Poem, 7/8:30
Darr, Ann: Two Poems, 9/10:56
Darr, Ann: Poem, 14/15:50
Davey: Poem, 9/10:23
Davie, Donald: Poem, 16/17:20
Davison, Peter: Poem, 16/17:21
Derleth, August: Poem, 2:24
Deutsch, R.H.: Poem, 16/17:23
Dischell, Stuart: Poem, 16/17:24
Doxey, W.S.: Poem, 7/8:51
Drum, Maria: Poem, 9/10:23
Duffy, Maureen: Poem, 16/17:25
Dwyer, Frank: Poem, 12
Dwyer, Frank: Poem, 14/15:62

Edgcomb, Gabrielle: Poem, 14/15:135
Edmond, Peter Van: Poem, 5/6:4
Elgin, Larry: Poem, 5/6:54
Erlanger, Linda: Poem, 5/6:12
Euripides: (tr. by Henry Taylor & Robert A. Brookes), 14/15:105

Feick, M. Mather: Poem, 4:43
Fisher, Roy: Poem, 16/17:27
Fishman, Charles: Poem, 18/19:49
Flaherty, Doug: Poem, 16/17:28
Flint, Roland: Poem, 12
Flint, Roland: Nine Poems, 14/15:7-20
Flint, Roland: Poem, 18/19:26
Forrey, Robert: Poem, 16/17:29
Forsythe, Richard: "Sense and Sentences: On Getting a Computer to Write Poems," 7/8:16
Foster, Susan: Poem, 9/10:22
Foster, Susan: Cover design, 18/19
Fowler, Gene: "Letter," 5/6:24
Fowler, Gene: Two Poems, 5/6:26
Fowler, Hilary: Poem, 5/6:52
Fox, Gail Seely: Poem, 5/6:52
Fox, Janet: Poem, 5/6:38
Fox, Larry: Two Poems, 14/15:138
Fox, Lora: Poem, 9/10:23
Frank, Barbara: Two Drawings, 14/15:2 & 34
Fries, Susan: Poem, 2:26
Fries, Susan: Poem, 3:35
Frisch, Catherine: Cover art, 1

Galvin, Martin: Poem, 2:9
Galvin, Martin: Two Poems, 7/8:48
Garcia, Luis: Poem, 12
Garzotto, Leonard R.: Poem, 1:18
Gatenby, Greg: Four Poems, 18/19:28, 32, 48, & 56
George, Emery: Two Poems, 18/19:19 & 47
Gibson, Margaret: Two Poems, 14/15:96

Girouard, Robert: Poem, 3:32
Girouard, Robert: Three Poems, 4:40
Girouard, Robert: Poem, 5/6:19
Gold, Edward: Poem, 5/6:14
Gold, Edward: Poem, 14/15:130
Gold, Edward: Bogomil Gjunzel translation, poem 14/15:86
Gold, Edward: Blaze Koneski translation (w/Graham W. Reid), Poem, 14/15:88
Goldblatt, Kenn: Cover photo, 13
Goranson, Eric: Three Poems, 14/15:136
Gordon, L. Suzanne: Poem, 2:10
Gordon, L. Suzanne: Two Poems, 5/6:60

Hall, Ted: Poem, 18/19:24
Hand, John Thomas: Poem, 2:27
Harmon, William: Poem, 16/17:30
Harris, Marguerite: Guest Editor, 16/17: *A Tumult for John Berryman*
Harris, Marguerite: Poem, 16/17:33
Haseloff, Charles: Poem, 16/17:33
Haynes, Bas: Three Poems, 4:18
Heath, Hunter: Poem, 1:40
Hecht, Roger: Seven Poems, 14/15:119
Hecht, Roger: Poem, 16/17:37
Heffernan, Michael: "Programs for Survival," (Review), 7/8:38
Heffernan, Michael: "Hounds of Intuition," (Review) 9/10:68
Heffernan, Michael: Poem, 12
Heffernan, Michael: "Promissory Notes: The Poems of Morton Marcus," 13:40
Heffernan, Michael: Poem, 16/17:38
Heffernan, Michael: Two Poems, 18/19:18 & 57
Heller, Anita: Poem, 16/17:39
Henderson, Archibald: Poem, 18/19:31
Holland, Barbara A.: Poem, 16/17:42
Holland, Bill: Two Poems, 2:15
Holland, Bill: Poem, 3:30
Holland, Bill: Two Poems, 5/6:42
Holton, Milne: "Contemporary Macedonian Poems," 14/15:84
Holton, Milne: Blaze Koneski translation (w/Vasa D. Mihailovich) 14/15:89
Howden, Michael: Poem, 1:38
Hulbert, John R.: Two Poems, 3:36
Hummer, T.R.: Three Poems, 18/19:33

Ignatow, David: Poem, 16/17:43

Janevski, Slavko: (tr. Milne Holton & Vasa D. Mihailovich) 14/15:89
Jason, Philip K.: Four Poems, 14/15:72
Jason, Philip K.: "Miracles In The Plains Style: Roland Flint's *And Morning*," 14/15:21
Jason, Philip K.: Guest Editor 18/19, *Shaping: New Poems In Traditional Prosodies*
Jauss, David: Poem, 18/19:17
Jellema, Rod: Three Poems, 1:11
Jellema, Rod: Two Poems, 4:10
Jellema, Rod: Two Poems, 5/6:20
Jellema, Rod: Two Poems, 9/10:60
Jellema, Rod: Issue 11, *Something Tugging the Line* (book)
Jellema, Rod: Petre Andreevski translation (w/Graham W. Reid), 14/15:85
Johnson, Dennis: Poem, 16/17:44
Johnson, Kathleen Jeffrie: Poem, 18/19:27
Jones, Margaret A.: Three Poems, 1:22
Jones, Margaret A.: Poem, 3:34

Kamenetz; Rodger: Poem, 18/19:21
Keithley, Goerge: Poem, 18/19:53
Keller, David: Poem, 16/17:46
Koneski, Blaze: (tr. by Edward Gold & Graham W. Reid), 14/15: 85
Kooser, Ted: Poem, 16/17:47

Kostelanetz, Richard: Poem, 14/15:33
Kozik, Peter L.: Poem, 16/17:48
Kroll, Ernest: Poem, 16/17:49
Lane, Rosemary: Three Graphics, 7/8:44
Langton, Daniel: Poem, 5/6:58
Lattimore, Richmond: Poem, 16/17:50
Lawson, Robert: Poem, 12
Lax, Robert: Three Poems, 4:2
Lax, Robert: Poem, 5/6:34
Lax, Robert: Four photos, 5/6:36
Lax, Robert: Poem, 9/10:34
Leary, Paris: Poem, 16/17:51
Lefcowitz, Barbara F.: Poem, 16/17:52
Lefcowitz, Barbara F.: Poem, 18/19:41
Leffler, Merrill: "Since You're So Depressed," (Review), 4:44
Leffler, Merrill: Poem, 5/6:50
Leffler, Merrill: Found Poem (w/Neil Lehrman) 5/6:67
Leffler, Merrill: "Avoid the Bad Poets," (Review), 7/8:59
Leffler, Merrill: "O Children, Think About The Good Times," (Review) 7/8:52
Leffler, Merrill: Poem, 9/10:44
Leffler, Merrill: "Poles Apart," (Review) 9/10:62
Leffler, Merrill: "A Small Cellar of Poets," (Review) 9/10:66
Leffler, Merrill: Poem, 12
Leffler, Merrill: "The Poetry of Sensuous Middle Age," (Review), 14/15:125
Leffler, Merrill: Poem, 16/17:53
Lehrman, Neil: Found Poem (w/Merrill Leffler) 5/6:67
Lehrman, Neil: "Pictures of a Reading," 7/8:43
Lehrman, Neil: Interview with Morton Marcus, 13:34
Levexier, Carlos: Photo, 7/8:9
Litewka, Jack: Poem, 16/17:57
Logan, John: Two Poems, 12
Logan, John: review of *In the Sleep of Rivers* by Joseph Stroud, 14/15:43
Logan, John Jr.: Two John Logan Poems Set to music on 45 record, 12
Loonie, Janice Hays: Poem, 5/6:22
Loonie, Janice Hays: Poem, 7/8:22
Lopes, Michael: Poem, 16/17:58
Lott, Clarinda Harriss: Poem, 12
Lott, Clarinda Harriss: Two Poems, 14/15:35
Loucheim, Katie: Poem, 14/15:49
Lowe, Loland: Two Photos, 7/8:23
Lowell, Robert: Poem, 16/17:59
Luba, Danny: Poem, 9/10:22
Lucas, John: Two Poems, 1:26
Lucas, John: "A Dialogue Concerning Poets," 2:28
Lucas, John: Two Poems, 7/8:47
Lynch, Michael: Poem, 16/17:61

Malanga, Gerard: Two Poems, 14/15:29
Maley, Saundra: Poem, 12
Marcus, Adrianne: Three Poems, 3:8
Marcus, Mordecai: Two Poems, 18/19:29 & 51
Marcus, Morton: Poem, 12
Marcus, Morton: Twenty Poems, 13
Marcus, Morton: Interview (int. by Neil Lehrman), 13:34
Marx, Arthur: Poem, 16/17:63
Mattheson, Frederick: Poem, 14/15:118
Matthias, John: Poem, 16/17:68
Matthews, Richard: Poem, 16/17:65
Matthews, William: Poem, 16/17:67
Mauch, James: Poem, 4:13
Maxon, H.A.: Poem, 18/19:23
McElroy, Laurie: Poem, 18/19:50
Meinke, Peter: Poem, 16/17:69
Meredith, William: Poem, 16/17:70
Merlihan, James: Poem, 14/15:26
Mew, Tommy: Poem, 1:21
Mihailovich, Vasa D.: Slavako Janevski trnaslation (w/Milne Holton): Poem, 14/15:89
Miller, A. Mca.: Poem, 18/19:45

Minty, Judith: Poem, 16/17:72
Moody, W.V.: Poem, 18/19:14
Morgenstern, Christian: (tr. by Herbert Schaumann): Two Poems, 4:8
Morris, Herbert: Poem, 16/17:73
Murray, Pauli: Poem, 4:24
Musgrave, Dick: Poem, 14/15:132

Namias, Sandra Slayton: Cover art, 2
Namias, Sandra Slayton: Cover art, 3
Namias, Sandra Slayton: Three Graphics, 5/6:31
Namias, Sandra Slayton: Cover art, 7/8
Newman, Paul Baker: Poem, 3:33
Norton, Peter: Two Poems, 5/6:46

O'Grady, Tom: Poem, 18/19:39

Palma, Ralph: Poem, 16/17:78
Pastan, Linda: Four Poems, 3:2
Pastan, Linda: Three Poems, 5/6:28
Pastan, Linda: Five Poems, 7/8:3
Pastan, Linda: Two Poems, 9/10:42
Pastan, Linda: Poem, 12
Pastan, Linda: Two Poems, 14/15:64
Peterson, Bob: Cover photo, 16/17
Petroski, Henry: Poem, 18/19:51
Pfingston, Roger: Poem, 5/6:48
Posen, David: Poem, 18/19:22
Pybus, Rodney: Poem, 16/17:79

Ramsey, Paul: Poem, 18/19:44
Randall, Belle: Poem, 12
Reid, Graham W.: Petre M. Andreevski translation (w/Rod Jellema): Poem, 14/15:85
Reid, Graham W.: Blaze Koneski translation (w/Edward Gold): Poem, 14/15:88
Ringgold, Nancy Rainier: Cover art, 4
Ringgold, Nancy Rainier: Two photos, 4:22 & 23
Ristau, Harland: Graphic, 4:5
Ritchie, Elisavietta: Poem, 14/15:93
Roberts, Percival: Poem, 16/17:80
Robin, Ralph: Poem, 3:38
Robin, Ralph: Poem, 5/6:53
Robin, Ralph: Two Poems, 14/15:70
Rodway, Allen: Four Poems, 2:14
Rogoff, Jay: Two Poems, 18/19:12
Rompf, Kraft: Poem, 12
Roseliep, Raymond: Poem, 16/17:82
Rosner, Arpad: (tr. by Peter E. Rosner): Two Poems, 9/10:48
Rosner, Peter E.: Arpad Rosner translation, Poem, 9/10:48
Ryan, Richard: Poem, 16/17:83

St. John, Primus: Two Poems, 4:35
St. John, Primus: Three Poems, 5/6:39
Schaumann, Herbert: Wilhelm Busch translation, 1:14
Schaumann, Herbert: Poem, 2:18
Schaumann, Herbert: Christian Morgenstern translation, 4:8
Schwartz, Howard: Poem, 9/10:76
Scully, James: Poem, 2:6
Sister Mary Ellen S.S.N.D.: Poem, 5/6:3
Sklarew, Myra: Three Poems, 9/10:52
Sklarew, Myra: Two Poems, 14/15:30
Slaughter, Adele: Poem, 14/15:32
Slayton, Ann: Poem, 5/6:23
Slayton, Ann: Four Poems, 7/8:11
Smith Joel: Photo of Morton Marcus, 13:2
Smith, Newt: Two Poems, 4:39
Solyn, Paul: Two Poems, 14/15:116
Sonde, Susan: Poem, 14/15:100
Sparenberg, David: Poem, 1:28
Spielberg, Peter: Two Poems, 1:34
Stafford, William: Two Poems, 2:4

Stark, Marianne: Cover art, 12
Stead, William Force: Poem, 2:25
Steinberg, Louis: Poem, 12
Stepanchev, Stephen: Poem, 16/17:85
Stroud, Joseph: Poem, 14/15:46
Sulkin, Sidney: Poem, 14/15:94
Sussaman, Aaron: Poem, 7/8:10

Tagliabue, John: Two Poems, 4:6
Tagliabue, John: Poem, 5/6:18
Tagliabue, John: Two Poems, 7/8:25
Tagliabue, John: Two Poems, 14/15:114
Taylor, Henry: Euripides translation (w/Robert A. Brooke): Poem, 14/15:105
Teitelbaum, Paul: Poem, 1:36
Thompson, Phyllis: Poem, 14/15:82
Todd, Ruthven: Poem, 16/17:86

Venable, Nancy: Two Poems, 2:20

Walker, David: Poem, 5/6:8
Walsh, Chad: Three Poems, 1:2
Watkins, Clyde: Poem, 4:38
Weiss, Irving: Poem, 5/6:49
Weiss, Theodore: Poem, 3:13
Whittemore, Reed: Three Poems, 5/6:5
Wickless, Robert: Two Poems, 14/15:66
Wild, Peter: Poem, 5/6:55
Will, Frederick: Two Poems, 5/6:15
Williams, Harry: Two Poems, 14/15:78
Williams, Ralph: Poem, 3:39
Wilner, Irving: Three Poems, 14/15:140
Witt, Harold: Two Poems, 1:16
Witt, Harold: Poem, 2:22
Witt, Harold: Poem, 18/19:42

Contributors Notes

Daisy Aldan lives in New York City. Her books include the novella *A Golden Story* (Folder Editions, 1978), a collection of poetry *Between High Tides* (Folder Editions, 1978), and *The Art and Craft of Poetry* (Caroline House Books).

Roger Aplon lives in San Francisco. His book of poems is *Stiletto* (Dryad Press, 1976). He was also included in *Young American Poets* (Follet, 1968). Roger was on the staff of the literary magazine *Choice*.

Philip Appleman lives in New York City. His books include the novel *Shame the Devil* (Crown, 1981), *Open Doorways* (W.W. Norton, 1976), and *In the Twelfth Year* (Putnam, 1970).

Eric Baizer was born in 1950 and now lives in Washington, D.C. He co-edited the magazine of *The Museum of Temporary Art* for many years, and recently published *Literaturegate*, a critical newsletter on the National Endowment for the Arts. Eric was co-host of the "Garfield Street" radio program on WPFW/Pacifica from 1978 to 1980. His books include *Bent* (Mannequin City Editions, 1979), and *In the Museum of Temporary Art* (White Murray Press, 1979).

Carolyn Banks lives in rural Virginia. She holds an M.A. from the University of Maryland, and her book reviews are often in the *Washington Post Book World*. Her novels are *Mr. Right* (Viking, 1979), and *The Darkroom* (Viking, 1980).

Ben Belitt was born in New York City in 1911. Educated at the University of Virginia, he has taught for many years at Bennington College in Vermont. His books include *Adam's Dream: A Preface to Translation* (Grove Press, 1978), *The Double Witness: Poems 1970-1976* (Princeton University Press, 1977), *The Enemy Joy: New and Selected Poems* (Univ. of Chicago Press, 1964), *Selected Poems of Pablo Neruda* (Grove Press, 1962), and *Poet in New York, Frederico Garcia Lorca* (Grove Press, 1956).

Michael Biddle was born in 1934 and now lives in Croton-on-Hudson, NY. He studied at Harvard, the Akademie der Bildenden Kunst in Vienna, and the Central School of Arts and Crafts in London. He works principally in oil paint now, with an occasional etching in between. His work is in public collections at the Library of Congress, Walter Chrysler Museum, Rosenwald Collection, Boston Public Library, Metropolitan Museum of Modern Art, Philadelphia Free Library and others. Michael has taught at Pratt Graphic Center, Skowhegan School of Painting and Sculpture, and NY City Community College. His work has been exhibited in more than 44 shows at places as diverse as Muscoot Park, NY and the Society of American Graphic Artists 46th Annual Exhibition.

Adelaide Blomfield lives in Anchorage, Alaska. Her poetry books are *The Sound of Breathing* (Solo Press, 1977), and *White Ash* (Charas Press).

Jorge Luis Borges was born in August of 1899. He has lived in Argentina since the end of WWII. In 1955, blindness ended his many years of teaching at the University of Buenos Aires. His many awards include the Prix Internationale des Editeurs (Prix Formentor) with Samuel Beckett. His books include *Six Problems For Don Isidro Parodi*, in collaboration with Andolfo Bioy Caesares (Dutton, 1981); *Extraordinary Tales*, also with Caesares (Souvenir Press, 1977); *A Universal History of Infamy* (Dutton, 1979); *Ficciones* (1962); *Labyrinths* (1962); *Dreamtigers* (1964); *Personal Anthology* (1967); *The Aleph and Other Stories 1933-1969* (1970); *Doctor Brodie's Report* (1971); and *Selected Poems 1923-1967* (1972).

Denis Boyles was born in 1946 and lives in New York City, where he works as a freelance journalist. He helped found the Maryland Writer's Council in Baltimore, has worked as an editor at *Crawdaddy* magazine and *The New York Times Magazine*, and is currently working on a book about Vietnam War Veterans for Simon & Schuster. His previous books are *An Introduction to Design Poetics* (Assembling Press, 1976), and *Maxine's Flattery* (Dryad Press, 1978).

Gwendolyn Brooks lives in Chicago. She won a Pulitzer Prize in 1950 for *Annie Allen*, a book of poems about black life in Chicago. In 1968 she was named Poet Laureate of Illinois. Her other books include *Selected Poems* (Harper & Row, 1963), *Maud Martha: A Novel*, (1953), *In the Mecca* (Harper & Row, 1968), and *The World of Gwendolyn Brooks* (Harper & Row, 1971).

Charles Bukowski was born in 1920 in Andernach, Germany, came to the States in 1922, and was raised in Los Angeles. He currently lives in San Pedro, CA. Bukowski published his first short story in 1944. He now has over 20 books in print, including the novel *Women* (Black Sparrow Press, 1978), *Shakespeare Never Did This* (City Lights, 1979), a collection of columns he wrote in the 60s for *Open City* called *Notes of a Dirty Old Man* (City Lights, 1973), plus *Mockingbird Wish Me Luck; Love is a Dog from Hell: Poems 1974-1977; Erections, Ejaculations, Exhibitions and General Tales of Ordinary Madness; Factotum; Post Office; South of No North; The Days Run Away Like Wild Horses Over The Hills; Burning in Water, Drowning in Flame: Poems 1955-1973*; and numerous other collections of poetry and stories.

Robert Carlson, a graduate of Catholic University, has had a number of group and one-man shows. When not painting in his basement studio, he works for the Labor Department as a computer programmer.

Siv Cedering is a Swedish poet who lives in Harrison, NY. Her books include *The Blue Horses* (Seabury, 1979), *Mother Is* (Stein & Day, 1975), *How To Eat a Fortune Cookie* (New Rivers Press, 1976), and *Cup of Cold Water* (New Rivers Press, 1973). As we go to press she has a novel and a book of translation about to appear.

Marvin Cohen lives in New York City. His books include *The Inconvenience of Living* (Urizen Books, 1977), *How the Snake Emerged from the Bamboo Pole But Man Emerged from Both* (Oasis Books, 1978), *Baseball is Beautiful* (Ultramarine Press, 1974), *The Department Store of Global Confinement and other Entities* (Seagull Pub., 1978), and *The Moody Rhetoric of the Love Club and other Parables* (New Directions, 1973).

Jane Cooper lives in New York City. Her books include *Maps & Windows* (Macmillan, 1974), *Threads: Rosa Luxemburg from Prison* (Flamingo Press, 1979) and *The Weather of Six Mornings* (Macmillan, 1969) which won the Lamont Poetry Prize for 1968.

Imogen Cunningham was born in Portland, Oregon, in 1883. In 1910 she established a portrait studio in Seattle, WA after taking a B.S. in Chemistry from the Univ. of Washington. In 1915, she photographed her husband nude on the slopes of Mt. Ranier. (Possibly the first nude male photos every taken by a woman.) In 1932, she founded the f/64 Group along with Ansel Adams, Willard Van Dyke, Edward Weston, and others. She continued taking photos right up to her death in 1976. Collections of her work are *After Ninety* (Univ. of Wash. Press, 1977), *Imogen Cunningham: Photographs* (Univ. of Wash. Press, 1975), *Imogen! Imogen Cunningham Photographs 1910-1973* (Univ. of Wash. Press, 1974).

Philip Dacey was born in St. Louis in 1939 and now lives in Cottonwood, MN. He read locally at the Writer's Center and at Garvin's Grille in 1981. His books include *The Boy Under the Bed* (Johns Hopkins Univ. Press, 1981), *Gerard Manley Hopkins Meets Walt Whitman in Heaven* (Penmaen Press, 1981), and *How I Escaped From The Labyrinth and Other Poems* (Carnegie-Mellon Univ. Press, 1977).

Ann Darr was born in Bagley, Iowa and now after many years in the D.C. area is living in Cambridge, MA. After graduating from the University of Iowa, she went to NYC and wrote and performed radio scripts for NBC and ABC. During WW II she served in the Women's Airforce Service Pilots. Her books include *Cleared For Landing* (Dryad Press, 1978), *The Myth of a Woman's Fist* (Wm. Morrow, 1973), and *St. Ann's Gut* (Wm. Morrow, 1971). The Alice James Poetry Cooperative in Cambridge, MA. recently published her new book, *Riding with the Fireworks*.

John Elsberg was born in New York City in 1945. He presently lives in Arlington, Virginia, and works as a history editor for the military. John was fiction editor for *Gargoyle* from 1977-1980, and currently edits *Bogg*, a magazine of British and American writing. White Ewe Press is planning to publish his first full-length poetry collection, *Home-Style Cooking on Third Avenue*, in 1982. Recent chapbooks are *Walking as a Controlled Fall* (Kawabata Press, 1980), *The Limey and the Yank* w/George Cairncross (Bogg Pub., 1981), and *The Price of Reindeer* (White Ewe Press, 1979).

Niko Engonopoulos is/was a Greek artist; in the two years of research for this anthology, we were unable to locate any biographical information, past or current, and found no other examples of his work. Unfortunately our search for details on the life and work of Jean Moralis, also a Greek artist, proved equally fruitless. If anyone has access to this information, please contact us.

Josef Erhardy lives in Paris, France, and is represented by the Galerie Ariel and Galerie Bcanbourg in Paris. At one time he was Caresse Crosby's secretary.

Doug Flaherty was born in Lowell, MA in 1939. Doug is currently teaching English at the Univ. of Wisconsin-Oshkosh. His books include *Circle the Earth Before Noon* (sun rise fall down artpress, 1979), *Love-Tangle of Roots* (Ithaca House, 1977), and *To Keep the Blood from Drowning* (Second Coming Press, 1976).

Roland Flint is originally from Park River, North Dakota, but now lives in Washington, D.C., and teaches at Georgetown University. His books include *And Morning*, now in its fourth printing (Dryad Press, 1975), *Say It* (Dryad Press, 1979), and the chapbook *The Honey and Other Poems for Rosalind* (Unicorn Publ., 1976).

Richard Forsythe was a graduate student at Oxford in the early '70s.

Gene Fowler lives in California. His books include *Return of the Shaman* (Second Coming Press, 1981), *Fires: Selected Poems 1963-1976* (Thorp Springs Press, 1976), about to go into a third printing, *Felon's Journal* (Second Coming Press, 1975), *Her Majesty's Ship* (Grande Ronde Press, 1969), *Shaman Songs* (Dustbooks, 1967), *Field Studies* (Dustbooks, 1975), and *Vivisection* (Thorp Springs Press, 1974).

Barbara Frank was one of the five founders of the Washington Women's Arts Center in Washington, D.C. She has a B.A. from the University of Maryland in Studio Art and Spanish Language and Literature, plus an M.F.A. in painting and Art History. She has taught at the University of Maryland, Prince George's Community College, and Northern Virginia Community College (both Alexandria and Annandale campuses). Her work is currently touring in the "Representation and Realism" exhibition, from the Foundry Gallery in town, to the Delaware Museum, Richmond Museum, Ringling Museum in Florida, and on. She is represented in Washington by Gallery K.

Margaret Gibson was born in Philadelphia in 1944. She now lives in Norwich, Conn. Her books include *Lunes* (Some of Us Press, 1973), *On the Cutting Edge* (Curbstone Press, 1976), *Signs* (LSU Press, 1979), and *The Butterfly Ward* (Vanguard, 1980). Margaret also co-edited *Landscape and Distance: Contemporary Poets from Virginia* with Richard McCann (Univ. Press of Virginia, 1975).

Leonard R. Garzotto was last working as a vocational counselor in New Kensington, PA.

Edward Gold has been teaching English at the University of Maryland since 1969. A graduate of the Johns Hopkins University Writing Seminars in 1970, he's done many readings in the area, and had poems and translations published in *Poetry Now, Cape Rock, Tinderbox, New Orleans Review, Cimarron Review, Three Rivers Poetry Journal, Southern Poetry Review* and *Ishmael* among others.

L. Suzanne Gordon lives in Rockville, Md. She is a graduate of the University of Maryland (1968), and has an MA from the Johns Hopkins Writing Seminars (1969). Her work has been published in such periodicals as *Rolling Stone, Washingtonian, Poetry Northwest, Southern Poetry Review, Arts in Society, Women: A Journal of Liberation*, and others.

J.J. Grandville was the professional name of one Jean Ignace Isidore Gerard, a French illustrator and caricaturist who lived from 1803 to 1847. He was especially noted for his political cartoons. He also illustrated Beranger's chansons, La Fontaine's *Fables*, and Swift's *Gulliver's Travels*.

Hiram Haydn was born in Cleveland, Ohio, in 1907. He edited the *American Scholar* from 1944 until his death in 1973. He worked as an editor for Bobbs—Merrill Co., and Random House at one time, and later became co-founder of Atheneum publishers. His books include *Words & Faces* (Harcourt, 1974), *Counter-Renaissance* (Harcourt, 1967), and the novel *The Hands of Esau* (Harper, 1962). He also edited *The Portable Elizabethan Reader*.

H.R. Hays was born in New York City in 1904. He was known for his Brecht translations, including *Selected Poems of Bertolt Brecht* (Harcourt, 1972). Other books include the novels *Stranger on the Highway* (Little, Brown, 1943), and *In the Beginnings* (1963), plus *Portraits in Mixed Media* (Survivor's Manual, 1978), *Selected Poems of Jorge Carrea Andrale* (SUNY Press, 1972), and *Children of the Raven: The Seven Indian Nations of the Northwest Coast* (McGraw-Hill, 1975). He died in 1980.

Samuel Hazo was born in 1928 and lives in Pittsburgh, Pa. His books include *Quartered* (Univ. of Pitt. Press, 1974), *The Very Fall of the Sun* (Fawcett, 1978), *Smithereened Apart: A Critique of Hart Crane* (Ohio Univ. Press, 1977), *To Paris* (New Directions, 1981), *Once for the Last Bandit: New and Previous Poems* (Univ. of Pitt. Press, 1972), and the deck of playing cards *Shuffle, Cut and Look* (Rook Press, 1977).

Bill Holland has been a singer and songwriter for the last six years, and his third album, *Let It Go Live!* was released this spring. Before pursuing his musical career, he was a prize-winning writer for the *Washington Star* and also published many poems in quarterlies. In 1973, Some of Us Press published his book of poems *How Us White Folks Discovered Rock and Roll*. After college, he served as a Peace Corps volunteer in Liberia, and later as a staffer for Vista.

Roderick Jellema was born in 1927 and grew up in Holland, Michigan. He teaches literature at the University of Maryland and is also director of the Creative Writing program. In 1968-71 he directed and convened four conferences on Poetry and the National Conscience. His books are *Something Tugging the Line* (Dryad Press, 1974), which will be reprinted this year, and *The Lost Faces* (Dryad Press, 1979).

Kathleen Jeffrie Johnson lives in Rockville, Maryland. Her work has appeared in *Poet Lore, Long Pond Review*, and others.

Rodger Kamenetz was born in 1950 in Baltimore, where he now lives and teaches. His books include *The Station House* (Laughing Man Press, 1973), and *The Missing Jew* (Dryad/Tropos Press, 1979). Rodger currently has a radio show on writing on WBJC and publishes broadsides and books from his Rumor Press.

Wilfredo Lam was born in 1902 in Cuba. He was one of the later converts to Surrealism.

Robert Lax was born in New York in 1915. He's spent many years in Greece but is now living in Zurich, Switzerland. His books include *Color* (Exempla Press, 1979), a boxed book in silk-screen colors, *Selected Poems 1950-71* (Journeyman Press), and *Texts* (Zona Press, 1978).

John Logan lives and teaches in Buffalo, NY. His books include *The House That Jack Built* (Abbatoir Editions, 1974), *The Anonymous Lover* (Liveright, 1973), *The Bridge of Change: Poems 1974-1980* (Boa Editions, 1981), *Only The Dreamer Can Change the Dream: Selected Poems* (Ecco Press, 1981), *Poem in Progress* (Dryad Press, 1975), *Photographs/Poems* w/Aaron Siskind (Visual Studies Workshop, 1976), and *Ghost of the Heart* (Univ. of Chicago Press, 1980). For years he edited the literary magazine *Choice*.

Clarinda Harriss Lott lives in Baltimore, Maryland. She runs the New Poetry Series of readings and publications. Her own book, *The Bone Tree*, came out in 1972.

Saundra Maley is a graduate student in the English Dept. at the University of Maryland, College Park, where she teaches creative writing.

Thomas Merton was born in 1915 in Prades, Pyrennes-Orientales, France. He enlisted in the Trappist Monastery of Gethsemani, Kentucky, in 1941, and took his vows in 1947. His books include the autobiography *The Seven Story Mountain* (Harcourt, 1948), *No Man is an Island* (Harcourt, 1962), *Seeds of Contemplation* (1948), and poetry volumes *Thirty Poems* (1944), *Figures for an Apocalypse* (1948), and *Selected Poems* (1959). Selected work was published in *The Thomas Merton Reader* (Harcourt, 1962). He died in 1968.

Deena Metzger lives in California. Her books include a radio play, *The Book of Hags* (Black Box, 1977), a book of poems, *Dark Milk* (Momentum Press, 1978), and the novel *Skin: Shadows/Silence*. She was also co-filmmaker of a 1974 film on Chile.

Josephine Miles was born in Chicago in 1911. She has been a Professor of English at the University of California, Berkeley since 1940. She read at the Folger in April. Books include *To All Appearances: Poems New & Selected* (1974), *Kinds of Affection* (Wesleyan Univ. Press, 1967), *Fields of Learning* (Oyez, 1968), *Poems 1930-1960* (Indiana Univ. Press, 1960), *Style and Proportion: the Language of Prose and Poetry* (Little, Brown, 1967), and *Coming to Terms* (Univ. of Illinois Press, 1979).

Henry Miller was born in Brooklyn on Christmas Eve of 1891 and died last year. His first book, *Tropic of Cancer*, was published in 1934 and created a censorship battle which lasted for years. More than 50 books have since been published, including *Black Spring, Tropic of Capricorn, The Colossus of Maroussi, The Wisdom of the Heart, The Smile at the Foot of the Ladder, The Books in My Life, Remember to Remember, Big Sur and the Oranges of Hieronoymous Bosch,* and many more.

Morton Marcus lives in Santa Cruz, CA. His books include *Origins* (Kayak Press, 1969), *Where the Oceans Cover Us* (Capra Press, 1972), *The Armies Encamped in the Fields Beyond the Unfinished Avenues* (Jazz Press, 1977), *Big Winds, Glass Mornings, Shadows Cast by Stars* (Jazz Press, 1980), *The Brezhnev Memo* (Dell, 1980).

W.V. Moody lives in New Hampshire.

Harry T. Moore teaches at Southern Illinois University in Carbondale, Illinois. One of the premier D.H. Lawrence scholars, his books include *D.H. Lawrence: His Life and Works* (Irvington, 1964), *The Priest of Love: A Life of D.H. Lawrence* (Farrar, Straus & Giroux, 1974), *Age of the Modern and Other Literary Essays* (S. Ill. Press, 1971), and *Frieda Lawrence and Her Circle: Letters from, To, and about Frieda Lawrence* w/ Dale B. Montague (Shoe String, 1981).

Jean Moralis (see Niko Engonopoulos).

Sandra Slayton Namias is a graduate of the Boston Museum School of Fine Arts. Now living in New Jersey, she freelances as a graphics designer.

Pablo Neruda was born Ricardo Eliecer Neftali Reyes de Basoalto in Parral, Chile, on July 12, 1904. He took the name Neruda after the Czech short-story writer Jan Neruda. He submitted his first poem to a magazine at age fifteen and continued writing up to his death in 1973. He was awarded the Nobel Prize in literature in 1971. His books include *Twenty Love Poems and a Song of Despair* which was published in 1924 and has sold almost 2 million copies, *Residence on Earth*, which appeared in 1933, *General Song*, which many consider his masterpiece, in 1950, and many others. Two posthumous publications are *Song of Protest* (Wm. Morrow, 1976), and *Toward the Splendid City: Nobel Lecture* (Farrar, Straus and Giroux, 1974).

Robert Newcomb was born in 1933. He teaches Electrical Engineering at the University of Maryland in College Park. He's won Fulbrights to Australia (1963) and Malaysia (1976), and is the author of some 200 technical papers and four books including *Active Integrated Circuit Synthesis* (Also translated in Spanish). He has guided some 40 Ph.D's in electrical engineering and taught the freshman seminar "Anais Nin, Integrated Circuits, and the Poetics of Science." He also currently directs the international program "Microsystems and Generalized Networks."

Anais Nin was born in 1903 in Paris, France, and came to the US in 1914. Nin is perhaps best known for her diaries. The first volume covered the period 1931-1934 and was published in 1966 by Swallow Press. Since then, seven volumes have been published, along with *Linotte* (1978), a diary volume that predated the first volume. Nin was also noted for starting her own press and self-publishing many of her books. The six novels that made up the *Cities of the Interior* were published under that name, in one volume, in 1959. Other books include *The Novel of the Future* (Macmillan, 1968), *D.H. Lawrence: An Unprofessional Study* (Swallow, 1964), *Paris Revisited* (Capra, 1972), *House of Incest* (Swallow, 1958), and *The Anais Nin Reader*, ed. by Philip K. Jason (Swallow, 1973). Since her death in 1977, two volumes of erotic writings have been published, *Delta of Venus: Erotica* (1977) and *Little Birds* (1979).

Joyce Carol Oates was born in Lockport, NY, in 1938. She presently lives and teaches in Princeton, NJ, after years of teaching at the University of Windsor in Canada. A prolific novel, story, and poetry writer, she won the National Book Award in fiction in 1970 for her novel *Them*. Other books include *Contraries: Essays* (Oxford Univ. Press, 1981), *Angel of Light*, a Washington DC thriller (Dutton, 1981), *Bellefleur* (Dutton, 1980), *Angel Fire* (1973), *Triumph of the Spider Monkey* (1976), *With Shuddering Fall* (1964), *Marriages & Infidelities* (1972), *Wonderland* (1971), *Do With Me What You Will* (1973), *The Seduction and Other Stories* (Black Sparrow, 1974), and *The Hostile Sun: The Poetry of D.H. Lawrence* (Black Sparrow, 1974).

Tom O'Grady was born in Baltimore in 1943. He is presently Poet-in-Residence at Hampden-Sydney College in Virginia, and editor of the *Hampden-Sydney Poetry Review*.

Linda Pastan was born in 1932. She graduated from Radcliffe and Brandeis and now lives in Potomac, Maryland. Her books are *A Perfect Circle of Sun* (Swallow, 1971), *Aspects of Eve* (Liveright, 1975), *The Five Stages of Grief* (W.W. Norton, 1978), which won the Poetry Society of America's di Castagnola Award, and *Waiting for my Life* (W.W. Norton, 1981). She's also had several chapbooks published: *On the Way to the Zoo* (Dryad Press, 1975), *Even As We Sleep* (Croissant & Co., 1980), and *Setting the Table* (Dryad Press, 1980).

Richard Peabody was born at Georgetown University Hospital in Washington, D.C. in March 1951. He holds a B.A. from the University of Maryland, and an M.A. in literature from American University. He co-hosted the radio series "Garfield Street" on WPFW/Pacifica from 1978-1980, and has edited *Gargoyle* magazine since its founding in 1976. He's published a book of poems, *I'm in Love with the Morton Salt Girl* (Paycock Press, 1979), and a chapbook of stories, *Monaural* (Kawabata Press, 1980).

Pablo Picasso was born in Malaga, Spain in 1881 and died in 1973. He founded Cubism with Georges Braque and participated in most of the artistic styles and movements of the Twentieth Century. Indisputably one of the most prolific, gifted, and influential artists who ever lived.

Eliot Porter has published many volumes of his magnificent photographs, among them *Antarctica* (Dutton, 1978), *American Wilderness* (Dutton, 1981), *Summer Island* (Ballantine, 1976), *Intimate Landscapes* (Dutton, 1979), *Baja California* (Ballantine, 1969), *Birds of America: A Personal Selection* (Dutton, 1972), and the *Eliot Porter Calendar* (Dutton, 1981).

Theodore Roethke was born in 1908 in Saginaw, Michigan. He won the National Book Award and Bollingen Prize for *Words for the Wind* (Indiana Univ. Press, 1958), and a Pulitzer Prize for his *The Waking: Poems 1933-1953*, plus another National Book Award awarded posthumously in 1965 for *The Far Field*. Roethke died in 1963. Other books are *On the Poet and his Craft: Selected Prose* (Univ. of Washington, 1965), *Selected Letters of Theodore Roethke* (Univ. of Washington Press, 1968), *The Collected Poems of Theodore Roethke* (Doubleday, 1966), and *The Contemporary Poet as Artist and Critic* (Little, Brown, 1964).

Francis Coleman Rosenberger was born in 1915 and lives in McLean, Virginia. He worked for years as an attorney at the U.S. Senate but is now retired. He edited the annual *Records of the Columbia Historical Society of Washington, D.C.* from 1961-1973, plus the anthology *Washington and the Poet* (Univ. Press of Virginia, 1977). His own poetry volumes include *XII Poems* (Gotham Book Mart, 1946), *One Season Here: Poems 1943-1976* (Univ. Press of Virginia, 1976), and *An Alphabet* (Univ. Press of Virginia, 1978).

Henry H. Roth lives in South Nyack, NY. His books include *In Empty Rooms* (December Press, 1980), and *Jackdaw* (Beyond Baroque Pub., 1976).

James Scully lives in Willimantic, Delaware. His books include *Santiago Poems* (Curbstone Press, 1975), *Scrap Book* (Ziesing Bros., 1977), *The Marches* (Ziesing Bros., 1967, reprinted 1979), which won the Lamont Poetry Prize in 1967, and *May Day* (Minn. Review Press, 1980).

Myra Sklarew teaches at American University in Washington, D.C. Her poetry books are *The Backyard of the Diaspora* (Dryad Press, 1976), for which she shared the Poetry Society of America's di Castagnola award with Erica Jong, and *in the basket of the blind* (Cherry Valley Editions). Dryad has just reprinted *Diaspora*, and Myra has a new chapbook, *Blessed Art Thou, No-One*, coming from Chowder Press, and a new book, *The Science of Goodbyes*, from the University of Georgia Press.

Ann Slayton has published poems in a number of literary magazines, among them, *Ms.*, *Southern Poetry Review*, *Poetry Now*, *Washington Review* and *Dryad*. She was one of the founding members of the Washington Women's Arts Center. Dryad Press will publish a book of her poems, *Naming Our Wisdom*, in Spring, 1982.

Richard Snodgrass, brother of W.D. Snodgrass, is a hard man to track down. We finally located him in Beaver Falls, PA. Richard has been on the road for the past five years but will spend some time this year at the Wurlitzer Foundation in Taos, New Mexico.

Martin Steingesser was born in New York City in 1937. A poet and photographer, his recent book is *The Apple Star* (Kickingdance Press, 1980).

Brian Swann was born in England in 1940, and is currently an Associate Professor of English at Cooper Union University in NYC. Among his many books are a novel, *The Runner* (Carpenter Press, 1979), and the poetry books *Unreal Estate* (Toothpaste Press, 1980) and *A Book of Voices* (Latitudes Press, 1980). He has five volumes of translation coming out this year, including, Melih Cevdet Anday's *Rain One Step Away* translated w/Talat Halman (Charioteer Press, 1981), and Vittorio Bodini's *The Hands of the South* translated with Ruth Feldman (Charioteer Press, 1981). Swann knew Caresse Crosby at Roccasinabalda.

John Unterecker was born in Buffalo, NY, but now lives in Hawaii where he teaches at the University of Hawaii at Manoa. His books include *Voyager: A Life of Hart Crane* (Farrar, Straus & Giroux, 1969), which was nominated for a National Book Award, *Dance Sequence* (Kayak, 1975), *Stone* (Univ. Press of Hawaii, 1977), *The Dreaming Zoo* (a book for children), and the forthcoming *The Dark Vineyards*, in which the essay reprinted here will appear in a slightly rewritten form. He is now planning a book on ballet that will focus on the work of George Balanchine and the New York City ballet. He has also written or edited numerous books on Yeats, Durrell, and Elizabeth Bishop.

Mark Van Doren was born in 1894 in Hope, Illinois. He taught for over 39 years at Columbia University, where he was long noted as a great teacher. Allen Ginsberg and Jack Kerouac were two of his students. He was also a lecturer at St. John's College in Annapolis, Maryland, from 1937 to 1957. Van Doren wrote drama, poetry, fiction, children's books and non-fiction. He wrote his autobiography in 1958, and edited or wrote books on Dryden, Thoreau, Hawthorne, Wordsworth, Whitman, Cowper, and Aaron Burr. His poetry volumes include *Good Morning: Last Poems by Mark Van Doren* (Hill & Wang, 1973), *Mark Van Doren: 100 Poems* (Hill & Wang, 1967), and *Collected and New Poems 1924-1963* (Hill & Wang, 1963). Van Doren died in 1972.

David Wagoner has been nominated three times for the National Book Award. He teaches at the University of Washington, and edits *Poetry Northwest* and the Princeton University Poetry Series. He has published over ten collections of poetry and ten novels including *The Hanging Garden* (Little, Brown, 1980), *Collected Poems 1956-1976* (Indiana Univ. Press, 1978), *In Broken Country* (Little, Brown, 1979), *Whole Hog* (Little, Brown, 1976), and *Sleeping in the Woods* (Indiana Univ. Press, 1974). Francis Ford Coppola is now filming one of his earlier novels, *The Escape Artist*.

Chad Walsh is a former Fulbright lecturer, now Episcopal Priest, who teaches at Beloit College in Beloit, Wisconsin. His books include the classic study *From Utopia to Nightmare* (1962), *The Literary Legacy of C.S. Lewis* (Harcourt, 1979), a children's book, *Nellie & Her Flying Crocodile* (Harper & Row, 1979), and the poetry volumes *End of Nature* (Swallow, 1969), *The Unknowing Dance*, and *Garlands for Christmas*. His new book, *A Rich Feast* (Harper & Row, 1981), is a guide to the *Bible*.

Irving Weiss lives in New York City. He recently edited the 2nd revised edition of Malcolm De Chazal's *Sens-Plastique* (Sun, 1980), and the *Thesarus of Book Digests 1950-1980* (Crown, 1981).

Reed Whittemore was born in New Haven, Connecticut, in 1919. He is presently teaching at the University of Maryland in College Park. He was Poetry Consultant to the Library of Congress from 1964-65. His books include *The Mother's Breast and the Father's House* (1974), *50 Poems 50* (Univ. of Minn. Press, 1970), a forthcoming volume of poems from Dryad Press, plus *The Poet as Journalist: Life at the New Republic* (New Republic Books, 1976). He was editor of the *Yale Literary Magazine*, his own magazine, *Furioso, a Magazine of Poetry* (from 1939 to 1953), and *The Carleton Miscellany* (from 1960 to 1965).

Harriet Zinnes was born in Massachusetts and is a Professor of English at Queens College of the City University of NY. Her books include *Entropisms* (Gallimaufry, 1978), *Ancient Ritual* (Seagull Publ., 1979), and *I Wanted to See Something Flying* (Folder Editions, 1976). She is also the editor of *Ezra Pound and the Visual Arts* (New Directions, 1980).

D.C. Magazines: A List in Progress (1784-1981)

Inclusion was determined by location in the area between the four points: South of Baltimore, Md.; North of Fredericksburg, Va.; East of Front Royal, Va.; and West of Annapolis, Md.

Selected Early Magazines & Papers Georgetown laid out—1751. Incorporated—1789. Washington, D.C. founded—1800

1784

Alexandria Gazette, 1784-ongoing.

1789

The Times and Potowmack Packet, 1789-? Georgetown Wkly.

1800

National Intelligencer, 1800-1870. Publisher: Samuel Harrison Smith.

1801

National Magazine; or Cabinet of the United States, 1799-1802. (moved from Richmond to DC in 1801) (8 issues)

1810

Agricultural Museum, 1810-1812. Editor: Reverend David Wiley.

1811

Hive Repository of Literature, 1811-?
Washington Gazette, 1811-? Editor: James A. Bayard.

1822

Weekly Literary Messenger, 1822-? Editor: A.S. Colvin.

1823

National Journal, 1823-? Editor: Peter Force.
Washington Quarterly of Arts, Sciences & Literature, 1823-24. Editor: Robert Little

1825

African Repository, 1825-1892. Publ. by American Colonization Society. Monthly

1831

Paul Pry, 1831-1836. Editor: Anne Royall

1832

The Metropolitan: A Miscellany of Literature, Science & Music, 12/5/1832-1/29/35. Weekly. Editors: Duff Green & James W. Simmons. (after 9/20/34, under name *Washington Literary Gazette*)

1836

The Huntress, 1836-1854. Editor: Anne Royall
Niles' Weekly Register, 1811-1839. Editor: William Ogden Niles (moved to DC from Baltimore in 1836. Moved back to Baltimore in 1839. Last issue in 1849.)

1837

The United States of America and Democratic Review, 1837-? Editors: John L. O'Sullivan and S.D. Langtree. (Later name changed to *Democratic Review* and moved to New York)

1847

The National Era, 1847-1860. Editor: Dr. Gamaliel Bailey.

1852

The Evening Star, 1852-1981. Founded by William A. Page

1871

Sunday Capital, 1871-1890.

1872

Georgetown College Journal, 1872-1970. Georgetown Univ. Student Editors

1877

The Republic: Sunday Journal of Literature and Events, 1877-1899.
The Washington Post, 1877-ongoing. Founded by Stilson Hutchins

1882

Family Fiction, 1882-? Weekly. Editor: ?

1883

Washington Hatchet, 1883-1906

1888

National Geographic, 1888-ongoing.

1892

Buff and Blue, 1892-? National College for the Deaf, semi-monthly.

1893

Howard University Quarterly, 1893-?

1894

Washington Times, 1894-1906

1895

The Bauble, 1895-1897 (ceased with vol. 3, no. 5 though vol. 3, no. 3 was purposely not published). Editor: William A. Page.
Southern Literary Messenger, 5/1895-7/1895. Publ.: Mrs. A. Truehart Buck

1897

The Washingtonian, 6/1897-11/1897

1899

Southern Magazine, 6/1899-12/1899. (Manassas, Va.)

1900

Realization, 1900-1903
Washington Mirror, 1900-1905. Editor: James H. Frazier

Literary Magazines (1901-1981)

1901

Columbian University Magazine, June 1901-? Editor: Litt P. Dryden Pre GW.—the Columbian Univ.
The Universit, 11/1901-6/1902. Editor: Stanton Canfield Peelle (8 issues) The Columbian Univ.

1903

Washington Life, 1903-1906

1907

Red Letter Magazine, 1907-? monthly. (literary)
Trinity College Record, April 1907-ongoing. Student Editors

1911

The University Symposium, 1911-11/1921. Editor: William Maguire. Catholic Univ. Monthly.

1915

The Minaret, 11/1915-7/1915 and again from 4/1923-10/1926. Editor: Herbert Broncken.

1921

The Ghost, 1/1921-5/1922 and again from 1/1927-5/1928. G.W. Univ. Student Editors

1924

The Pendulum, 1924. Editor: Wm. Northrup Morse. G.W. Univ. Student Editors (2 issues)

1925

The Lash, 1925-2/15/1926. Ed.: John R. Bromell G.W. Univ.

1927

Colonial Wig, 1927-1929. Editor: Wanda Webb. G.W. Univ. (6 issues)

1928

Sonnet Sequences, 1928-1959. Editors: Murray and Hazel L. Marshall.

1929

The Carillon, 1929-1933. Editors: Caroline Giltnan, Anne Robinson, Catherine Cate Coblentz and Courtland Baker (17 issues)
Janus, 1929. Editor: Solon R. Barber (1 issue)
Star-Dust, 1929-1932. Editor: Edith Mirick (and John Lee Higgins Fall 1929-Sprg/Summer 1930)

1930

The Colonial Review, 1930. Ed.: Miriam De Haas. (7 issues) Supplement to G.W. *University Hatchet.* Vol. 27, no. 9-Vol. 27, no. 31.
The Old Line, 1930-?. University of Maryland magazine.

1931

Manuscripts, 1931-1932. (a.k.a. *Fifty Manuscripts* and *Author's Forum*) Editor: Unknown
The Washington Review, 11/1931-12/1933. Editor: Justin Herman

1932

Measure, 12/1932-12/1934. Editors: Gerard Manley Hopkins Society—James C. Hendrickson, Theodore Maynard, John Shields, and others. (3 annual issues)

1934

The Centaur, 1/1934-12/1934. Editors: Diana Kerany Powell, Henrietta Randolph Wirt, and John Dillion. (3 issues)

Blue Moon Quarterly, 1932-1958? Editor: Inez Sheldon Tyler. (Moved to D.C. 1934)
The Fourth Decade, 1/1934-8/1934. Editors: Lee Alexander, James Whiting Saunders, Benjamin Klein Schwarta, Helen Swick and others. (Bimonthly)
The Loom, 1934. Omicron Epsilon Pi magazine, American Univ. (2 issues)

1935

The Eyrie, 1935-1937. American University (4 issues)

1937

The Beak, 5/1937 Editor: Frank Diggs. American Univ. (1 issue)
Inward Light, 1937-? Editor: Elined Kotschnig
The Silver Star, 1937-1940? Editor: Emory C. Pharr

1939

Foothills, Sprg. 1939-Fall 1940. Editors: Jack Zeigler (Sprg. 1939)/Jack Deasy (Fall 1940) (2 issues) Mimeo.

1940

Whispers, 11/1940-1942? Editor: Katherine W. Fulton (8 issues a year)

1941

Helicon, Editor: Albert Tate, Jr. G.W. Univ. Literary Club Mimeo. (1 issue)

1944

The Bookfellows, Summer 1944-1946. Publ. by The Federal Poets before they changed their name from The Bookfellows.
Maryland Quarterly, 1944. Editor: Norman Macleod (3 issues) Univ. of Maryland

1945

Portfolio: intercontinental review of art and literature, 1945-1948. Editor: Caresse Crosby (6 issues)
Strange Harmony, 1945. Omicron Epsilon Pi magazine, American Univ. (1 issue)

1946

The Federal Poet, 1946-ongoing. Publ. by the Federal Poets. Editors change as club members change.

1947

The Envoy, 1/1947-? Publ. by Gtown Univ. School of Foreign Service
The Grind, Jan. 1947. Editor: Sherie Simon. (1 issue) G.W. Univ.
The Surveyor, Winter 1947. Ed.: Louis Munan. (1 issue) G.W. Univ.

1949

Colonial Review, Fall 1949-Sprg. 1950. (3 issues) G.W. Univ.

1952

The Courier, Fall, 1952-Spring, 1971 (*Foreign Service Courier* until 1966) Georgetown Univ.

1955

American University Writer, Sprg. 1955-1965. Student Editors. (17 issues)
The Literary Review, Sprg., 1955. Catholic Univ. Student Editors

1956

Nexus, Sprg. 1956-1959. Catholic Univ. Student Editors
Seasame, Ed.: Murray Arndt, S.D.S. Divine Savior Seminary, Lanham, Md.

1957

Expression, 5/1957-1963. Univ. of Md. Student Editors
Off the Record, 5/1957-Sprg., 1965. Trinity College Student Editors

1958

The Bald Eagle, 1958-1965. Editor: Vic Sussman. Founded by: W.R. Kraemer & F.J. Sellers (American Univ. Humor magazine) (8 issues?)

1959

The Potomac, Sprg., 1959-Sprg., 1970. G.W. Univ. Student Editors (23 issues)

1961

Daesin, 1961-1962. (moved to NYC) Editor: Percy Johnson

1962

Outcry, 1962-1963. Editor: Lee Holland (3 issues)
Poems for Peace, 1962-? Editor: Jeanne S. Bagby

1963

Views, 1963-?

1964

The Idler, 1964-? Editor: Sam Smith
Penfeather, 1964 (1 issue) American Univ. Freshman English mag.

1965

American Magazine, Sprg., 1965-1977. American Univ. Student Editors (notably William F. Ryan, Ann Beattie, and Harrison Fisher) Merged *Bald Eagle* and *A.U. Writer*. (20 issues)
Black Bread, 1965-1968. Editor: Christopher Toll Catholic Univ.
Graffiti, 1965. Editor: Steve Stern (2 issues)
The Other Side, 4/1965-5/1965. Editor: Margaret Singleton. G.W. Univ. (2 issues)

1966

The Argonaut, 1966-70? Honors Journal of Cambridge A Dorm. Editor: Art Young. Univ. of Md.
Anubis, 1966-1968. Editor: Paul Willis
Promethean, 1966-1968? Howard Univ.

1967

Dryad, 1967-1978. Editors: Merrill Leffler & Neil Lehrman (19 issues)
Kauri, 1964-1971. (Moved to D.C. from NYC in '67) Editor: Will Inman (33 issues) Mimeo
Mana, 1967-? Editors: Hellar Grabbi & Sodra Vagen
Mind Fucke, 1967-1969. Editor: Joe Stewart (5 issues)
Spectrum, 7/1967-9/1967. (11 issues)
Voyages: A National Literary Magazine, 1967-1973. Editor: William F. Claire (15 issues)
Washington Quarterly, 1967-1968

1968

Afro American Review, 1968-1970. Editor: Paula Gittings and Stan Ferdinand. Howard Univ.
Aquarius, 1968-1969. Catholic Univ. (2 issues)
Artisan, 1968-? Editor: Charles Dorn
Castalia, 1968-1970 Montgomery College.
The Circle, 1968-1969. Editor: William E. Garrison (3 issues)

1969

Calvert Review, Fall 1969-ongoing. Univ. of Maryland, College Park. Student Editors.
Ivory Gate, 1969-1976. Catholic Univ. Student Editors
Takoma, 1969-1970. Editor: David Sawyer. Montgomery College, Takoma Park, Md. (2 issues)
The Wig, Sprg., 1969. (1 issue) G.W. Univ.

1970

Abbey, 1970-ongoing. Editor: David Greisman. Peter Blush Co-Editor
Buffalo Stamps, 1970-1975. Editors: Simon Schuchat with Alec Bernstein and Matt Stover (7 issues)
Dialog, Fall, 1970-Winter/Sprg., 1970. Editor: Edmund Ghareeb. Georgetown Univ. (4 issues)
The Duet, 1970-1972 Montgomery College.
Forefront, 1970-? Editor: Carl L. Shears
Modus Operandi, 1970-1980. Editor: Sheila R. Jensen
None Such, 1970-? Editors: Peter Savitsky and Carolyn Hopewell? (2 issues?)
People On The Streets, 1970. Editors: Rick Margolies, Vernard Gray, Peter Noterman and others. (1 issue)
Phoebe, 1970-ongoing. George Mason University. Student Editors (Notably Richard Bausch, Jim Everhard, and Joyce Renwick)

Portfolio, 1970-1971. Editors: Kenneth Arnold and Eleanor Wilner.

Rock Creek, 1970-1978. G.W. Univ. Student Editors

1971

Higginson Poetry Journal, 1971-ongoing. Editor: Fred Morey.

Mythos, Editor: Thomas Zelaney Catholic Univ. (1 issue)

Three Sisters, Fall 1971-ongoing. (verged *Viewpoint, Georgetown Journal,* and *Courier*) Georgetown University. Student Editors. (1st editor: Greg Orfalea)

1972

Black Box, 1972-ongoing. Editor: Alan Austin (cassette magazine)

Edcentric, 1972-?

Feminist Studies, 1972-ongoing. Woman's Studies Program, Univ. of Maryland.

Northwoods Journal, 1972-1980; 1981-ongoing. Editors: Robert W. Olmsted and Paul Hodges.

Poet, 1972. Editor: Peter Coates (3 issues)

Proteus, 1972-1978. Editors: Frank and Cathy Gatling. (7 issues)

Strange Respects, 1972-1973. Editor: Michael Lally

Transition, 1972. Editor: E. Ethelbert Miller (2 issues) Howard University

Vort, 1972-1976. Editor: Barry Stevens Alpert (9 issues)

1973

Asylum, 1973-ongoing. Mount Vernon College. Student Editors.

Hoo-Doo, 1973-ongoing. (Came to D.C. in 1973, left in 75?) Editors: Ahmos Zu-Bolton, E. Ethelbert Miller, and Jerry Ward.

Mass Transit, Summer 1973-Fall 1974. Editors: Terence Winch, Michael Lally, Ed Cox, Tina Darragh, Beth Joselow, and P. Inman. (5 issues)

Old Friends, 1973-1974. Editors: David Allen, Anne Becker, Kelp Homburg, William Mayville, and Jacky Potter. (4 issues)

Saxifrage, Sprg., 1973-ongoing. Georgetown Univ. Student Editors

1974

ArtWash, 1974-? Madam's Organ Art Collective.

Eel (everybody's ex-lover), 1/1974-1977. Editor: Peter Inman. (4 issues)

Joint Conference, 1974-ongoing. Editor: Kathryn King

Quest: A Feminist Quarterly, 1974-ongoing. Editors: Arleen Rogan, Sara Shepard, Jackie MacMillan, Marilyn Lerch, Lynn Gorshove, Gerri Traina, Tracy Thiele, Sara Begus, Lisa Hoogstra and Isabelle Thabault.

Soundings, 1972-1976 (moved to DC from Calif. in 1974) Editor: Peter Garland

Washington Review of the Arts, 1974-ongoing. Editors: Jean Lewton, Patricia Griffith, Clarissa Wittenberg, Mary Swift, Bernard Welt, and others.

1975

Aleph, 1975-1979. Editors: Larry Fox and Mel Raff (7 issues)

Bogg, 1968-ongoing. (US supplement to British magazine started in Arlington, VA. in 1975. In 1980 the magazine became a US-based mag published locally with a British section.) Editors: John Elsberg (USA)/ George Cairncross (UK)

MOTA, 1975-1979. Magazine of the Museum of Temporary Art. Editors: Eric Baizer and Janet Schmuckal. (17 issues)

Sibyl-Child, 1975-ongoing. Editors: Candyce Homnick Stapen, Doris Mozer, Susan B. Shannon, Joan Wood, Mary Louise O'Connell, Carey Groom, and others.

1976

Chimera, 1976 (1 issue) Univ. of Maryland. Editors: Carol M. Dupre, D. Marc Kever and Carol Peck.

Gallimaufry Journal, 1973-1979. (moved to DC from Berkeley, Calif. in Spring 1976) Editor: Mary MacArthur; Asst. Editors: Mary Mackey and Jonis Agee. (14 issues)

Gargoyle, 1976-ongoing. Editors: Richard Peabody and Gretchen Johnsen. (w/Russell Cox, Paul Pasquarella, John Elsberg, Lynn Sheridan, and David Hickman).

La-Bas, 1976-1979. Editor: Douglas Messerli (12 issues) Mimeo.

The Mill, 1976-ongoing. Editor: Kevin Urick

Poet Lore, 1889-ongoing. (Moved to DC from Boston in Spring 1976) Editors: Philip K. Jason and Kevin Madden.

Proteus, Sprg., 1976 Catholic Univ. (1 issue)

Readout Poetry, 1976-1977. Editor: John R. Woodward. (4 issues)

Rustlings, 1976-ongoing. Editors: Marina Rogers-Flores and Diane Pierce.

Sun and Moon: A Journal of Literature and Art, 1976-ongoing. Editors: Douglas Messerli and Howard N. Fox.

Window, 1976-1980. Editors: Paul Deblinger, Dan Johnson, Trisha Tatum, and Nan Barbour. (9 issues)

1977

Cerberus, 1977 (1 issue) Editor: Joseph Lerner

Dog City, Summer 1977-ongoing. Collective editing by contributors: Lynne Dreyer, Chris Mason, Joan Retallack, Donald Britton, Julie Brown, Diane Ward, Connie McKenna, Bernard Welt, Doug Lang, Phyllis Rosenzweig, Bob Zimmerman, Marshall Reese, and Kirby Malone.

Little Patuxent Review, 1977-ongoing. Editors: Ralph and Margot Treitel.
Manassas Review: Essays on Contemporary American Poetry, 1977-ongoing. Editor: Patrick Bizzaro.
Omowee Journal, 1/1977-ongoing. Student Editors. Howard University.
OO-sh'Bop, 1977. Editor: Calvin Reed (1 issue)
Transmutant, 1977-1978. Editor: Desmond O'Brien. (3 issues)

1978

Abortion, 1978-? Editors: Bruce Weber
As Is, 1978-ongoing. Editors: Leland Gamson and Paul Parsons.
Asanteh Airloom Alo, 1978 (1 issue) Editor: Frank O. Matheis-Nichol.
Nethula Journal, 1978-ongoing. Editors: Kathy Elaine Anderson and Essex Hemphill.
Nucleus, 1978. Editor: Paul Trimble. (2 issues)
The Phoenix, 1978 Editor: Peggy Simons. Montgomery College/Takoma Park Campus.
Piano, 1978. Editors: Patti Chambers and Walt-Christopher Stickney. (1 issue)
Plum, 1978-ongoing. (Moved to NYC after 1st issue) Editors: Harvey Lillywhite and Eileen Silver-Lillywhite.
Sirannon, 1978-? Editor: Ira Craig.
Verbena: Bilingual Review of the Arts, 1978-ongoing. Editor: Barbara Mujica.
Washington Book Review, 1978-1980; 1981-ongoing. Editors: Joseph Lerner (Kevin Bezner for issue no. 8)
Watermelon, Sprg., 1978-? Georgetown Univ. Arts Hall Project Lit. Group
Wooden Teeth, 1978-1981. G.W. Univ. Student Editors (5 issues)
Working Cultures, 1978. Editors: Gabriella Edgcomb and E. Ethelbert Miller. (1 issue)

1979

The Bushwhacker (a.k.a. *American University Journal of Contemporary Literature*), Spring 1979-Spring 1980. Editors: Kimble Kokich, Richard Flynn, and Herbert Guggenheim. (2 issues)

Ethos, Sprg. 1979-ongoing. Dept. of Engl., Univ. of Md. Editor: Jack Greer
Mutant Journal, 1979 Editor: Larry Navat (3 issues).
Outlet, 1979 (1 issue) Editors: P.R. Brosowin, M.L. Kao, Judith Lundlin, E.G. Maxwell, Margaret Richardson, and Robert F. Whisler.
Visions, 1979-ongoing. Editor: Bradley R. Strahan.

1980

Columbia Road Review, 1980-ongoing. Editor: Kathryn King
Crop Dust, 1980-ongoing. Editor: Edward C. Lynskey, Wayne Kline, and Cameron W. Yeatts.
Dirt, 1980-ongoing. Editor: Chasen Gaver.
Green Poetry, 1980-? Georgetown Univ. Arts Hall Project Lit. Group
Just Three Guys, Sprg., 1980-ongoing. Editors: Eugene DiPaola, William O'Conor & Robert Sandri.
The Montgomery Review, 1980-? Editor: Samuel R. Blate. Montgomery College, Rockville, Md.
Northeast Rising Sun, 1976-ongoing. (moved to Wheaton, Md. from NY in 1980) Editor: Pamela Beach Plymell.
Re:Visions, 1980-ongoing. Catholic Univ. Student Editors
Rock Creek Review, 1980 (1 issue insert in *Rock Creek Monitor*) Editors: Brian Doherty and Linda Botimer.
Sagala, 1980-ongoing. Semi-annual. Editor: Stephen Henderson.
Water Pik, 1980 (1 issue) Editor: Gretchen Johnsen.
Wingspread: A Feminist Literary Journal, 1980-? Women's Center, Univ. of Md. College Park. Student Editors.
The Writ, 1980-ongoing. Editor: Elizabeth M. Williams.

1981

Alph Null, 1981-ongoing. Editor: Larry Navat.
DEROS, 1981-ongoing. Editors: Lee-lee Schlegel and Ken Rose. (Vietnam Veteran Literary Mag)
The Eyrie, 1981-ongoing. American Univ. Editor: Linda Farwell.
G.W. Review, 1981-ongoing. George Washington Univ. Student Editors
Up Against The Wall, Mother, 1981-ongoing. Editor: Lee-lee Schlegel (Women-in-crisis mag)

Alternative Newspapers and Arts Magazines (Some of which published fiction or poetry)

1966

Washington Free Press, 3/22/1966-12/1969. Poetry Editor: Peter Novick

1967

Washington Independent, 1967-1968. Editor: Thomas DeBaggio

1969

Quicksilver Times, 1969-1972
Woodwind, 1969-1973. Editors: Richard Harrington and Mike Schreibman. Poetry Editor: Deirdra Baldwin

1970

The Colonial Times, 1970-1971
D.C. Gazette, 1970-ongoing, Editor: Sam Smith.
Off Our Backs, 1970-ongoing. Editors: Vickie Leonard, Carol Anne Douglas, Mary Klein, Alice Henry, Janie Kelly, Fran Moira, Tacie Dejanikus, Lin Jansen, and Wendy Stevens.
Pace! 1970-? Editor: Richard L. Schlegel

1971

The Daily Rag, 1971-1973

1972

Black Stage, 1972-ongoing.
Fly By Night, 1972-?
Good Times, 1972-? Editor: Richard Branciforte

1973

First Folio, 1973-? Editor: Jay Alan Quantrill
First Things First
Neversell Monthly, 1973-? Editors: Bob Griffiths, Jethro Soames, and Roger Ordway
Unicorn Times, 1973-ongoing. Publisher: Elliot Ryan
Washington Scene, 1973-? Editor: Robert England

1975

Marquee, 1975-? Editor: B.S. Ryder Quarterly
Washington Times, 1975-? Publ.: Frank Bolling; Editors: Teddy Vaughn and Richard Covington

1976

Newsworks, 2/1976-10/1976 Publisher: Dorothy McGhee. Editor: William S. Kowinski.

1977

Bread & Roses, 1977 (2 issues) Bread & Roses Collective
Washington Tribune, 1977-ongoing. Founder: Donald Smith. Editors: Charles Paul Freund and Mark Jenkins.

1978

Black Arts Review, 1978 Pub.: Vernard Gray & Ronald Sharps.
The Mag, 1978 (1 issue) Cathy London, Melissa Bell, Crispin Sartwell, Buzz McClain, John Messina, Jr., & Steve Blevins.
Rock Creek Monitor, 1978-1981. Editor: Brian Doherty

1979

Art Ink, 1979-ongoing. Project Director: Janet Schmuckal
It, 1979-1980. Editor: Dana Sohr (13 issues?) Monthly

1980

Encore (a.k.a. *City Life*) 1980-ongoing. Publ.: Deborah Dean. Editor: Kevin Chaffee

1981

1981, 1981-ongoing. Editors: Russ Smith & Michael Mariotte

Other Anthologies with an Emphasis on Area Poets & Writers

District of Columbia Poets, ed. by Edith Mirick, Henry Harrison Publ., 1932.

Poetry from the Potomac, ed. Emes MacVeagh, 1948.

Poems from the Capital, ed. by Ron Arcque, 1972.

Synergy, ed. by E. Ethelbert Miller & Ahmos Zu-Bolton, 1975.

Landscape and Distance: Contemporary Poets from Virginia, ed. by Margaret Gibson & Richard McCann, University Press of Virginia, 1975.

Hoo-Doo No. 5 (Women's Issue), ed. by Lucille Clifton, Audre Lorde & Amma Khalil, 1976.

The Washington Sound: Love and Death in Demon City (issue no. 8 of *Black Box* magazine), ed. by Alan Austin & Ahmos Zu-Bolton, PO Box 50145, Washington, DC 20004, 1976.

City Celebration '76, ed. by Octave Stevenson, DC Public Library & DC Bicentennial Commission, 1977.

Rye Bread: Women Poets Rising, ed. by Walter H. Kerr & Stacy Tuthill, SCOP Publications, 5821 Swarthmore Dr., College Park, MD 20740, 1977.

Washington and the Poet, ed. by Francis Coleman Rosenberger, Columbia Historical Society & University Press of Virginia, 1977.

Women Surviving Massacres and Men, ed. by E. Ethelbert Miller, Anemone Press, PO Box 441, Howard University, Washington, DC 20059, 1977.

A Sampling of Poems by Poets-in-the-Schools, Maryland, ed. by Eric Cheyfitz, Maryland Arts Council, Baltimore, MD, 1977.

Carry Me Back: An Anthology of Virginia Fiction (issue no. 12 of *Gallimaufry* Journal), ed. by Mary MacArthur, 1978.

The Unicorn and the Garden, ed. by Betty Parry, The Word Works, Inc., PO Box 4054, Washington, DC 20015, 1978.

Seeds & Leaves, ed. by Exenia Butler, Esther Colvin, Ed Cox, Lee Howard & Elizabeth Pendelton, The Roosevelt Hotel Poetry Group, 2101 16th Street, NW, Washington, DC 20009, 1979.

Centerwords: an anthology of poetry and prose from the Washington Women's Arts Center, ed. by Barbara Berman & Margaret Litchfield, 1821 Q St., NW, Washington, DC 20009, 1978 & 1979.

Free DC, ed. by A.B. Spellman, D.C. Writer's Workshop, 10201 E St., NE, Washington, DC 20001, 1979.

Positively Prince Street, ed. by Dalton Delan, Irene Rouse Bookseller, 905 Duke St., Alexandria, VA 22314, 1979.

The Poet Upstairs: A Washington Anthology, ed. by Octave Stevenson, The Word Works, Inc., PO Box 4054, Washington, DC 20015, 1979.

The Other Side of the Hill, The Capital Hill Poetry Group & The Capital Hill Arts Workshop, Sandy Point Press, PO Box 50089, Washington, DC 20004, 1979.

Second Rising, ed. by Stacy Tuthill, SCOP Publications, 5821 Swarthmore Dr., College Park, MD 20740, 1979.

The Ear's Chamber: 50 Metro Poets, ed. Stacy Tuthill, SCOP Publications, 1981.

Takoma Park Writers, 1981, ed. by Suzanne Rhodenbaugh, Downcounty Press, c/o 53 Walnut Ave., Takoma Park, MD 20012. 1981.

Baltimore Anthologies which Feature some Area Poets

Poetry at the Angel, ed. by Kenneth Baldwin, Mary Jane Lupton, Susanne Moore & William Lupton, Bloomery Books, 3115 N. Calvert St., Baltimore, MD 21218, 1978.

Baltimore Renaissance: Poetry, ed. by Stephen Ciesielski, The New Poets Series, 541 Piccadilly Rd., Baltimore, MD 21204, 1980.